BACKSTORY

BACKSTORY

INSIDE THE BUSINESS OF NEWS

KEN AULETTA

THE PENGUIN PRESS

New York

2003

THE PENGUIN PRESS

First published in 2003 by The Penguin Press,
a member of Penguin Group (USA) Inc.

Copyright © Ken Auletta, 2003
All rights reserved.

All of the selections in this book first appeared in *The New Yorker*
with the exception of "Synergy City," which appeared in *American
Journalism Review,* and "New York's Tabloid Wars," which is
being published for the first time in this volume.

LIBRARY OF CONGRESS CATALOGING-IN-PUBLICATION DATA

Auletta, Ken.
Backstory : inside the business of news
p. cm.
Includes index.
ISBN 1-59420-000-9
1. Journalism—United States—History—20th century.
I. Title.

PN4867.A94 2003
071'.3'0904—dc21   2003050675

Printed in the United States of America
1   3   5   7   9   10   8   6   4   2

This book is printed on acid-free paper. ∞

BOOK DESIGN BY AMANDA DEWEY

For Abe Lass,
a high school principal who helped
save lives, including mine.

CONTENTS

INTRODUCTION

I was first infected with the idea of becoming a journalist while studying political science in graduate school. The bylines I remember belonged to Murray Kempton, David Halberstam, Homer Bigart, Gay Talese, I. F. Stone, Lillian Ross, among others. Why not, I thought, extend school through my life and get paid to learn, travel, and meet people? Journalism also held some allure as a profession where independence was prized. Didn't reporters brave Bull Connor's dogs to report on the struggle for civil rights? Didn't the *New York Times* face down President Kennedy when he wanted Halberstam yanked from Vietnam? Didn't the *Washington Post* back two cub reporters over an incident known as Watergate? I saw how Lillian Ross—and then years later, Gay Talese, Norman Mailer, and Tom Wolfe—perfected something called the New Journalism, a way to marry narrative fiction techniques to nonfiction. This was a profession that could educate and entertain. It could inspire change. True, it conferred power without responsibility, and thus was a wonderful way to prolong adolescence. But it was also a noble calling, a vital public service in a democracy where citizens rely on information to vote and to form and freely express opinions.

I'm still a sucker for the romance of journalism, but I'm also a realist. My adult lifetime graduate course has taught me that my métier's virtues, like those of the Greek heroes, often become its vices. Its very successes—illuminating the civil rights revolution, helping open America's eyes to Vietnam or Nixon's depredations or financial mismanagement—induced excess. Reporters wanted to be famous, rich, influential. As a media writer, I've reported on a new generation of windbags, of callow people who think they become investigative reporters by adopting a belligerent pose without doing the hard digging, of bloviators so infatuated with their own voice they have forgotten how to listen, of news presidents who are slaves to ratings, and of editors terrified they may bore readers. As in any profession, some folks take shortcuts.

The shortcut I worry most about today falls under the rubric of "business pressures." I worry about the owners of journalistic properties making business decisions that harm journalism. Recall the oft-told story of the wasp with a crippled wing that pleads with a frog to carry him across a pond. After promising not to sting him, the wasp finally induces the frog to lug him across. Arriving on the other shore, alas, the wasp stings him. As the frog is expiring he plaintively asks, "Why'd you sting me?"

"What can I tell you? I'm a wasp. It's my nature."

As a reporter, I've learned it's the nature of corporate executives to extol the virtues of synergy, profit margins, the stock price, cost cutting, extending the brand, demographics, ratings, and getting on the team. Journalists rarely share these concerns, so we often denounce what we see as dumb corporate decisions that do violence to journalism. We would do better to recognize that this is the nature of the business culture and figure out how to translate our journalistic concerns into language corporate executives can understand. Since they write the checks, somehow journalists must persuade our corporate chiefs to broaden their too narrow definition of success.

This won't be easy. The cultural divide between us is vast. The corporate buzzword *synergy* is rarely journalism's friend. The business assumptions that animate synergy—cost savings, "team culture," "leverage" of size—are often a menace to journalism. Take, for example, the proposed merger of CNN and ABC News that surfaced in the latter half of 2002. The key argument for "consolidating" CNN with a network news division was that upward of $200 million in cost reductions could be realized. This "synergy" would sweeten the bottom line and maybe provide CNN with the use of more visible ABC stars, but it's hard to see how it would improve news coverage. ABC would have access to CNN's more extensive bureaus overseas, but ABC, except in national emergencies, has continued to shrink international news. Early in 2002, ABC tried to replace its luminous internationalist newscast—Ted Koppel's *Nightline*—with David Letterman. The merging of CNN and ABC means that two competing newsrooms would be replaced by one.

Sometimes, the "independent" news division shows off its team spirit. In the spring of 2003, a news executive at CBS dispatched a proposal to the family of Pfc. Jessica Lynch, who had been captured and wounded in Iraq, offering her exposure on various news programs. But the news executive didn't stop there. She noted that Viacom, the corporate parent, owned Paramount, which could make a movie of Lynch's heroics, and Simon & Schuster, which could offer a book, and MTV, a popular cable network, which might make her a cohost of a video show, and Infinity Broadcasting, the second largest radio network. The news executive put in the proper qualifications about how she could not speak for the movie or book or any other division. Nevertheless, a CBS News executive was making a pitch for the Viacom team. Similar synergistic proposals were received from other big media companies, including the HarperCollins publishing division of News Corp.

A corporate preoccupation with cost synergies is, of course, not new. Mark Willes, when he became the CEO of Times Mirror in the first half of the 1990s, lashed the company's newspapers, which included the *Los Angeles Times,* to lift profit margins from 8 percent to 16 percent. And Knight Ridder ordered its two Philadelphia papers to double profit margins. Gannett saw its stock soar partly because it enjoys double-digit profit margins. Editors at some Gannett, and other, newspapers have sometimes ordered reporters to skip press conferences and in-person interviews and instead sit at their computer terminals and retrieve information, thus improving "productivity" by filing more stories. It is old news that news-magazines boost sales by dressing up their covers with celebrities, and despite the boom following 9/11, international news continues to be downsized.

For many years, media companies have succeeded in generating profit margins of 50 percent at their TV stations, the principal reason media gi-ants want government to relax rules on how many stations they may own. Owners skimp on costs, particularly the cost of local news, which is usu-ally a station's profit locomotive. So in succeeding in earning more than fifty cents on each dollar of revenue, they usually fail to produce worthy local newscasts. Similarly, distant group owners who now dominate local radio stations—like Clear Channel Communications—raise their margins by lowering local news costs, producing centralized, homogenized news that is pumped out to various stations.

As happened with network television, which became more preoccupied with ratings as it lost market share, so it goes with print journalism. Pub-lishers ask why we need such expensive bureaus in D.C. and state capitals. Why so many seriously boring stories on government? Why tie up our best reporters and writers on long investigative reports on poverty or race or housing when they could monitor services our readers use—like mammograms—or write vivid features? Why, nervous executives ask, can't we pepper the mix with more gossip, more marketing-driven and friendly news, more news readers or viewers can use, more features that will please our advertisers? Why, the question recurs with depressing fre-quency, do journalists have to be such scolds?

At the same time, as media companies get bigger, the role of the jour-nalist within them is diminished. Inside a behemoth like Disney, Time Warner, Viacom, or Clear Channel, news rarely matches the profit margins of other divisions, such as cable or programming, and thus loses internal clout. And as media companies converge, a premium is placed on *team-work*. Occasions for journalistic conflicts of interest thus proliferate. To a Disney or GE executive, synergy is achieved when ABC's *Good Morning America* broadcasts from Disney World or when NBC's *Today* show features stars from its entertainment division. To AOL Time Warner, synergy was achieved when Warner Books won the right to publish retiring GE chairman and CEO Jack Welch's memoir, promising to enlist the support of its various divisions to promote the book.

GE, which has huge business interests in China, leaned on its NBC Sports to apologize to China for Bob Costas's perfectly reasonable mention of human rights abuses during the opening ceremonies of the 1996 Summer Olympics. "We wanted to make it clear that we didn't intend to hurt their feelings," said an apologetic NBC spokesman. Nor, presumably, did NBC want to get off the team and hurt the business interests of its corporate parent, General Electric. Rupert Murdoch, the CEO of News Corp., Sumner Redstone, the chairman of Viacom/CBS, and Gerald Levin, the former CEO of AOL Time Warner, each went out of his way to attack critics of the Chinese government, hoping to win entrée to the world's largest market.

The cultural gap between the business and news divisions at media companies is as wide as the gap between scientists and government that C. P. Snow wrote about nearly a half century ago. Media corporations prize teamwork to create a "borderless" company that eliminates defensive interior barriers among divisions, strive to use leverage to boost sales, and push synergy. But journalists are meant to prize independence, not teamwork, and to value distance from advertisers or sources, not synergies with them. We journalists need borders—that is to say, a degree of independence—to do our jobs. We don't aspire to a "borderless" company because we want the advertising department to stay the hell out of the newsroom. The "leverage" journalists seek is the kind that pries loose the story, not the kind that boosts the parent company's other "products."

It frustrates those on the business side that journalists often fail to recognize that they are part of a business. If the business fails to make money, how attract investors or justify squandering the pension moneys invested by widows or giant shareholders? The Times Mirror Company can be faulted for the way it killed a fine newspaper, but if *New York Newsday* really hemorrhaged more than $100 million and had no prospect of earning a profit, then Times Mirror eventually had no choice but to put it to rest. General Electric can be faulted for the way it treated NBC News when it took over that network in 1986, but not for seeking to learn why nearly half the stories assigned by the news desk never aired.

If journalists hope to bridge the cultural divide, they might start by understanding the value of earning a profit. More profits can mean hiring more reporters, or more time to report stories. They might also learn to advance business reasons to support journalistic claims. There are, for example, sound business reasons to zealously guard the credibility of journalism. *USA Today* has gained credibility—and awards—by relaxing strictures on story length and by offering more in-depth reports. In turn, these are touted in advertisements to build up its *brand value.* A TV reporter perceived as a gunslinger will lose both viewers and potential interviews. The *Los Angeles Times's* credibility was tarnished by its secret advertising deal with Staples, making it harder to attract top editorial talent, at least for a while. Ditto the *Wall Street Journal* after Foster Winans or the *New York Times* after Jayson Blair. Sully the credibility and you damage the brand. These may not be easily quantifiable, but they are nevertheless real.

Journalists also have to confront the profit margin argument. They need show how a 20 percent profit margin (versus, say 15 percent) may mean cutting bone, not fat; how the higher target means the newsroom will not be able to launch the kind of investigative stories that win respect and awards, and that bureaus will be shuttered. Business executives like to quantify things, and so journalists will have to get specific: *You want more coverage of Islam or Korea, or a series on immigration? You can't have it and still achieve a 20 percent profit margin—unless you want us to eliminate our bureau in the state capital. Yes, I know shareholders want a 20 percent margin—but not if in the long run it means they own a diminished asset.* The next time a media executive like Michael Eisner of Disney expresses pride in the work of ABC News and insists that costs can be curbed without harm to the journalistic mission, someone has to ask him: Do you really believe ABC can effectively cover the world—as it did in the fall of 2002—with only five overseas correspondents? When the networks buy footage from an overseas picture service, they usually tack on a voice-over and claim they are covering a hot spot, but a picture is no substitute for reporting. It does not provide the *context* or *authority* that media executives always insist sets network news apart. Usually only a reporter on the ground who speaks the local language and has mined various sources and is familiar with the nation's culture and traditions can provide such context. Similarly, the wire service dispatches relied on by many Tribune papers and other chains cannot set those newspapers apart.

The public is no mere spectator to this dialogue. If readers don't trust journalists, if they cynically believe we're all in the tank, or make things up, or push our own political agendas, politics will become even more shrill and uncivil with no trusted referee to sort out the facts. We would be perceived as partisans, the way too many European journalists are. If journalism was not about more than profits, we would not receive special protections under the First Amendment. We receive such sanction because in a democracy voters get much of their information from the press. While journalism is about concrete things like reporting facts, it's really about fulfilling a public trust. That trust can't be synergized or quantified, but you know it when you lose it.

Synergy and public trust are two of several themes explored in this collection of articles. With one exception, each was written for *The New Yorker,* and in one case—"Tabloid Wars"—I include a piece *The New Yorker* did not run. I have sometimes added material excised at the time for space reasons. The Howell Raines profile, for example, adds about five thousand words that were cut from the original piece, which ran at seventeen thousand words. After each piece I add a postscript, including an analysis of post-Jayson Blair controversies at the *New York Times.* The pieces start at the top of the profession with the *New York Times,* then plunge into the synergy abyss, go on to explore various news business strategies, trying to sketch where journalism was back once, where it has gone since then, and where it is going next.

The process of compiling and editing this collection happened to coincide with membership on President Lee C. Bollinger's task force to explore the future of the Columbia School of Journalism. Over the course of six dinners, the thirtyplus members of the task force delved into what was wrong with contemporary journalism and what the country's foremost journalism school might do to better train journalists.

As we went around a large rectangular dinner table at a club in New York City, task force members discussed the varied ills of modern journalism—business pressures to achieve ratings or circulation gains and how this often trivializes news and produces infotainment; the journalistic game of Gotcha! and how this spurs reporters to chase headlines without understanding what they're after; the bimbo factor of dumb reporters (or dumb questions) without a clue what to ask or who pursue mindless stories without context; reporters who are full of attitude, not information, who think it is okay to be cynical, as opposed to skeptical, and who adopt a fake adversarial pose without having done the legwork; the conformity of pack journalism; the lack of time that leads to hurried stories.

An inescapable truism about journalism is that form dictates content. The form of journalism—gimme a headline, gimme a story in the next hour or two, and gimme it in 500 or 250 words—subverts the content. It's easy for someone who is allowed 20,000 words and months to report a *New Yorker* story to say this, but it's nevertheless true that most editors don't allow reporters enough time or space to get a story's facts and context right. One hopes that a journalism education would address these ills, would induce students, as historian Alan Brinkley said at one meeting, to aspire not to get a job but to be a great journalist.

Shaping a journalism curriculum, we all learned, is no simple feat. Questions came at us with machine-gun speed. Is journalism to be taught as a craft? Do you offer separate craft courses—how to write a lead or include the *who, what, when,* and *where* of a story? Or do you include the craft elements in each course? Is there a body of knowledge a journalist should possess? How much time should be devoted to mastering writing as opposed to mastering reporting? Should on-the-job training be emphasized or study? Should a journalist be trained as a specialist in a given field or as a generalist? Should it take one year or two to receive a degree? And if two, can students afford the steep tuition? How does one teach what task force member Mike Oreskes called a journalistic way of thinking—a mind-set that helps a reporter become what another member, Karen Elliott House, called a truth seeker, sorting truth from a welter of "facts"?

Each of these questions flows back to what I think of as the tree-trunk question: How best to train a professional journalist? In turn, this core question assumes that while someone can be a fine journalist without a journalism degree, journalism is not a walk-on profession. It requires training, just as a split end and quarterback repeatedly practice pass routes or a violinist again and again rehearses a concerto. This is a vital assumption for it justifies the special role journalists play in a democracy. While we are not licensed as lawyers or doctors, and not as extensively trained, we are, in effect, accredited to sort out fact from fiction, to decide what is news and what is not, what is more and also less important, what the public needs to know to make decisions in a democracy. The myriad questions about what to include in a journalism school curriculum are all mere branches of this tree.

There is at least one other critical question a journalism school should ask, and it is one that President Bollinger and the task force member he boldly induced to become dean, Nicholas Lemann, asked of this task force: Do you design a journalism school curriculum to prepare journalists to function in the commercial world as it is or for the way you wish journalism to be? Do you train journalists to excel at the way the game is played today or do you train them to reform the way the game is played? I believe a journalism school should be a beacon, not a reflection, educating not just its students but their prospective employers.

The acorn of good journalism is humility. Humility is more essential than good writing or hard work—though these are obviously vital. Humility is required to use two of a journalist's irreplaceable tools: the curiosity to ask questions and the ability to listen to the answers. Each requires modesty because each requires us to assume we don't already know the answers. Asking and listening assume an ability to understand someone's position, to empathize. Sources talk to journalists for many reasons—because they have something to say; because they are vain and believe in themselves; because they wish to protect themselves should we be talking to adversaries; because they honestly believe they have something to sell; because the publication, or the journalist, carries some weight. But sources also talk if they sense that a reporter genuinely seeks understanding (and not just a headline). Sensing this, they are more likely to open up and to help a journalist to better sort truth from fiction.

Criticism helps keep journalists—like politicians—humble, as we were all reminded in the spring of 2003 when the *New York Times* was convulsed by the Jayson Blair scandal. After the paper published a 7,200-word account of how reporter Blair had stolen the work of others and tricked his editors into printing lies, the staff of the *Times* went into an uproar. Management called a mass meeting at a nearby movie theater whose entrance was guarded by an army of competing reporters and cameras. To enter the theater, *Times* journalists had to pass a phalanx of preying reporters and flashing bulbs. Most shunned eye contact and pretended not to hear their names called; some shielded their faces, like mobsters entering a police station. For the first time in most of these reporters' lives, they experienced what it must feel like to be on the other side of a story—to be embarrassed, to duck questions or worry about what they might say, about whether their quotes would get garbled, about how they might look. *Should I talk? Did I say the right thing? Will my words get me in trouble? Is that snide bastard going to do me in?*

Should he return to editing, Howell Raines—the departed executive editor of the *Times*—would probably be a more sensitive and empathetic editor after the awful experience he endured. His humbling experience became a universal experience. Those of us in journalism were reminded that when our foremost paper is sullied, so are we. Nor was what happened at the *New York Times* the usual "inside baseball story" editors deride when they say no one except other journalists are interested in what goes on in a newsroom. New York's two tabloid newspapers, the *News* and the *Post,* each plastered the ouster of Raines and his deputy on their June sixth front pages. It was big news because every citizen is reliant on news and the "facts" journalists disseminate. No journalistic institution's facts are more relied upon than those in the *New York Times.*

But the backstory behind these headlines is about the humility Raines and his publisher and most journalists—or anyone else infected by power—often lose. In their embarrassment, they learned what defeated candidates, disgraced politicians, indicted officials, or aging sports stars must: Nothing breeds humility like independent scrutiny, the "check and balance" of rigorous criticism or competition. The work that follows is meant to serve that end.

BACKSTORY

THE HOWELL DOCTRINE

A MAN WHO TAKES the subway wearing the white panama hat of a plantation owner is either blithely arrogant or irrepressibly self-confident, and in the nine months that Howell Raines has been the executive editor of the *Times* both qualities have been imputed to him. Raines is fifty-nine, and has worked for the *Times* for a quarter of a century; he has been praised and derided for the sometimes coruscating editorial page that he ran from January of 1993 until August 2001. But until last year his acquaintance with the newsroom was only passing, and to most of his *Times* colleagues he was an alien—as the metropolitan editor, Jonathan Landman, characterized him, a "Martian."

Raines is built close to the ground (he is five feet eight), with short, stocky legs that churn rapidly—like those of "a Tasmanian devil," one female reporter affectionately says. He has neatly brushed back, wavy black hair flecked with gray, a wardrobe of dapper sports jackets and pastel shirts, a courtly manner, an engaging wit, and he is fond of quoting the former University of Alabama football coach Bear Bryant, or Yeats, or what he learned from his father, growing up in Birmingham, Alabama—sometimes all three, and sometimes trying the patience of his listeners.

Raines's eyes are nearly black; in photographs, even when he's half smiling, they convey an unsmiling intensity. That intensity has excited and occasionally alarmed the inhabitants of the world's most powerful newsroom, who often ask if this son of hill-country Alabamans is comfortable leading a newspaper staffed by Ivy Leaguers. They see that he enjoys power and is unafraid to use it, but wonder why he is often hostile to others who hold it. What is clear, a little more than a year since it was announced that he would succeed Joseph Lelyveld in the top job, is that Howell Raines is quickening the pulse of the *Times*.

Raines has been waiting for this chance for years. His friend R. W. (Johnny) Apple, Jr., the paper's political sage, recalled a trip they took to South Africa in 1995, when Raines talked about one day becoming executive editor. "'I'm not at all sure I'll get it. But I'll be ready if I get it. I'm going to prepare myself,'" Apple remembers Raines saying. In early 2001, Lelyveld told Arthur O. Sulzberger, Jr., the *Times*'s chairman and publisher, that he planned to retire as executive editor; and when Sulzberger decided that his choice was between Raines and Bill Keller, the managing editor, Raines had indeed prepared. "I knew that I wanted to raise the competitive metabolism of the paper," Raines said to me during a series of interviews this winter and spring. When Sulzberger asked him what he might do as executive editor, he told the publisher that he "wanted to enliven the front page with more exclusive breaking news—original stories." He knew that, unlike almost every other newspaper in America, the *Times*'s daily circulation was growing—by April of 2001 it had reached 1.15 million—but that this growth came from the national edition, introduced in 1980, which now accounted for nearly half of the paper's readers.

To continue its expansion, Raines argued, the *Times* had to become "a must-read" for new customers, and he described the paper in somewhat military terms: Just as the "Powell doctrine," promulgated by General Colin Powell, declared that American troops should be sent into battle only if they had enough force to overpower the enemy, so Raines proposed covering big stories with the overwhelming force of the newspaper—some twelve hundred editorial employees who work in newsrooms on the third and fourth floors of the Times Building, on West Forty-third Street, and in offices scattered throughout the building, as well as in twenty-eight foreign and ten domestic bureaus. He believed the *Times* was competing for eyeballs with every newspaper and magazine. In particular, he saw the *Journal* taking aim at the *Times,* and he rejected the "dangerous mind-set at the *Times* that we can't compete with the *Wall Street Journal* on business news. My view is that I want to be General Giap to their Westmoreland." He would move faster, work harder, catch rivals by surprise.

The newsroom was introduced to its editor-to-be on May 21, 2001. For Raines, the victory was total. He did not have to contend with his rival, Keller, because Keller was given a biweekly column, alternating Saturdays with Frank Rich, and became a senior writer for the *Times Magazine.* With Sulzberger's prior approval, Raines picked a somewhat reserved deputy managing editor, Gerald Boyd, to be his managing editor; they had worked together in the Washington bureau in the mideighties. A decade later, Boyd had been in the running for the managing editor's job, but was rejected by Lelyveld; Boyd, in turn, described Lelyveld and Keller as not "inclusive," a word with deep meaning for a fifty-one-year-old black man. Unlike Keller, Boyd was invited to join the regular Wednesday lunch that serves as the paper's steering committee, along with Sulzberger; Raines; Gail Collins, whom Raines had hired, and who succeeded him as the editorial-page editor; and the *Times*'s president, Janet L. Robinson.

Raines spent the summer getting to know the newsroom. Earlier in his *Times* career, he had been based in Atlanta, Washington, and London; now he spent evenings visiting various desks, and took an assortment of editors to coffee, lunch, and dinner, all in preparation for taking over, after Labor Day. He met with the sports editor, Neil Amdur, and said that he wanted more college sports, particularly football and basketball. He met with Margaret O'Connor, the picture editor, and Mike Smith, her deputy, and heard that *Times* photographers felt like "second-class citizens" because they weren't sent out often enough on breaking stories; their best photographs were often unused. The photo department, Raines learned, had put these unused photographs up on a wall, under the words "The Ones That Got Away." Raines assured O'Connor and Smith that things would be different. He and Boyd flew to Atlanta in August for a dinner with southern bureau chiefs and told them they should be on the road more, capturing "the pulse" of America.

Sometimes, Raines revealed his tough side. That spring Lelyveld had made several appointments, including Berlin bureau chief Roger Cohen as deputy foreign editor, to start in September. Lelyveld thought he still had a paper to run; Raines worried that he barely knew Cohen and that Lelyveld was saddling him with people he might not have chosen. In August, the soon-to-be executive editor summoned Cohen back from Berlin. Cohen wrote Raines that he would land at 4:00 P.M. at JFK on a Monday, and suggested they meet the next day. Raines insisted that they dine the night Cohen arrived. "There were no references at dinner that it was the day I arrived and maybe I was jet lagged," recalls Cohen with a laugh. "He doesn't like wimping. This was clearly someone who doesn't want to waste time. I had been in the country two hours!"

Raines promised to manage the newsroom in the collegial way that he'd run the editorial board, which has fourteen members. But he can also be autocratic—some say bullying. In a sharp and, to those inside the paper, controversial departure from the Lelyveld era, Raines said that he wanted what is known as the masthead to be more engaged in shaping stories and coordinating news coverage. (The masthead consists of the managing editor, his deputy, and the seven assistant managing editors whose names appear under the executive editor's on the *Times* editorial page. The department editors, whose names do not appear, actually run the various sections of the paper.) "Howell has thought about this job a long time, and he loves it," said John Huey, the editorial director of Time, Inc., who worked with Raines on the *Atlanta Constitution* in the early seventies. "Some people who held that job wore it like a hair shirt." (Huey mentioned Lelyveld and his predecessor, Max Frankel.) "Howell Raines expected to have fun." His energy was obvious, and the newsroom was probably more excited than anxious in the months before he took over. There was little indication of just how fast Raines intended to move.

A WEEK
IN SEPTEMBER

The Raines era began on September 5, 2001. When Raines arrived at his office, in the northeast corner of the newsroom, his favorite image was already on the wall behind his desk. Taken by a *Times* photographer, George Tames, it is a sequence containing seven black-and-white photographs of Senate Majority Leader Lyndon Baines Johnson cajoling Senator Theodore F. Green, of Rhode Island; in each succeeding frame, LBJ shrinks his colleague's space until Green is bent backward over his desk and LBJ is hovering just inches from his face. Implicitly, these photographs suggest how Raines intends to bend the *Times* to his will. And those who might miss this signal are provided another, for he placed on the edge of the small round desk where visitors sit across from him a copy of the novel *Stay Hungry,* by his college classmate Charles Gaines, as a reminder of his desire for a hungry newsroom.

"I just like the tribal culture of a newsroom," Raines told me one day as we sat in a small sitting room behind his office. "I'm—in some sense—home. The populist side of me is very much about my identification with the culture of a newsroom." He explained what he meant by citing Bear Bryant. "Coach Bryant had a lot of flaws—he was late to support integration," Raines said. "But he was a very influential figure for any student of leadership. . . . When Coach Bryant walked onto a football field, everybody in that stadium knew that football would be played here today."

September fifth, a Wednesday, was a relatively slow news day; the front page had stories about the New York mayoral primary, about administration officials defending Bush's budget, about immigration policy. But the new editor's presence could be felt. The Washington bureau chief, Jill Abramson, remembers that Raines called her and said, "I want something with pop for the Sunday paper." To assure more "pop," he initiated, that first day, a 10:30 A.M. meeting of the masthead, to supplement a noon meeting, originated by Lelyveld, of the department and masthead editors, and a 4:30 P.M. page-one meeting. The morning session, Raines said, was meant "as a teaching device for me" and as a way to "include the masthead" in shaping the paper.

On Monday, September tenth, Raines announced that Andrew Rosenthal, the foreign editor, was being promoted to assistant managing editor, and would serve as Gerald Boyd's principal news deputy, and that Roger Cohen would become acting foreign editor. With less fanfare, he made his first reporter assignment, switching media reporter Alex Kuczynski to the style section, where she would write the sort of pop-feature pieces that would appeal to the *Times*'s national audience. "It was no accident that the first transfer I made when I got down here was to move Alex Kuczynski from media to style," Raines said. "I did that to set a standard."

On the morning of September eleventh, Raines rose at around seven o'clock and prepared a pot of tea for Krystyna Stachowiak, thirty-eight, an attractive, self-possessed Polish-born public relations executive who shares a Greenwich Village town house with him. Then he read the *Times* and sent e-mail. He wasn't yet dressed when he heard that a plane had crashed into the World Trade Center. Arthur Sulzberger, Jr., called immediately. Minutes later, Raines grabbed his hat—since having a cancerous lesion removed from his nose he always wears a hat—and was on Seventh Avenue, gaping at the smoldering North Tower to his left, and to his right, at the staff of St. Vincent's Hospital, in their green scrubs, mobilized for victims that never came. Uptown, Gerald Boyd was in a barber's chair at 104th Street and Amsterdam Avenue when a passerby poked his head in the door with the news. "I leaped out of the chair," Boyd recalls, and he hurried to the subway, which had already suspended service, before hailing a gypsy cab and getting to the office at 9:10 A.M., about forty minutes before Raines arrived.

Roger Cohen had just dropped off his son at school in Park Slope when he heard an explosion and looked up and saw orange flames billowing from the Trade Center and the sky raining paper. He raced to catch the No. 2 train, which ran under the World Trade Center site. "That train must have been the last one to run," he said. Other members of the masthead never made it to the office that day. Andrew Rosenthal couldn't get across the Hudson from New Jersey; the ferry that Al Siegal, an assistant managing editor, was taking from Hoboken was turned back by the Coast Guard.

A few blocks from Boyd's barbershop, Jonathan Landman, the metropolitan editor, was at a gym on 106th Street when he looked out the window and saw his wife running toward the building. She told him of the attacks. He hurried home and started calling some of his hundred-odd reporters, directing traffic to Ground Zero. The police reporter Christopher John (C. J.) Chivers was already downtown. It was primary day in the city's mayoral election, and he had been assigned to the Board of Elections headquarters. He was wearing his best suit. When his beeper went off, he ran half a mile to Ground Zero, approaching Liberty Street just as the second plane hit the South Tower. As desks and concrete and steel beams plunged to the street, he dived into the entrance of a liquor store near Trinity Church, and soon began interviewing people huddled nearby.

Chivers tried calling the metropolitan desk, but his cell phone didn't work. To escape falling debris, he moved under the Liberty Street Bridge to another building, stepping in dust "that was like fine powdered snow." He had reached a building that housed a day-care center, where children were fretting over the whereabouts of their parents, when he heard a "high-pitched, twisting, grinding, metallic screeching" that "sounded like an enormous train collision" and felt like an earthquake. The South Tower had collapsed. His cell phone still didn't work, so he found a telephone and called Landman, who told him, "I don't really know what to tell you to do, but you have good judgment, so follow it." Chivers spent the next twenty-four hours at Ground Zero, feeding information to *Times* reporters in the newsroom.

Gerald Boyd was in the newsroom. "The dimensions kept growing," he recalled. "We heard Congress had closed and the airlines were shut down. We discussed what would happen if the *New York Times* were attacked. Could we put out a paper?" John Geddes, the deputy managing editor, who was at his desk when the first plane crashed into the Trade Center, said, "This was a story we had been training all our lives for."

Raines likened his role to that of Ulysses S. Grant: Before attacking the biggest story of his career, he would concentrate his forces. Never once, Raines says, did he think to call the publisher, Sulzberger, or the president, Janet Robinson, about the extra costs of covering this story or about his instinctive decision to banish advertising from the main A section of that day's newspaper. "I don't think any editor in the world could do what I did that day," Raines would recall, "which was just walk into the newsroom and go to work without any question in my mind that the publisher would throw out a half million dollars in ads to bring our kind of journalism to this massive and traumatic story." All day, Raines and Boyd moved back and forth from their neighboring offices, sometimes ministering to distraught staff members. Sometimes they comforted themselves. They were not, of course, mere witnesses. Their city and their families and friends were jeopardized. "The toughest thing for me was in a personal sense," Boyd said. "I had dropped my son at school and couldn't reach my wife and son until 5:00 P.M." Late in the afternoon, Krystyna Stachowiak left her midtown office and made her way to the *Times,* where she greeted Raines with a hug.

For its September twelfth edition, the *Times* deployed some three hundred reporters, thirty staff photographers, and two dozen freelance photographers. Eighty-two thousand five hundred words were devoted to the attacks on the World Trade Center and the Pentagon; there were seventy-four bylines accompanying sixty-seven stories, filling thirty-three pages of a ninety-six-page paper. Nearly 1.7 million copies were printed, almost half a million more than normal. At the top of the front page, which is now framed on Raines's wall, was a headline—U.S. ATTACKED—set in ninety-six-point type, a size used only twice before: to announce Neil Armstrong's walk on the moon, in 1969, and the resignation of President Nixon, in 1974. In the center of the page was a two-column tree trunk of four color photographs, showing the Twin Towers ablaze and the destruction at Ground Zero. Symmetrically branching down either side of page one were four stories, not the usual seven. In a September twelfth e-mail to the newsroom, Raines wrote, "Thank you one and all for a magnificent effort in putting out, in the midst of a heartbreaking day, a paper of which we can be proud for years to come. . . . In a different context of violence, Yeats wrote that 'a terrible beauty is born.'"

Long before September eleventh, Raines had given much thought to ways of conveying a sense of command. He says that he learned the importance of this from his father, who never finished high school but built a store-fixture business in Birmingham that eventually made him a millionaire. He often told colleagues the story of one summer after he graduated from Birmingham-Southern College and had gone to work for his father, who warned him that sooner or later an employee would challenge him, and told him that, when he did, "you've got to win that fight." Now, in September of 2001, Raines wanted to challenge his editors, to get into the fray before assignments were made.

Raines became what Assistant Managing Editor Michael Oreskes referred to as "the reader-in-chief," meeting constantly with the assistant managing editors. To better penetrate the Pentagon and the national security agencies, he brought the defense-and-intelligence expert Michael Gordon back from London. He asked Patrick Tyler, a trusted friend, to return from Moscow, where he was bureau chief, to write "lead-alls"—stories meant to bring together the different strands of a news event, like the stories that Johnny Apple had written during the Gulf War. Each move stirred hurt feelings and aroused some opposition. So, too, did Raines's insistence on working directly through the masthead editors rather than through the department editors, as Lelyveld had done. Raines wanted his assistant managing editors to demand more of the department heads. "How come something we discussed at the page-one meeting didn't get in the paper today?" he would ask, according to Soma Golden Behr, an assistant managing editor. He started asking for stories that offered "all known thought" on a subject—what was known about Osama bin Laden's finances, or about anthrax. "Hunt big game, not rabbits," he would say. He was impatient with complaint, and in truth there was little time for it. One complaint he would not abide was that he didn't respect borders between departments—that he shouldn't parachute in his "star" writers to cover stories.

Criticism that he favored stars had attached itself to Raines when he ran the Washington bureau, and it was a criticism, Sulzberger told those he confided in, that would have blocked Raines's promotion if Sulzberger had not been convinced that he had changed. Raines, however, believes that an editor's first obligation is to the readers; he wanted to use distinctive writers, such as Rick Bragg, in Pakistan. Bragg, a roving national correspondent with a taste for elegiac, sometimes purple prose, had scant overseas experience and was, in the words of John Geddes, "not an easy writer to handle" but "one of our best tellers of stories." Raines asked Bragg to come off a tour for a new book, which had just appeared on the *Times* best-seller list; Raines says that Bragg, who is a friend, volunteered. Raines went to the foreign desk and told Roger Cohen to send Bragg overseas, which Cohen did reluctantly.

"He wanted to own all parts of this story," Abramson, the Washington bureau chief, said of Raines. He wanted the *Times* to be first. "Target selection is key," Raines said. "And then you have to concentrate your resources at the point of attack. Geddes has another term for my style, which is 'flood the zone.' I've been in journalistic contests where I was up against real formidable opposition"—with the *Washington Post,* when he worked in the Washington bureau. "If I'm in a gunfight, I don't want to die with any bullets in my pistol. I want to shoot every one."

He also wanted the *Times* to be accessible, but there was too much information about the September eleventh attacks, in too many different sections, interrupted by too many ads; and there were too many stories containing unrelated but vital news. At one masthead meeting, Raines turned to Al Siegal, a production expert, and asked, "Can we make a section?" Siegal said they could, and Sulzberger quickly agreed to spend the extra money. "A Nation Challenged" appeared on September eighteenth, giving the story its own section.

The 10:30 A.M. masthead meeting became the executive editor's management tool. "We were inventing not just procedures but a philosophy of how to put out this newspaper," said Siegal, whose responsibilities include drawing up the front page. Raines, he went on, wanted to give masthead editors and himself a new kind of role. "We were essentially elbowing our way into the process." It was not unusual, certainly, for an editor to take command, as A. M. (Abe) Rosenthal did with the Pentagon

Papers, or as Lelyveld did during President Clinton's impeachment. (Michael Oreskes, who was Washington bureau chief under Lelyveld, says that he heard from Lelyveld "four times a day.") But, if Lelyveld tended to take over the editing of individual stories, Raines was relying on his masthead to manage—some said micromanage—the entire paper.

One of the talents to emerge from the coverage of September eleventh was C. J. Chivers. Reared in Binghamton, New York, Chivers enrolled in an ROTC program at nearby Cornell. After graduating, he was commissioned a second lieutenant in the Marine Corps; he stayed in nearly seven years, served in the Gulf War, and left as a captain. "I wanted to be a writer, but I had no money," he said. "Journalism was the only writing job with a union card." Chivers is a wiry man with broad shoulders, black hair only slightly longer than a marine brush cut, a cleft chin, and beguiling modesty. "Praise is kryptonite," he said, attempting to steer me to interview another reporter. After the Marine Corps, he enrolled at the Columbia School of Journalism; later he got a job with the *Providence Journal,* where he wrote a nine-thousand-word series on the imperiled fishing industries of Nova Scotia and Newfoundland, for which he won the 1996 Livingston Award for International Reporting, given to journalists under the age of thirty-five. (Raines and I are two of eight national Livingston judges.) Raines, an avid fisherman, was particularly enthusiastic about Chivers's entry, and in 1999 he helped to engineer his hiring by the *Times.* "I had in mind that if I ever came down here he'd be a great guy to cover a war," Raines recalled.

Chivers, who is thirty-seven, had been assigned to the so-called police shack, at police headquarters, downtown; his breakout assignment was as a Ground Zero correspondent, where his marine background proved invaluable. When he came uptown twenty-four hours after the towers collapsed, his feet were bleeding. He went to the office to brief his editors, then to his apartment, on the Upper West Side, where he threw out his suit and shoes, showered, and slept. That night, he went back downtown, wearing work boots, jeans, and a marine T-shirt. He stationed himself next to a Verizon truck just outside the security zone; he bought several cups of coffee and, looking like a marine volunteer, got past security and through to Ground Zero. Once there, he lay down beside sleeping police

officers and firefighters, "so when I woke up I was one of them." He became what he calls "the garbageman" at the site, setting up and emptying
trash receptacles. "No one asked if I was a reporter," he said. "I took dis-
creet notes on scraps of paper." After several days, the metro editor,
Landman, called him and asked if he wanted to come out. No, he said;
security had tightened and he'd never get back in. When the National
Guard started checking IDs, a sergeant, who like Chivers had attended
ranger school, helped sneak him past security.

Chivers stayed at Ground Zero for twelve days, writing a page-one di-
ary of this emerging "village":

> The inhabitants of ground zero ate together in abandoned restau-
> rants and beside piles of putrid garbage, they fell asleep together
> wherever they could, they sobbed and prayed together, and, as they
> became familiar with Lower Manhattan's emerging new landscape,
> they shared directions to working phones and bathrooms that were
> not splattered with vomit. . . . Now and then a body, or some part
> of a body, would emerge, and the firefighters would bag it and be-
> gin the long march to the morgue tent.

In October, Chivers was assigned to cover the war, first from Uzbek-
istan, before slipping into Afghanistan in November. Although he had
never been a war correspondent, he did not feel at any disadvantage.
"It's just journalism," he said. "You go around asking people what
happened. . . . It's no different over there than here. Same stuff. Slightly
worse living conditions. And lighter editing."

The *Times,* to be sure, was not alone in its brilliant 9/11 coverage. The
Washington Post won a Pulitzer Prize for national reporting. The *Wall Street
Journal,* whose headquarters were wrecked by the collapse of the Twin
Towers and whose managing editor, Paul E. Steiger, was briefly missing,
published a newspaper the next day; it won a Pulitzer for breaking-news
reporting. The *Daily News,* a Pulitzer finalist, produced vivid accounts
from Ground Zero, and the *Los Angeles Times* excelled in war coverage.
But among America's newspapers, none matched the reach of the *Times.*

Reporters like Chivers, Barry Bearak, Dexter Filkins, John F. Burns,

David Rhode, and Amy Waldman, from the war region; Judith Miller, William J. Broad, and Stephen Engelberg, on bioterrorism; and Landman and some of his reporters—including Jim Dwyer and the metro columnist Clyde Haberman, who wrote an elegant daily summary of the news, from Ground Zero to Kabul—are just a few of the reasons that the *Times* was celebrated for its coverage of September eleventh and afterward.

Perhaps the most talked-about stories were the short, unsigned biographies of the dead that appeared each day under the rubric "Portraits of Grief." The idea had originated in part with the metro reporter Janny Scott, who was frustrated with an assignment to write about victims when no one would concede that there were any. Scott, who is forty-six, has a rare talent for making other people want to confide in her. She kept expecting to receive a list of victims, but it never came. Her September thirteenth story, co-written with Jane Gross, was about the flyers being handed out on street corners with pictures of the missing. The next morning, Scott headed to the metro section, where she spoke briefly with Landman and two of his deputies, Christine Kay and Susan Edgerley. Scott thought that the families she had interviewed would love to talk about their missing relatives as if they were alive, and she wanted to tell the stories in the voice of the person who told them; Kay suggested that each story focus on a single anecdote.

"Among the Missing" first appeared on September fifteenth—the next day, the title was changed to "Portraits of Grief"—and eventually 110 reporters contributed to 2,100 profiles, none of which carried a byline. "People pull me aside now on the street," Scott said, and tell her how "it really helped them and made them understand things they didn't understand before, made them experience this and recover from it almost, or begin to recover from it, in a way."

The *Times,* wrote William Powers, the media critic for the *National Journal,* "is a magnificent paper," but also "a somewhat cold paper, a lofty institution crippled by its loftiness. . . . It's never been terribly comfortable with real people, or the emotional content of everyday human lives. When I've put the paper down in recent years after a bracing morning read, I've often mused: If only it had a heart. And now it does." He went on to talk about "Portraits of Grief" and how because of it "You could almost feel the paper awakening from its icy trance, realizing that a great obit doesn't require a 'great' life. It requires a belief that all lives are great."

THE AGENDA

The imperatives of September eleventh slowed Raines's agenda but also speeded some changes. Among early casualties were some of his predecessor's appointees. Raines worried that Lelyveld had saddled him with people whom he might not have chosen, such as Nicholas Kristof, the associate managing editor responsible for the Sunday newspaper, the most read paper of the week and the one Raines calls "the key to our national edition." Raines admired Kristof's work as an overseas correspondent (he and his wife, Sheryl WuDunn, shared a Pulitzer Prize in 1990 for their coverage of China) and his profiles of Bush during the 2000 presidential campaign. But Raines and Kristof didn't see things the same way because, Raines felt, their metabolic rates did not match. "What was happening was that weekend stories were ordered up early in the week," says managing editor Boyd. Raines wanted more timely news.

Matters came to a head at a late-October page-one meeting over a story from Pakistan about a deformed woman whom worshipers treated as if she possessed healing powers. Kristof was dubious; he said the piece, by Rick Bragg, was gripping, but he thought that it lacked significance, and he pushed another story for the front page.

"Are you telling me it's too good a story?" Raines asked, his eyes menacing Kristof. "What's wrong with putting on page one a story everyone will talk about?"

The Bragg story ran on the front page that Sunday. A few weeks later, with a nudge from Raines, the publisher gave Kristof a one-year assignment as a twice-weekly international columnist. (In an e-mail, Kristof declined to comment on "internal exchanges.") Raines also reversed Lelyveld's appointment, last summer, of the Los Angeles bureau chief, Todd Purdum, to replace, in due course, Adam Clymer as chief Washington correspondent. Purdum had been one of the newspaper's White House correspondents during the Clinton administration, but Raines thought that he lacked the foreign policy and national security experience required for the new job. He made Purdum the State Department correspondent.

Raines pressed Glenn Kramon, the business editor, to cut down on "soft features" and get more news on the front of the business section. Kramon had been business editor since 1997, and had some sixty reporters at his disposal, the second-largest pool of reporters, after metro. At meetings, Kramon recalled, Raines would badger him to move more quickly, not to wait until they nailed down every last detail of a story, a delay that could give competitors a chance to beat the *Times*. "It's like taking your best shot after the buzzer," Raines said. He was at first so exasperated by Kramon that he thought of replacing him. "He pushed us hard," Kramon said. Raines wanted more news not just from Wall Street but from Hollywood, the fashion world, and the media.

Sometimes Raines imposed his own views on a story. In December, when Gerald Levin announced that he would step down as CEO of AOL Time Warner and that his protégé, Richard Parsons, would replace him, editors were puzzled by the meaning of the move. Suddenly, from one end of the long conference table, Raines asked, "It's obvious, isn't it?"

The others weren't so sure that it was.

"The old company won," Raines said. "That's the story!" The former political reporter, who is proud of being able to anticipate stories, was convinced that Levin and the Time Warner side of the company had won a battle with the AOL side. This editor-driven account appeared the next day, and it upset several business reporters who thought the analysis was simplistic—and wrong.* Perhaps emboldened by the nearly flawless news decisions that he had made since September eleventh, Raines could now halt a conversation by exclaiming, "Isn't this what's really going on?" One senior editor worried that Raines was too opinionated—not in an ideological sense but as an editorial-page editor must be, and in a narrow,

---

*In the end, Raines proved to be correct, as Time Warner people now run the company. Whether he was correct at the time is debatable.

perhaps cynical view of those in power—and that this certitude was going unchallenged.

The 10:30 A.M. masthead meeting became a source of newsroom unhappiness. Soon after the editors walked down what one reporter called "the DMZ staircase" (it separates most of the third-floor newsroom from the area where many of the masthead editors have offices and where the foreign- and national-desk staffs sit in rows), orders would be issued. Katy Roberts, the national editor, recalls getting instructions from Boyd or Rosenthal: "'OK, these are the five stories we want to get done.'" She was not happy with this system, which the newsroom characterized as "top-down management." Roberts said, "Joe Lelyveld always used to say that the best ideas come from reporters. I grew up with that at the paper. . . . And I always believed that was true." She had once worked for Raines on the op-ed page, and they were friendly. But now she complained loudly, sometimes tearfully, about having to undo assignments she had already made.

These complaints did not deter Raines, who knew that laments about intrusive editors were nothing new. In a 1971 memoir, *My Life and the Times*, the former executive editor Turner Catledge describes one of his innovations, the daily 4:30 P.M. meeting, which many editors opposed: "I think some of the editors felt that these daily meetings were a threat to their long-standing autonomy (I certainly regarded them as such)."

In October 2001, the *New York Observer* reported "tensions" between the masthead and the Washington bureau—another seasonal phenomenon at the *Times*. (Tension between Washington and New York was at the center of Gay Talese's majestic 1969 book on the *Times, The Kingdom and the Power*.) In this latest round, Jill Abramson was initially anxious because Michael Gordon and Patrick Tyler were brought in by Raines to enhance her bureau, and because the masthead now included three former Washington bureau chiefs—Raines, Craig R. Whitney, and Oreskes—and a former deputy, Rosenthal. It was well-known that Tyler had been a fishing buddy of Raines's going back to the seventies, when they worked together at the *St. Petersburg Times,* and that Raines had hired him away from the *Washington Post,* in 1990; and many suspected that Raines wanted to install him as bureau chief. Raines says that his hope was to persuade

Abramson eventually "to move to New York as part of the masthead or as a department head." But Abramson had become bureau chief only the previous January, and her son was still in high school. Abramson is a friend of the columnist Maureen Dowd, who had been as close to Raines as any reporter on the paper is; a portrait that Raines once drew of Monica Lewinsky is on her office wall. Dowd laced into Raines for demeaning Abramson.

Raines went out of his way to praise Abramson, and to say that he saw her in a larger role at the paper, and she and Dowd were somewhat mollified. "She's very good at something Howell loves—she is tough," the editorial-page writer Steven Weisman, a Raines friend who has an office in the Washington bureau, said of Abramson. "Hemingway is one of Howell's favorite writers," Weisman went on. "There are Hemingway people and there are Fitzgerald people. Howell is a Hemingway person." So, in this view, is Abramson.

Raines believed that, with Johnny Apple, who is sixty-seven, about to become an associate editor, the paper needed other authoritative voices in Washington; he was sure that Patrick Tyler, at fifty, was his man. Tyler had headed bureaus in Cairo, for the *Washington Post,* and in Moscow and Beijing, for the *Times;* covered the Pentagon and national security and defense for the *Post;* spent a year and a half as a visiting fellow at Stanford; written two books; and briefly hosted a show about Congress for PBS. Other people had serious doubts. "Tyler is an extremely talented guy," someone who has worked closely with him says. "He has a motor and you can hear it purr. He's got raw energy. But is he wise enough?" *Times* reporters pointed out that Tyler had little experience covering the White House, or campaigns, or much politics at all, and whispered that their editor was guilty of cronyism.

In the end, Abramson accepted Tyler's move to Washington, but she did complain that Raines would bypass her and call Tyler about a lead-all. Her greatest frustration came when she and her editors were on the speakerphone to New York, outlining stories they were planning. "It was humiliating," someone who watched this unfold said. "It wasn't 'Jill, what do you have in the Washington report?' It was 'Jill, this is what we think should be in the Washington report.'" Abramson did not dispute the substance of most of the ideas from New York editors; her quarrel was with the "dictatorial style." A Washington friend of Raines's said, "Howell and his people are making the mistake everyone makes. They have this new toy and they are arrogant." The Washington bureau started referring to the masthead as the Taliban, and to Raines as Mullah Omar.

In mid-October, Gerald Boyd flew to Washington for what was to be a relaxed brown-bag lunch in the bureau's conference room. Boyd is a formal man, and an imposing figure, balding, and built like a linebacker. He is meticulously organized. He chews gum, but so slowly that his mustache hardly moves. "The most important thing I do is serve as an adviser to Howell," Boyd said in describing his job. "And by *adviser* I mean someone who tells him the bad and the good news." That day, Boyd said, his mission was to be a "troubleshooter," to "reassure them how valuable they were."

The lunch was a debacle. The staff wanted to know why the best stories were assigned to reporters whom Raines had worked closely with when he ran the bureau, like Tyler. They felt insulted, particularly when Boyd said that the New York editors weren't playing favorites; they were picking the best people. Or when he said that they wanted more Johnny Apple analysis stories, because "no one does it better than Johnny." Eyes darted to Adam Clymer, then sixty-four, who was sitting directly across from Boyd. Although Clymer had the title Washington correspondent, he had not been given a major assignment since September eleventh. In trying to describe the 10:30 A.M. masthead meeting, Boyd kept saying, according to several participants, "We decide."

Boyd was shaken. "The issue of the heavy-handedness was a lot more personal than I certainly realized," he told me. "I didn't defuse it. I probably added to it, which wasn't good." After lunch, Abramson and Boyd walked across the street and sat on a park bench facing the White House. She told Boyd that she felt "disrespected" and said that if there wasn't a change, she would quit. Perhaps it was her invocation of "disrespect" that broke the ice, for the conversation soon became human, that of a black man and a woman connecting on the common ground of what condescension feels like. "That was an important lesson for us," Boyd said. "It was a stylistic issue of how we were operating."

The next day, Raines apologized, told Abramson that she was "a star," and promised to abandon the speakerphone dictates. "I learned several things in that," Raines told me. "I was genuinely taken aback to learn that she was uncomfortable in those speakerphone meetings." And he was reminded that the message he intended to send was not always the message received. The next time they were on the speakerphone, Abramson said she wanted to speak first. The first time the masthead interrupted, she declared, "I'm not finished." When she did finish, Raines and the masthead broke into applause.

By the end of 2001, relations between Washington and New York had become less strained. But Raines remained what Soma Golden Behr admiringly calls "a guy in a hurry. I see a pretty determined guy who sees he has a limited lifetime at the top of this paper. He's not wasting a minute." To other *Times* employees, Behr's "guy in a hurry" was someone who had become a little too eager to show who was in charge.

THE ALABAMAN

Howell Raines's ancestors were farmers who owned neither plantations nor slaves. Many joined the Union Army, and called themselves Lincoln Republicans. They became Roosevelt Democrats during the New Deal. "Herbert Hoover had brought the hillbillies hunger and a firm economic policy," Raines wrote in his book *Fly Fishing Through the Midlife Crisis,* in 1993. "Franklin D. Roosevelt had brought electric lights and the best crappie fishing in the world."

"That outsider mentality influenced me," Raines told me. His father, W. S. (Wattie) Raines, dropped out of school when he was fourteen and went to work in a horse-collar factory, and later as a cabinetmaker for the A&P. Wattie Raines was a handsome man with a storyteller's gift. He met Bertha Walker at church when they were teenagers. Her father was a farmer, a postmaster, and a justice of the peace, and after high school she attended a state teachers' college and taught first grade for a year. They were married in 1929, when they were twenty-two. "She was a country girl who had a sense of style," Raines said. In 1931, their first child, Mary Jo, was born, and two years later their first son, Jerry. The family moved to Birmingham, where, in 1937, Wattie Raines and two of his brothers opened a lumber-and-woodworking business, Raines Brothers.

By the time Howell was born, in 1943, the store-fixture business was thriving. The family did not live on the side of town with the mansions and country clubs; his father built a three-bedroom bungalow on a fifty-foot lot not far from the steel mills. Eventually, they had a nanny, a Cadillac, and cottages on the Gulf in Panama City, Florida, an area that Raines would later popularize as "the Redneck Riviera." Raines had what he calls a "sunny" childhood. He was a good student and a skilled baseball player; he was popular, and was elected vice president of his senior class. He often went fishing with his father.

Because of his mother, he said, he read Hemingway and Steinbeck and his mind first opened to the possibility of being a writer. His father taught him to sympathize with the underdog and to compete hard. Once his Birmingham Little League team played an important game against a rural team, and Howell and his teammates dismissed their opponents as "the rednecks." His dad, who had helped drive the team to the game, pulled Howell aside and admonished, "I want you to remember something: A hungry ballplayer will beat you." That advice, he says, has stayed with him forever. As did something else: a disdain for sloth. He remembers his father sneering, "That man is so lazy it would not be worth the lead it would take to kill him."

Grady Hutchinson, who went to work for the Raines household when she was sixteen and Howell was seven, had a big influence on young Howell. His mother was out during much of the day, his father working, and his teenage siblings at school or with friends, and Grady became a surrogate parent. Howell had curly hair, which he hated, so Grady would heat a straightening comb on the stove and pull it through his hair. He was insecure about his appearance and his height, and she would tell him how good he looked. He wrote stories, and she was full of praise for these efforts. She read him Hemingway's *The Old Man and the Sea.*

Most of all, Grady Hutchinson opened Raines's eyes to race. He was about nine, he wrote in "Grady's Gift," a 1991 article for the *Times Magazine,* when she began to speak to him "of a hidden world about which no one has ever told me, a world as dangerous and foreign, to a white child in a segregated society, as Africa itself." In the magazine piece, which won a Pulitzer Prize, Raines wrote that Grady "taught me the most valuable lesson a writer can learn, which is to try to see—honestly and down to its very center—the world in which we live." He came to see that his hometown, Birmingham, where four young black girls had been killed in a 1963 church bombing, was the true evil heart of segregation. Birmingham was where Raines became imbued with what he called "the choking shame" of racism. To this day, racism remains a simple evil to Raines. (In early May, the *Times* sent Rick Bragg to cover the trial of Bobby Frank Cherry, an ex-Klansman accused of the church bombing; later, Raines himself went. "To paraphrase Faulkner's Dilsey, I saw the first and I wanted to see the last," Raines wrote in an e-mail a few days before Cherry was convicted. "This is a story that I've been living with since my senior year in college and reporting about since 1974." When Bragg had to leave the courtroom, Raines took notes.)

Grady moved up north in 1957, when Howell was fourteen. More than three decades later, in 1994, she returned to Fairfield, just outside Birmingham, to the house her mother had owned. She is sixty-eight, and keeps in touch with Raines by phone and sometimes sees him; she thinks of him "as more like a brother." She told me that when she informed him that she was moving back, "He had my whole house done over—the roof, the kitchen—the whole house. He paid for all of it. . . . He's the best thing that ever happened to me."

Raines graduated from high school in January of 1961 and enrolled at Birmingham-Southern College, just a few blocks from his home. "It was a great stroke of luck for me," he said. "I was able to be a small fish in a small pond, which is what I needed at that time. It had a great English department, and that's where I met Richebourg McWilliams, the most important influence on my life as a writer." It was also the height of the civil rights movement—the time of the Birmingham police chief Bull Connor—but only two of the college's thousand students, Raines recalls, were "brave enough" to demonstrate. (Raines was not one of them.) A mixture of shame and a belief that he was witnessing a momentous event sparked his interest in journalism.

After graduating, in 1964, he planned to attend Florida State's Tallahassee campus, where a graduate teaching assistantship awaited. "My plan was to teach English and write novels," he said, yet he knew that if he pursued a doctorate he would get stuck on a campus. At about that time, a friend told him that the *Birmingham Post-Herald,* the smaller of the two dailies in the city, was hiring reporters. Raines landed a job there, and in November he got his first byline when he volunteered to write a feature story on an Alabama football game. He spent half the game standing behind Bear Bryant, which for him was "like watching John Wayne." In January of 1965, Raines was assigned to cover first the county school board, then Governor George Wallace's visits to Birmingham. Watching Wallace, he says, prompted in him a rage at lying—he "warped an entire society with what he knew as lies."

Later that year, a local TV station, WBRC, offered Raines a job—with a salary increase from $100 to $125 a week—and he accepted. For almost two years, he covered and wrote stories to be read by TV anchors, and wrote documentaries, including one on child abuse. He had joined the National Guard in 1965, when the Vietnam War was starting to escalate, to avoid being drafted. He was ordered to active duty for six months in 1967, a tour that ended his television career.

Then he enrolled in a master's program in English at the University of Alabama. He ran out of money but stayed in school and took a job at the *Tuscaloosa News,* covering city hall. He started work on the same day, in January 1968, as a layout artist named Susan Woodley. She was two and a half years younger, and also from Alabama; she had been reared in Tuscaloosa and had just graduated from Randolph-Macon Woman's College, in Lynchburg, Virginia. At first, she found him odd. What man brought fresh gardenias to the office and placed them on his desk? What southern gentleman asked a woman to come to his apartment on a first date? "He had been trying to get me to go out with him," she recalled. "He wanted me to come to his house and watch *Laugh-In.* I was offended and wouldn't go out with him."

In the spring of 1968, Robert Kennedy was scheduled to speak at the University of Alabama. Raines had something that Susan Woodley wanted: a press pass to the speech. They went on their first date with what newspaper reports say were ten thousand other Alabamans, most of them white, and after that they were inseparable. Raines believed that Kennedy could unseat President Johnson, end the war in Vietnam (which he says he found "misguided from the start"), and fight hard for equal rights. He said he was "a big believer in the possibility of rapid social change." Susan Woodley was struck, she recalled, "with Raines's self-confidence," with "how he didn't have a chip on his shoulder." They were roughly the same height, but to her he seemed taller. Within weeks, two of their heros—Kennedy and Martin Luther King, Jr.—were assassinated. They would be married at her family's home in March of 1969.

They moved to a carriage house on twenty acres in Birmingham; every morning at five o'clock, Raines would go to the screened porch to work on a novel, tentatively titled *The Death of Bluenose Trogdon.* "He had a lot of drive," Susan Raines told me. In the photographs that she took of Raines on their porch or with his fishing gear, one immediately notices his dark, brooding eyes. He had reason to brood: Money was short, particularly when their son Ben was on the way. (He was born in 1970; a second son, Jeff, was born in 1972.) To earn more money, Raines left the newspaper to join the family store-fixture business as a plant foreman.

In late 1970, Raines returned to newspapers, as a reporter on the *Birmingham News.* He stayed just nine months, and then found a job with the *Atlanta Constitution,* whose former editor, Ralph McGill, had dared to denounce segregation; on weekends, he tried to work on the novel. A lover of movies, he became the paper's movie reviewer. At night, he tried to work on his novel, which Susan would type. Nick Taylor covered county government, and they became friends. Whether about movies or politics, recalls Taylor, who today writes books and lives in New York and is president of the Author's Guild, "I do remember he always knew what he thought." When another young reporter, John Huey, joined the *Constitution* in early 1974, he remembers, journalists dreamed of emulating such national icons as Tom Wolfe and Hunter Thompson. To Huey, they were distant figures. "Locally," he says, "Howell stood out. He seemed very mature and undaunted by authority. He was the one management would talk to if they had a problem with the worker bees. And he was a very eloquent writer. He wrote about popular culture in an eloquent way. He always had an air that he had been around—and he hadn't." Raines became the paper's political editor in 1974. Later that year, he was given an advance by Putnam to write an oral history of the civil rights movement. He quit the paper to devote himself to the history and to his novel.

The novel was "turned down by virtually every major house in New York," Raines said. He kept writing and rewriting it. His retirement from journalism was short-lived, and in 1976 he was recruited by another southern newspaper legend, Eugene Patterson, to become the political editor of the *St. Petersburg Times,* where he began his friendship with Patrick Tyler. Raines was determined, however, to be an important novelist, and when, in 1976, Viking bought the novel, for six thousand dollars, he was ecstatic. "We had dreams of living in Europe, and he'd be writing novels and I'd be taking photographs," Susan Raines said.

Both books got good reviews when they were published, in 1977. Of *My Soul Is Rested,* the oral history, Anthony Lewis wrote, in the *Times Book Review,* "No book for a long time has left me so moved or so happy." If this book captured Raines's hopeful, idealistic side, the novel captured his darker side. *Whiskey Man,* as the novel was retitled, is a bleak story about an idealistic young man, Brant Laster, who returns from college to his beloved father and a tiny hill town that he invests with bright hopes and gauzy memories, only to encounter the Snopes-like prejudice of hypocritical preachers and spineless politicians. Its citizens, including his father, live a life of "doubleness," their faces masked by "eyes as flat and unfathomable as poker chips." Late in the novel, Raines's narrator says:

> Then I was back in the car and the car was rolling for home again, down past the church looming skull-like in the darkness, past the graveyard where Bluenose lay in the absolute silence and darkness and time-without-end of that pine box, the smell of the whiskey poured on it already smothered and absorbed by the compact earth.

After a brief moment of savoring his fine reviews and selling paper-back rights to both books, Raines faced reality. It had taken years to finish and publish *Whiskey Man;* no one would advance him the kind of money he wanted for a second novel, and he had a family to support. "Doors always seemed to open for Howell in journalism and not in the literary world," Susan Raines said. He continued his work at the *St. Petersburg Times.*

His writing attracted the notice of editors in New York, among them Bill Kovach and Dave Jones of the *Times.* In 1978, Raines and his wife came to the city and stayed at the Algonquin Hotel. He interviewed with editors at *Time* and at the *Times.* He was at "a fork in the road," feeling a need to choose between rolling the dice on a second novel and entering "the big leagues" of journalism.

Abe Rosenthal, the executive editor of the *Times,* remembers reading Raines's books before his interview and doing "something I rarely did, which is say, 'I want this guy on the paper.' Even before he was inter-viewed. The books were clear and strong, and what interested me was the catholicity of the books. This guy had more than one story."

CHOOSING
JOURNALISM

Raines was hired by the *Times* as a national correspondent, based in Atlanta, and in 1979 was made bureau chief there. During the 1980 presidential campaign, he was drafted by Bill Kovach, the new Washington bureau chief, to cover Reagan, and soon afterward Kovach offered him the White House beat, which he shared with Steven Weisman. Susan Raines, who had become a successful freelance photographer, was not happy to leave Atlanta, but the *Times,* and Howell, came first. Susan counts thirteen moves over the first eleven years of their marriage.

Raines was taken with the Tennessee-born Kovach, who had an open-door policy and brown-bag lunches with the staff each Friday. Once a

year, on the reporter's birthday, he sat with each for a two-hour evalua-
tion. In New York, Abe Rosenthal was respected but feared; in Washington, Kovach was respected and beloved. Kovach was smitten with Raines.
"He was a very gifted writer," he says. "And very smart, and articulate in
his smartness. We had a lot of very smart people at the *New York Times,*
but they were not as methodical in their thought process. His thought
process was as methodical as any lawyer, and as subtle as any psychologist.
When he talked about Reagan's mind he didn't dismiss him as Big Dumb
Dutch or a movie actor. He talked about a quality of mind that was more
than intellect; it included beliefs. . . . He likes politicians because they're
so complex. He loves trying to figure people out." In the Washington bureau, Howell met, for the first time, Arthur Sulzberger, Jr., who was training to one day be publisher—just as his father had trained—and serving
as a reporter in the bureau.

By 1983, Raines was weary of covering the White House—like many
before him in that job, he felt like a stenographer. He was promoted to
national political correspondent, to the great displeasure of the Walter
Mondale campaign, which complained that he dwelled on campaign gaffes;
after Reagan's reelection, Raines became Kovach's deputy. He prided himself on forcing the Washington reporters to "start thinking of their stories
earlier in the day" and to have their thoughts clear by 4:00 P.M., Gerald
Boyd recalled. "His approach to management was meticulous," Kovach
said. "He was meticulous in explaining what needed to be done." It was
in this period that Arthur Sulzberger, Jr., became more aware of Raines.
Sulzberger had admired Raines's stories, but remembers hearing that he
was a "harsh" manager.

Meanwhile, Abe Rosenthal was about to turn sixty-five, the mandatory retirement age for masthead editors at the *Times.* Kovach had hoped
one day to succeed him, but he was thought, even by his friends, to be
too rigid—he didn't want to work overseas, and he found it hard to be
diplomatic with those he held in low regard. After Frankel became the
Times editor, in the fall of 1986, Kovach left the paper to become the editor of the *Atlanta Journal-Constitution.*

When Frankel visited Washington, Raines asked about being appointed
bureau chief. He did so with apprehension because, of all the editors he

had known at the *Times,* Frankel—who, like Rosenthal, had a sweep of experience at the paper—was the only one who made him feel insecure. Raines recalled, "He explained to me patiently and kindly that he was not making me Washington editor because I didn't have foreign experience and was not as deeply experienced in economic issues as I was in national political issues." Frankel offered Raines a choice of three jobs: Paris bureau chief, London bureau chief, or national editor—all plums, but not what Raines wanted. He thought about going to Atlanta with Kovach, and that night he talked about his options with Johnny Apple. Apple, who had been London bureau chief for ten years, recalled telling Raines that from London he could "write about anything," and could move around Europe. There was another, social advantage: The Sulzberger family passed through London regularly; Raines would get to know everyone who mattered to his career. "He's a man of intense, if not always acknowledged, ambition," Apple said of Raines.

Raines told Frankel that he would accept the London job. Yet he was not happy; he had given up fiction, although he continued to imagine a literary career for himself, and, at the same time, he fretted that his journalistic career had been sidetracked. He was forty-three. He needed to learn a new skill—foreign correspondence. Susan Raines had been working in a gallery in Washington and was thriving, and now she imagined having to become a London hostess. She was miserable; the marriage was fragile. Raines describes his mood at the time as one of "generalized restlessness . . . a general sense of life passing and one not having great joy." In many ways, his work in London reflected his ennui.

Senior people at the paper say they cannot remember a single memorable story that Raines did from overseas. Joe Lelyveld, who was then the foreign editor, told friends, "I did not lean on him. He was a little bruised." However, Raines had not given up hope of one day moving up the masthead. He had spent time with the Sulzbergers on their visits, and Philip Taubman, who had worked alongside Raines in Washington and had become Moscow bureau chief, kept in touch. Over a long lunch in London, where Taubman was on vacation, they discussed their careers. "We sort of agreed at that lunch that we'd try and work together if it worked out that we became editors," Taubman recalled. "He was very confident in declaring, 'I'm going to be an editor here and I want to find like-minded colleagues.'"

Perhaps Raines knew by then that Frankel's choice to run the Washington bureau, Craig Whitney, assisted by deputies Judith Miller and Johnny Apple, was not working out. Among Whitney's first acts was to suddenly announce that he was transferring six senior staffers from the bureau. "I made too many moves too fast. It caused morale problems," admits Whitney. In addition, he lacked a feel for politics, and Miller lacked a feel for managing other people. "Craig had no eyes in the back of his head," observes Apple, "and Judy had too many eyes." What he left out was that he himself was usually blind to everything but his own writing. After Raines had been in London less than two years, Frankel asked if he would like to trade jobs with Whitney. In July of 1988, the Raineses returned to Washington, where the bureau welcomed him.

The marriage, however, did not survive. In *Fly Fishing Through the Midlife Crisis,* Raines wrote of reaching a time of "a largely unspoken sense of finality and divergence." He added, "The winding down of any long marriage is a complicated story and a sad one, too, if the marriage has been a very good one for a very long time." Susan eventually remarried, and today is friendly with her former husband; he called her just before his appointment as executive editor was announced, she told me, and said that he "could never have done it without me." (The Raines children are married; Ben is a reporter at the *Mobile Register,* in Alabama, and Jeff plays guitar and composes for the funk band Galactic.)

Raines pushed the staff in Washington. "Howell came in and energized a lot of the reporters who needed it," the columnist William Safire, who is an avuncular presence in the bureau, recalled. He made unusual assignments. Andy Rosenthal, who had worked for the AP in Moscow and covered politics in Washington, was assigned the Pentagon. "I don't know anything about the Pentagon," Rosenthal remembers protesting.

"That's why I'm putting you on the Pentagon!"

Raines wanted an outsider there, a fresh set of eyes. "It was a great idea, except I sucked at it," says Rosenthal. It seemed that at every interview he attended, the brass asked whether he had served in Vietnam. One day Raines told his staff he needed someone to cover the economy who knew politics. David Rosenbaum got the assignment and still marvels that Raines granted him three months to study economics. Raines had an ability to see around corners, an instinct for the real story. In 1991, he summoned reporter Maureen Dowd to his office and told her to check whether the Senate Judiciary Committee's brusque questioning of Anita Hill during the Clarence Thomas confirmation hearings was detonating female rage. When she wrote it and was celebrated for spotting the story "with a woman's eyes," she laughed. Years later she wrote, "Howell saw it with his good ole boy eyes."

But there were complaints. Taubman, who became Raines's deputy in Washington and is now the deputy editor of the editorial page, recalls that Raines "had a management style that was very hard driving." One embarrassing story, often told, is that Raines once asked a news clerk to take his plants outside so they could get "natural rainwater." It was, Raines says today, "a mistake in judgment that I never repeated."

The biggest complaint was that he had a coterie of pals, and saved the best assignments for them. They would congregate in a part of the newsroom that became known as Happy Valley, and others felt ostracized. At one staff lunch, Raines spoke of his A team and his B team, one participant recalled. "Some of the real talents in the bureau were not realized because they were not encouraged," he said. "I'm all for putting the best people on stories." It was only after Raines left that people like Michael Wines and David Johnston, whom Raines had pigeonholed as members of the B team, began to stand out. At the same time, Raines succeeded in ways that others hadn't; during his four years as bureau chief, there was less second-guessing from New York, and a universal sense that the *Times* was more than holding its own against the *Washington Post.*

By 1992, Raines was ready to move on. Arthur Sulzberger, Jr., had recently been named publisher, succeeding his father, and that spring Raines told him that the op-ed page needed a liberal columnist in Washington, to counterbalance Safire. "Arthur Jr. found Raines beguiling," Susan E. Tifft and Alex S. Jones recounted in *The Trust,* their authoritative 1999 history of the *Times* dynasty. Raines was "a kindred spirit: a contrarian whose values had taken shape during the sixties, who viewed the world as a moral battleground." Sulzberger wanted the editorial page to speak with his voice—a more pointed, less old-fashioned voice—and, when Raines suggested the column, Sulzberger made a counterproposal: become editorial-page editor, succeeding Jack Rosenthal. "It was a leap," Sulzberger said. "But I knew we needed passion."

Raines did not jump. "I had never thought about that," he told Sulzberger.

"Why don't you think about it?" the publisher replied.

When they talked later that summer, Raines was surprised that the publisher didn't ask about his views on the issues of the day. Sulzberger felt no need to. He knew that Raines, like him, took liberal positions on affirmative action, capital punishment, abortion rights, health insurance, welfare, the environment, and the role of an activist government. Sulzberger said that he saw the editorial-page editor and the executive editor as partners in the *Times*'s future. They would have lunch every Wednesday; they would discuss business as well as editorial policy. Although Raines knew that he would become what he calls "a staff officer," commanding not an army of correspondents but a platoon of fourteen editorial writers and thirty staffers, he also knew what awaited him if he said no. "The next hierarchical move for me would have been to be an assistant managing editor," he said, a position that would have diminished his chance of ever becoming executive editor or managing editor when Max Frankel retired. "I felt that he wouldn't offer me that kind of job unless he saw me as a potential executive editor," Raines said. He knew that Frankel, too, had been editorial-page editor before moving to the top newsroom job.

Raines would not take over until January of 1993, but, as he thought about filling the new post, he grandiosely chose a president as his model: Harry Truman. "I was probably more influenced by Harry Truman than by anyone else," Raines told me. "Truman wanted to find a one-armed economist so he wouldn't say, 'On the one hand, on the other hand.'" Nor did Raines believe in using precious space to outline opposing views. "My view was, let's use our space to make our arguments," he said.

Raines's politics were formed, as Tifft and Jones suggest, by the sixties, and also by his upbringing. He was proud of his own populism; in *Fly Fishing,* he wrote bitterly about "reporting on President Reagan's success in making life harder for citizens who were not born rich, white and healthy"—as if Raines himself had not been born in all three categories. Over the next eight and a half years, he used the editorial page to rail against favorite targets: what he saw as a corruption of politics by money; the despoiling of the environment by oil and gas interests; the poor treatment of the less fortunate by HMOs and insurance companies; the excesses of corporate America. Raines was certainly not antibusiness—he grew up in a businessman's family and works for a company whose profits are essential to the well-being of its employees. But he was quick to attack what he saw as predatory practices or, in the case of Microsoft, monopolistic practices—all very much in the liberal tradition. He could also be provocative, as when, in a signed piece, he scolded the filmmaker Oliver Stone for inventing history and, in *JFK*, for making a hero out of the New Orleans district attorney, Jim Garrison, who had accused the CIA of complicity in the Kennedy assassination. What was startling was that the *Times*'s editorial-page editor went on to suggest another, "more likely" conspiracy theory: that the Mafia, not the CIA, may have been behind the murder.

In the past, the *Times* editorial page had been criticized for being too predictable, too fastidious. Raines's critics now found it becoming too shrill, particularly in its portrayal of the Clinton administration, which Raines saw as ethically lax and politically corrupt, an enormous disappointment of early hopes. One member of the editorial board says that Raines showed more "rage" toward Clinton's obfuscations and outright lies than he did "toward genocide." Officials in the Clinton White House were furious; they thought that Raines was jealous or resentful of fellow southerners who succeeded as Clinton had. Raines said, "It was always surprising to me the degree to which the Clinton people saw things in personal terms"—an odd observation, since Raines had changed the tone at the *Times* but still expected the editorial page to be treated as if it maintained a detached voice.

If there is a common theme in Raines's commentaries—and his politics—it is a detestation of hypocrisy and lying, even in matters of lesser moment, such as a 1998 commentary, signed by Raines, in which he attacked the *Boston Globe* columnist Mike Barnicle for plagiarism, and then the *Globe* (which is owned by the *Times*) for not firing Barnicle at once.

The commentary Raines is proudest of was an unsigned piece in 1995 on former Secretary of Defense Robert McNamara and his book *In Retrospect,* in which he confessed to maintaining silence about his deep misgivings while sending Americans to die in the Vietnam War. Raines wrote:

> His regret cannot be huge enough to balance the books for our dead soldiers. The ghosts of those unlived lives circle close around Mr. McNamara. Surely he must in every quiet and prosperous moment hear the ceaseless whispers of those poor boys in the infantry, dying in the tall grass, platoon by platoon, for no purpose. What he took from them cannot be repaid by prime-time apology and stale tears, three decades late.

Steven Weisman said that Raines "loved making a statement and standing up for the dead, for the people he grew up with. It was a great reflection of who he is. When you strip away all the layers of civility and graciousness, you get to his unforgiving soul, particularly about race and class."

On the tenth floor of the Times Building, where the editorial offices circle a quiet library, Raines nurtured a happy family. During his tenure, he replaced half the editorial board, and hired several women, including Tina Rosenberg, who won a Pulitzer for her 1995 book, *The Haunted Ground;* Eleanor Randolph, who had been a reporter with the *Washington Post* and the *Los Angeles Times;* and Gail Collins. In thrice weekly editorial meetings, said Gail Collins, whom he hired to write editorials and later helped promote to columnist, "He was unusually good at explaining things and how his own mind was working and how he got to things. . . . Editors in general, and people who go into journalism, are mainly people who don't want to interact. They want to watch. They tend to be shy and not center stage people. The surprising thing about Howell was that he had a real star presence or charisma." Brent Staples, who joined the board under Jack Rosenthal and stayed on with Raines and is today the only black member, said, "You never came away from a conversation with him feeling he played you cheap or he didn't respect your intelligence. Whether you wanted something or you argued with him, you came away feeling you'd been heard." Eleanor Randolph first met Raines when she covered the 1976 Jimmy Carter campaign for the *Los Angeles Times,* and kept in touch when she worked for Ben Bradlee at the *Washington Post.* Raines hired her to join the editorial board and she said, "He's very demanding. I loved working for him. You had to do your absolute best. He's a lot like Ben Bradlee in that way."

The most important audience, of course, was the publisher, and he was pleased with Raines's tenure. "There's a relentlessness about Howell that I admire," Sulzberger told me. "On the editorial page, he just wouldn't let Clinton off the hook. I would argue that he should not have." Sulzberger, who in 1997 succeeded his father as chairman of the company, hastened to add, "That is not a rap on Max or Jack, but I think what we saw with the editorial page under Howell is a ratcheting up of its level of staking out clearly defined ground"—of stating its views without a lot of shading. Sulzberger says he sometimes looked at draft editorials and maybe, once a month or so, "made suggestions." The publisher is being too modest, several members of the editorial board say. "Arthur sometimes edited our pieces and Howell never told us," one board member says, not in anger but in appreciation for Raines's diplomacy.

THE
COMPETITION

Raines's relationship with Joseph Lelyveld, who in July of 1994 succeeded Frankel as executive editor, was ostensibly smooth. Sulzberger told people he trusted that during seven years of Wednesday lunches, or at *Times* retreats and meetings, he never witnessed tension between them. Nor, he said, did either ever lobby him about the other. Raines and Lelyveld were aligned on certain issues, particularly against those on the business side who wanted to spin off the *Times*'s news Web site as a stand-alone company.

They agreed that such a move could undermine the paper's journalistic standards. At one *Times* retreat, Lelyveld invited Raines to spend the night at his weekend home, in Ulster County, New York.

But the relationship was never more than polite. When Frankel had announced, in early 1994, that he would step down a year before the mandatory retirement age, Raines partisans believed he did so to block Raines. They reason that Frankel, by leaving early—and little more than a year after Raines had moved to New York from Washington—made sure that his deputy, Lelyveld, would follow him. After Lelyveld was selected, he invited Raines to discuss the number-two job in the newsroom, the managing editorship. Corporate etiquette demanded the meeting, but it was an awkward encounter. Lelyveld had little interest in selecting Raines, and Raines had no interest in working under Lelyveld. "I had only been editorial-page editor for a year and a half," Raines said. "Also, if I came downstairs at the start of Joe's editorship, it would be unlikely that I would succeed him. You can pick up a lot of scar tissue in these jobs."

Lelyveld surprised the newsroom with his choice for managing editor: Gene Roberts, a retired *Philadelphia Inquirer* executive editor and a former *Times* national editor, who was sixty-one. In some ways, Roberts helped to crystallize the different management approaches of Raines and Lelyveld, who saw the masthead as Roberts did—as, in Roberts's word, "bureaucrats." Roberts added, "The whole point of Joe's administration, since Joe spent his life as a reporter there, was to keep his reporters from getting swallowed up by the bureaucracy and from getting second-guessed." Roberts and Lelyveld believed the only editors on the masthead that mattered to reporters and their line editors were the two at the top, and Roberts was particularly zealous. Under them, and to a somewhat lesser extent when Keller replaced Roberts in 1997, most masthead editors were miserable. They used to sit in a long row of desks behind what was disparaged as "the blue wall." Lelyveld treated it as if it were the Berlin Wall, and had it torn down, awarding chunks of it to those who worked in the newsroom. "I was a bad guy," remembers Al Siegal, who joined the paper in 1960 and was a powerful arbiter of what appeared on page one under Abe Rosenthal and Max Frankel. "I felt less gainfully employed under Joe than under Max."

Raines believed that the experience of the masthead should be tapped and that two people alone could not coordinate the various departments of the *New York Times*. In 1999, the *Times* embarrassed itself with a series of accusatory stories suggesting that a Los Alamos nuclear scientist, Wen Ho Lee, may have spied for China—coverage that eventually led to a long and mystifying editor's note. Raines told friends that many of the *Times*'s reporting mistakes sprang from infighting between the Washington bureau and the science desk. Washington believed that Lee was guilty; the science reporters were dubious—and, Raines thought, no one on the masthead adjudicated. (Raines's editorial page assumed that Lee was guilty.)

Lelyveld left a distinguished legacy. He resisted salacious stories about President Clinton's sex life. He hired strong reporters, and deployed an army of reporters to provide illuminating coverage of, among many stories, the Florida recount after the 2000 presidential election. But the differences between Lelyveld and Raines were substantive, and reflected two distinct personalities. Lelyveld wanted to publish longer pieces, one of his major efforts being a yearlong reporting project that involved more than fifty people and produced a fifteen-part series, "How Race Is Lived in America," in 2000, which won a Pulitzer; he pushed for what he called "not-a-today story." Raines also wanted long pieces, but above all he wanted them to trigger news. In political coverage, Lelyveld put more emphasis on the words of the candidates and the opinions of voters; he was less interested than Raines was in tactics and drama. Raines believed that Lelyveld's approach to political reporting missed the Florentine flavor of politics, as captured in the LBJ photo montage displayed in his office. The assistant managing editor, Andrew Rosenthal, probably reflected Raines's view when he said, "I may regret saying this—I don't want to come off as critical of Joe—but the Gore campaign was profoundly hurt by a series of small stupid lies, and you won't find them in the *New York Times*."

Lelyveld was a rabbi's son, a man more comfortable playing the rabbinical role of observer. He would never bluster, as the *Yale Daily News* reported after Raines spoke at Yale in 1995, "We should not give up on cynicism. Inquiry is our business, not cheerleading." (He later repeated the same thought to Cynthia Cotts of the *Village Voice*, who was in the

Yale audience and wrote of visiting him at the *Times.*) Lelyveld would have substituted a more neutral noun—*skepticism,* say. As an editor, Lelyveld's friends believe that he thought Raines was too passionate, too *hot;* Raines thought Lelyveld was too diffident, too *cool.*

For seven years, Raines and Lelyveld coexisted on their separate floors. Johnny Apple, who was friendly with both men, remembers that when he returned from the trip to South Africa with Raines, in 1995, Lelyveld "was very frosty to me."

"What's the matter with you?" Apple asked.

"I hear you were in South Africa," Lelyveld replied.

"That said to me that surely it was more than that I didn't call him," Apple observes. Lelyveld, who won a Pulitzer in 1986 for a book about South Africa, where he reported for the *Times,* may have been miffed at not being consulted about the trip, particularly since it was paid for out of his news budget. Lelyveld told some people that what annoyed him was "a Johnny Apple holiday dressed up as a reporting trip."

Apple can't explain the roots of the tension between two men he admires and feels close to. "I could never get either of them to confide in me," he said.

In the spring of 2001, Sulzberger invited Raines to dinner at Aquavit, a midtown restaurant that the publisher likes for its Scandinavian fare and a waterfall that prevents eavesdropping. Sulzberger had earlier tipped off Raines that Lelyveld had decided to retire in the fall, about six months before the mandatory age, and that Raines was a prime candidate to replace him. Now Sulzberger wanted to hear what Raines might do as editor.

Raines knew that his principal competitor was Bill Keller, the managing editor since 1997. Lelyveld had been best man at Keller's recent wedding, and Raines suspected that Lelyveld would champion his protégé's candidacy.

"The center of my plan for the paper," Raines told the publisher, "is to grow the national edition as our main vehicle for the future of the print paper . . . and also to move from passive to active cooperation in terms of extending our kind of quality journalism across digital, cable, and broadcast platforms"—from print to the *Times* Web site to television to radio. Raines knew that 87 percent of the paper's display-advertising revenue was coming from full-run national advertising, compared with just 34 percent in 1996. He also knew that the *Times* was far ahead of its ten-year goal to boost daily circulation by 250,000 and Sunday's by 300,000. And he knew that the Times Company owned seventeen daily newspapers, including the *Boston Globe,* eight TV stations in midsized markets, and two radio stations.

Raines saw the job as a management challenge, an assessment that appealed to Sulzberger. "I also felt that I would bring a style of closer personal engagement and interaction with the staff," Raines said. Above all, Raines concluded, his main task, like that of every previous executive editor, would be the "stewardship" of a great newspaper. He thought it could be a greater newspaper. He would be a reform agent.

Keller represented continuity. When he met with Sulzberger, he spoke of continuing what he and Lelyveld had started: a horizontal style of management that would reduce the size of the masthead and grant clear responsibilities to those who remained. Keller spoke of wanting a happy newsroom, and of expanding coverage of popular culture and the media. Sulzberger later confided to Lelyveld that, though he admired Keller as a newsman, he did not feel close to him. Lelyveld understood that Raines and Sulzberger had clicked on a personal level.

By May, Janet Robinson, the newspaper's president, whose office on the fourteenth floor is just down the corridor from Sulzberger's, had decided to support Raines, and told the publisher so. In addition to Robinson and Lelyveld, Sulzberger consulted his father, Arthur (Punch) Sulzberger, Sr.; his wife, Gail Gregg, an artist and a former journalist; his Times Company CEO, Russell Lewis; "one or two friends," including his 5:45 A.M. gym partner, the investment banker and former *Times* reporter Steven Rattner; and some members of the masthead. Sulzberger says he was so vexed by the choice that "I threw my back out" and took to bed. It was probably less difficult than he lets on. All along, Keller believed, and told friends, that Raines had the advantage.

"I chose Howell in the end because I decided we needed a new pair of eyes," Sulzberger told me recently. "Joe really had made Bill his partner. That's a good thing. And while Bill did lay out a vision for what the newsroom would be under him—and how it would differ—I thought the time was right for a different step. . . . Any organization needs change to continue to improve, and that's part of my job, to assure that this organization has regular change."

Raines's age was also an advantage. At fifty-eight—six years older than Keller—he could serve no more than seven years. Sulzberger believed that the last editor to stay more than a decade, Abe Rosenthal, had become too authoritarian, especially at the end. He knew that he could select Raines and still consider Keller—or Gerald Boyd, Andrew Rosenthal (who is Abe Rosenthal's son), Michael Oreskes, Jon Landman, or Jill Abramson—down the road.

After Raines's appointment was announced, in May of 2001, Apple and his wife, Betsey, invited the Lelyvelds and Raines and Krystyna Stachowiak to dinner at Esca, an Italian seafood restaurant near the Times Building. There were a few jokes, Apple recalls, but mostly there were awkward silences. "It was clear to me that they found it difficult to be together in such a small group after all these years," Apple said.

COURSE CORRECTIONS

By January of 2002, colleagues were used to seeing Raines, wearing a hat, enter the Times Building around 10:00 A.M., taking furious little steps up to the conference room on the fourth floor. Everyone had heard a Bear Bryant story, or his favorite exhortation: "Let's commit some journalism here!" Many had tried to peer into the two narrow glass panels of his office to see if he was at his desk; he rarely wandered around the newsroom. Sometimes, at the end of the day, editors, and occasionally reporters, were invited into the small room behind his office to share a drink—preferably bourbon, scotch, or gin. This practice, along with Raines's frequent sports and military references, had begun to make some women in the newsroom uncomfortable. "I'm not sure who Bear Bryant is, but I guess I have to learn," laughs Assistant Managing Editor Soma Golden Behr, who would prefer a glass of wine but says she still has "a great talk" every time she goes back there.

Raines believes that January marked the real beginning of his new job—when he could concentrate on his agenda at the paper. Joe Lelyveld enjoys high culture—opera, concerts, recitals—and he had the like-minded John Rockwell edit the Sunday Arts & Leisure section. Under Raines, the newsroom began to notice a greater emphasis on popular culture and lifestyle. An early hint of this change had come in December, when Rockwell was encouraged to step down. Rockwell is a gifted writer—and a former rock critic—but there was broad support in the newsroom for a section more balanced between high culture and popular culture. Even so, there was concern about Raines's tastes. "What makes the *Times* distinctive is foreign news, and cultural news," one senior editor says. "That's what people outside New York find missing from their own local newspapers." This editor worried that in its quest for a national audience, the *Times,* like the television networks, could end up making marketing-driven decisions.

The newsroom took notice of a page-one Botox story by Kuczynski, which followed by a week her page-one story about supermodels attending exclusive parties at the World Economic Forum. The Botox story described the cosmetic injections that erase both wrinkles and facial expressions. When it was first offered up as a page-one candidate by a female editor, recalls another female editor, there was "a surreal" scene. "Every man at the table was asking the most stupid questions. Alex's piece was great. But the women at the table"—usually at the noon and the 4:30 P.M. daily meetings about a dozen of the thirty or so editors are female—"were rolling our eyes. One question was, 'Do you get this done in a doctor's office?' It was almost a parody of a clueless discussion." The story placed Botox in a larger context—noting how more than one million Americans had the procedure in 2000, a number expected to grow by up to 50 percent in the next year, and how the drug was enriching pharmaceutical companies and preventing actresses over thirty-five from looking angry in movies. Being on page one, says Kuczynski, "is what being a journalist is all about. It's the most influential place to be." But there was audible snickering in the newsroom about how Raines was "sociologizing" stories onto page one, a complaint that had also been lodged when Abe Rosenthal fronted a story about pickles or Max Frankel a story about rising hemlines.

The newsroom took notice as well of the "flood the zone" coverage the *Times* gave to the contretemps between Lawrence H. Summers, the new president of Harvard, and the black studies department. Page-one stories told readers: *Professor Cornel West was insulted. He may leave. Was Harvard still committed to affirmative action?* When K. Anthony Appiah decided to leave, the *Times* headline above the fold on page one screamed: A HARVARD STAR IN BLACK STUDIES JOINS PRINCETON. The story placed Appiah's departure in the context of the dispute, even though the story quoted Professor Appiah insisting that he was leaving not "because he shared Dr. West's complaints" but because he was "tired of commuting weekly to Cambridge" from his New York City home. A few days later, when Harvard lured a prominent University of Chicago professor to join its program, the relatively brief story appeared on page sixteen. (When it was announced in mid-April that West was moving to Princeton, the *Times* splashed the story on page one.)

The suspicion spread: The way Raines played the Cornel West story suggested that he, and Sulzberger, were allowing their own views to intrude, particularly on racial matters. This notion gathered force within the *Times* after the March fifteenth page-one meeting. At this meeting, Jon Landman, the metro editor, proposed running on page one an exclusive story by David Kocieniewski about the controversial findings of a state-sponsored study in New Jersey concluding that black drivers are more likely to speed. The story cited testimony that racial profiling was real, but it added a level of complexity to the familiar narrative: Black drivers, the study reported, are stopped for speeding in disproportionate numbers because they are far more likely to speed than other drivers. Raines said that he was troubled that the *Times* did not have the actual study (though the newspaper has often published accounts of studies it hasn't seen), and after the meeting he stopped by Gerald Boyd's office to say that he had other problems with the story; he believed, as federal officials did, that the study's methodology was flawed, and he worried that the newspaper was being "spun."

By 8:30 P.M., Boyd reported back that there were, indeed, flaws in the story and that it would be put on hold. The exclusive did not appear for six days, or until March twenty-first, and then not on page one but on the first page of the metro section. I asked Landman if Raines was being politically correct by holding the story. Landman wouldn't answer. "You'll have to draw your own conclusions," he said.

Despite this obvious disagreement, Raines was enthusiastic about Landman and his metro staff; he did not feel that way about the national staff. To capture what Raines called "the pulse" of a region and the nation, he wanted reporters in the ten domestic bureaus to travel more. He saw a business reason for mobility as well. If the national edition was to grow, the paper needed more bylines from more places. Raines was frustrated with particular bureaus, especially Los Angeles, because he considered its coverage of Hollywood to be soft. By the spring, Raines had appointed a new L.A. bureau chief—John Broder—and added to the bureau one of his "stars," metro reporter, Charlie LeDuff.

This conflict with the national staff came to a head over Kevin Sack. Traditionally, bureau chiefs were rotated every three to five years. Kevin Sack, however, the Atlanta bureau chief, had been in his post for five years, and in the bureau for almost seven, and wanted to remain in the city. A popular, respected reporter, Sack had been hired away from the *Atlanta Constitution* twelve years earlier, partly on the say-so of Raines. Sack's byline graced the first of the fifteen stories of the Race in America series. When Raines, Gerald Boyd, and Katie Roberts had dinner in August with Sack and his deputy, David Firestone, and three other southern correspondents who flew in, they were put on notice that editors wanted them to be more mobile. Privately, before dinner Sack told Raines he couldn't move. He had just gone through a messy divorce and had an eight-year-old daughter whom he got to see only one night a week and every other weekend. The *Times* under Lelyveld had been sensitive to his plight and let him stay on. Sack was willing to give up the bureau-chief job, but asked to stay in Atlanta, perhaps until his daughter graduated from high school, in about ten years. Raines said that he thought the paper had made too many private deals, that fairness required him to rotate bureau chiefs and others so that promotion opportunities were available to less senior reporters. He and Lelyveld agreed on this point. The matter was not resolved then, and was placed on a back burner after 9/11.

Sack returned to a front burner in January, when Washington bureau chief Jill Abramson flew to Atlanta and over dinner made what Sack told friends was "a great job" offer. He would move to Washington and write political profiles off the news, and would back up the chief political correspondent, Richard Berke. Further, Abramson recalls, "I told him this was a big enough place that if he plans to go to Atlanta for the weekend, we would find someone to cover for him. I all but gave him a certain pledge that we could." He heard: *Maybe* they could. He said he dreaded not just giving up his weekly visit, but flying to Atlanta every other weekend and having his daughter stay in a hotel room. After mulling it over for a few days, Sack declined the offer. He sent Boyd an e-mail explanation, and said he would love to stay at the paper but he really needed clarity. Boyd sent back a brusque e-mail that said his next assignment would not be in Atlanta. Sack phoned, and Boyd said they could grant him four to six weeks to find another job.

Kevin Sack began looking around for other newspaper jobs, and as he did, word of his predicament traveled through the newsroom like a brushfire. Although the newsroom is populated by reporters, often facts do not intrude on their opinions. Few knew that Sack had been offered a very good job in Washington, with a pledge to be able to take off every second weekend. Few knew this was not an abrupt decision and that Raines had his first conversation with Sack in August. Nor did they know Sack might want to stay in Atlanta another ten years. Outrage filled the newsroom. Reporters who agreed with Raines that the rotation of correspondents was only fair nevertheless fretted that the *Times* was becoming unfriendly to families, that Raines didn't want to hear about a son's birthday or a daughter's soccer game, that he was Napoleonic, that senior people were getting pushed out to pasture, that Raines and Boyd were macho men. An outpouring of sympathetic letters and e-mails from *Times* colleagues cheered Sack.

One "star" correspondent thought the way Raines handled the Sack situation served as the perfect anecdote to summarize his own confused feelings about the new editor: "You can make an argument that he gave Kevin fair warning and that we need beefing up in our national bureaus, and people shouldn't have jobs forever. A lot of what Howell wants is good. The danger is how you go about it. That was the question when he was Washington bureau chief, too. Does he have enough heart?" Fortunately, this reporter has more clarity when writing his own stories.

"I don't want to burn any bridges at a place I love," Kevin Sack said into the phone when contacted in mid-February. He had not spoken to Raines since August, but he was determined not to fuel the controversy by granting an interview. Raines did reach out to him later that month, did praise his work to editors at the *Boston Globe* and the *Los Angeles Times*. "I told him," says Raines, "we'll keep a candle in the window for you." The problem is that the newsroom didn't hear any of this. Raines's real message, one editor said, was that there are no special deals, but "the message received was 'Nobody's safe.'" In April, Kevin Sack joined the *Los Angeles Times* as a national correspondent. "They'll allow me to stay in Atlanta indefinitely," he said.*

NO ONE NEEDS MORE TLC, or loves to complain more, than reporters. They moan when they don't make page one, when their copy is altered or cut, when they don't like an assignment, when a colleague gets a better one, or when they believe they are being lied to. Perhaps only those on welfare nurse a greater sense of grievance. To those outside the paper, they are kings, makers or breakers of reputations. Governors and mayors and White House staffers break appointments to bend a reporter's ear. Inside the paper, most are grunts, the ground troops editors send to cover stories. Editors are usually brusque with them, and reporters get to speak to the executive editor about as often as a White House correspondent for the *Tuscaloosa News* speaks to the president. The disparity between a reporter's reception outside and inside the paper helps fuel the anxiety found in any newsroom. Couple this with unforgiving deadlines, and

*Kevin Sack would, in April of 2003, win a Pulitzer Prize.

newsrooms can be pretty grim. Sure, there are lots of laughs, pranks, shared memories, and affairs. But as a general rule, newsrooms are wary precincts.

During the day, reporters' eyes anxiously follow editors in and out of their offices, up and down stairs, noticing when they enter and leave. Ben Bradlee, when he was the executive editor of the *Washington Post,* used to walk around the newsroom and call out, "Morale check, morale check!" He remembered, "I'd see two guys talking, and you wanted to know what the hell they were talking about. Sometimes you waited until the third guy joined them, because the two guys may be talking about you. You got to know what they're talking about. An editor is a lot like a coach. You wouldn't coach the football team without knowing that your guard is not talking to your tackle."

At the *Times,* the executive editor—including Howell Raines—rarely bounced around the newsroom like Bradlee. The only time he ever sees masthead editors cross the DMZ staircase and enter the third-floor metro section, says a senior metro reporter, "is when they want to look outside to see if it's raining." To induce reporters to look up from the desks, Abe Rosenthal once hired the New York State Police Band to march through the newsroom. "People looked up who I hadn't seen in ten years!" Rosenthal recalls. "I shocked everybody, which I wanted to do. It certainly woke them up!"

By late this winter, the anxiety level at the *Times* had grown. "There is enormous resentment, the likes of which I've never seen," someone who's been at the paper for thirty years told me. Perhaps not since Abe Rosenthal's last years had the din of newsroom complaint been as loud. Reporters joked that Raines "was southern-fried Abe." Arthur Gelb, who has just completed *City Room,* a memoir of more than fifty years at the *Times,* observes that every *Times* editor is criticized by the newsroom. When Gelb started at the paper, in 1944, as a nineteen-year-old copyboy, the complaint about the first top editor he knew, Edwin L. James, "was that he wasn't accessible and hid in his office so he didn't have to give raises. Next was Turner Catledge, and the complaint was that he was away from the office a lot. Next was Clifton Daniel, and the complaint was that he was haughty. Then came Scotty Reston, who people thought was pontifical. Then came Abe. He was thought to be too demanding. Then Max was perceived as too theoretical and not impulsive enough in jumping on news. Joe was perceived as too aloof. Now Howell is perceived as moving too fast. The pendulum is that you're either too tough and enthusiastic or too laid back and unenthusiastic."

Jon Landman, who respects Raines and the energy he has brought to the newsroom, is among those who were sometimes uneasy with the peremptory tone of the masthead's edicts to section editors. Landman is popular and respected because he is unafraid to speak his mind; Bill Keller has said that if he had been made executive editor, he probably would have picked Landman as his managing editor. Landman is also respected by Raines, for whom he worked in the Washington bureau. "There is nothing wrong with the executive editor having story ideas," Landman told me. "The problem is when these story ideas become commands and overwhelm everything else. . . . There's a feeling of a one-way windstorm." He worried that reporters and editors would become "tentative."

By late February, there was concern that Raines was trying to shake up a great institution so vigorously that he might damage it. "How hard can you shake it before it cracks?" one experienced correspondent asked. Every time Raines talked about speeding up "the metabolism" of the paper and attacking "complacency," many staff members felt they were under assault. Landman, like many others, interpreted Raines's comments as suggesting that the *Times* was somehow broken and needed to be fixed. "When you use phrases like 'metabolism' and 'complacency,' it's unmistakable," he said. Landman believed that the *Times* was a greater paper last year than it had been the year before, or the year before that. What many in the newsroom heard, he said, "was assaultive. It sounded contemptuous"—not, he thinks, the message Raines meant to send.

Word even filtered up to the fourteenth floor, to Sulzberger, who joked to friends, "I'm hearing 'Abe's back'!" Not that Sulzberger was displeased. When he became publisher, in 1992, he felt that a cultural revolution was needed at the *Times,* and he held retreats to advance his cause. "Any executive or manager has only two drawers in his desk," Sulzberger says. "One says 'Centralize,' and the other says 'Decentralize.' There is no third drawer. And there's no right or wrong. It's balance that you want. Different times need different approaches."

Raines' approach was to use his three daily fourth-floor conference room meetings—the 10:30 A.M. masthead meeting, the noon review, and the 4:30 P.M. page-one gathering—to place his own stamp on the paper. His stamp was most visible at the 4:30 P.M. meetings. Before each page-one meeting, senior editors receive a "frontings" memorandum containing drafts and summaries of stories that each department is working on that might qualify for page one. Raines sometimes read particular stories, and more often summaries of stories, before they went into the paper. But after the page-one meeting, his office was usually surprisingly tranquil. The machinery of the paper, under Assistant Managing Editor Craig Whitney, the night editor, took over and would put the first edition to bed around 10:00 P.M., long after Raines had left for dinner. Maybe two or three times a week, he says, he talks to Whitney late at night. Most days, he doesn't read what's in the *Times* until 7:00 A.M., when he gets up, and by 10:00 A.M., when he arrives in the office, he will have read it and other papers. He describes his role this way: "I don't want to become the executive copy editor of the *Times*. So I'm trying to play a shaping role at the noon meeting and at the 4:30 P.M. meeting. I also try to play the readers advocate—what do they need to know, or are curious or confused about?" He likened his role to that of Bear Bryant. On the morning of each game, he recalls, Bryant used to take a walk with his quarterback and say, "'In the third quarter this situation is likely to happen, and when it does, this is what we're going to do.' It wasn't clairvoyance. It was that he had been in so many football games that he was able to predict." His job was to look around corners.

In the conference room each day, Boyd, the managing editor, sits in the middle of a long table, and Raines sits to his far left at one end, under a white board used to display pictures. On the surface, these meetings seem relaxed—ties and makeup are uncommon—and begin when Boyd calls on each department head or a deputy to make his pitch. In truth, the editors are tense because they are fearful of being quizzed by Raines or another editor and of not knowing enough about their own story.

On Friday, February fifteenth, nearly three dozen editors crowded into the conference room. They all knew that Raines was keenly interested in the Winter Olympics. Before this year's skating scandal, he had demanded that the sports department produce a story about the subjectivity of the judges, and the February tenth story had run on page one. Rick Bragg's prescient piece began this way:

> If it were just a matter of performance, if a machine could capture the perfection of her motions the way a stopwatch decides the men's downhill or simple arithmetic decides a hockey game, she would seem unbeatable. But in the subjective sport of figure skating, the difference between gold and silver may not be a spin, but a smile. . . . Some coaches and skaters say that the subjectivity allows judges such a broad inconsistency of standards that an award-winning program one day may be substandard the next, depending on who sits on the panel of judges.

In all, the *Times* had sent twenty-four people to Salt Lake City, including four correspondents from outside the sports department. Now Boyd turned to Neil Amdur, the sports editor, who described the International Skating Union's decision to reverse the judges and award a second gold medal to a Canadian pair in figure skating, and to suspend a French skating judge for misconduct.

"What is it about this that broke the IOC's high level of tolerance for shenanigans?" Raines asked. "To me, this is a watershed time for the Olympics. . . . Somewhere, we have to get all that together for the reader." He wanted a news-analysis piece, and worried that sports did not know how to write a broad, authoritative account that would mix skating, politics, and diplomacy.

Boyd then addressed a couple of other editors before Raines said that he wanted to go back to sports. He referred to the news-analysis piece that he wanted, and asked, "Neil, can we write about the Olympics without using the word 'firestorm' anywhere in the story?"

"Ice storm?" Amdur replied, amid laughter. Raines laughed, too.

(Later, however, he said that he wanted a Johnny Apple-style analysis. "That's not something they're used to producing in that department," he said. Among themselves, members of the sports department complained that correspondents covering the Games had to wait until after the masthead met to get their marching orders.)

After finishing with sports, Boyd asked for the foreign-desk report, and Alison Smale, the British-born assistant foreign editor (who has since been promoted to deputy), offered several candidates, among them a story from Afghanistan about the assassination of a minister in the post-Taliban government. After addressing the other desks, including photo, Boyd looked at Al Siegal, who usually sits at the table across from him, and said, "All right, what do we like?" They were looking for seven stories worthy of the front page, including one especially interesting or well-written story. Most of all, they were searching for the one story to lead the paper—in the upper-right-hand corner.

Siegal appeared to have no doubts, and said that the Afghan story should lead the paper, and that is probably what most of the editors thought. Certainly it would be the traditional *Times* lead.

"The Olympics is the biggest story of the day," Raines countered. No one challenged him.

The skating story led the Saturday-morning front page, with an extraordinary four-column headline. There was also news about the murder in Afghanistan, the secret sale of a hundred million dollars in Enron stock by its CEO, and the use by China of mental hospitals to incarcerate dissidents. Later, however, one senior editor said that he was disturbed. "Never in a hundred years would that story have led the paper," he said. "It did because Howell thought it was the most interesting story. In the past, it would have been seen as not having enough gravitas." Siegal, he continued, "was trying to steer Howell to the most important lead, but he backed off." Why? Because editors—himself included—are afraid to confront Raines, he said.

The Enron scandal crystallized what the newsroom admired about Raines, and also what it found alarming, as he pressed editors to produce page-one stories. He wanted editors "to forget turf lines," the assistant managing editor, Carolyn Lee, says. "Howell wants speed." He wanted the Washington and the Houston bureaus, the national desk, and legal correspondents to get involved, as he asked for separate stories and also for long narratives that would give readers what Raines calls "one-stop-shopping pieces." He told his business editors, "The Enron story is going to be your World Trade Center story."

Others thought the coverage was excessive. On his Web site on January twenty-eighth, press critic Mickey Kaus totaled fourteen Enron stories, not counting two complete pages of reprinted transcripts, in what he labeled a "slightly intemperate, Raines-like crusade about Enron." One female reporter Raines admires saw him, in the Enron story, as macho man: "To say we're doing this to beat other people bothers me. One thing I love about the *New York Times* is that the things that were invoked to get us moving had to do with the highest principles of journalism. To cite other papers is a slightly less noble aspiration." People worried that "flooding the zone" could mean diverting resources from other stories, thus losing a sense of proportion; or that the *Times* would become so invested in Enron that, unconsciously, editors would push their investment; or that driven by a natural desire to be on page one and to catch their editors' attention, reporters might hype stories. In February, Raines held a lunch with Glenn Kramon and the business staff, and in his opening remarks talked only about Enron, mentioning none of the other stories they had produced.

The preoccupation with Enron sometimes overshadowed other business stories; for instance, at a page-one meeting in late January, Kramon argued that the "most important business story today" was not about Enron but about how HMOs were curbing health coverage for the elderly. Nevertheless, Enron made page one, and the sort of populist, people-getting-victimized story that Raines usually relishes—the type of story that would have produced an indignant Raines editorial—was buried only in the business section. One reporter observed that under Raines the *Times* "is a more exciting place to work," but she worried that there was "a lot of reporting on the moment." Raines, who has become a Kramon fan, defends himself from this sort of criticism. "Do I think we've had too much Enron in the paper?" he said. "It's a huge story, and it's a story of as much sociological significance potentially as the great populist reaction to the abuses of the Gilded Age."

IN EARLY MARCH, Raines became concerned that he needed to strike a better balance. He knew that he had to spend more time praising his predecessors and his editors, and that he had to reveal his thinking to more people in the newsroom. When he was told that editors believed his message was that the paper was broken, he responded, "That's delusional! The paper is stronger than it's ever been."

Raines started meeting the department editors and accelerated a practice, begun sporadically in the fall, of lunching with various departments. One of these lunches, held on March fifteenth in an eleventh-floor executive dining room, was attended by twenty-six members of the national and foreign staff. They gathered under three brass chandeliers in a bright yellow room. It was a formal setting for an informal occasion. A long table was draped with white linen and *Times* silver, and on it would appear a salad of artichokes, salami, and tomato; followed by filet mignon, risotto, and haricots verts; followed by fresh fruit in wine goblet glasses. Raines sat at one end of the table and draped his checked sports jacket over the back of his French armchair and began talking, ignoring the three courses that would be placed in front of him.

"The biggest lesson I've learned since I became the executive editor is that there is real value for me in talking to the staff and real value in having time to answer your questions," Raines said. He spoke of the accomplishments of his predecessors. "You hear me talking about raising our 'competitive metabolism.' That's not because I feel we've failed in any way. It's not an invidious comparison to anything that's gone on before." For the next hour and fifteen minutes he took questions from a staff that did not seem intimidated.

Did he think stories were too short? He said he agreed with something Max Frankel once said, which is that the newspaper should be "a buffet," because "if all stories were the same length there is no way anyone can judge the importance of a story." He feared that he was not always heard when he spoke: "One of the things I've learned in this job is if I utter the word 'shorter,' it comes back to me as, 'All he wants is shorter!' That's not true. One of the other things I've learned about my language is when I talk about breaking stories, people say, 'He's only interested in spot news!'"

Was he aware that sometimes late in the day masthead editors would order up a story that disrupts reporters who have started on another story? He blamed the masthead: "You can't have good journalism unless you have good management." He continued, "I feel no timidity if something is off the tracks in the middle of the day; I'll step in. But I am consciously trying to have my ideas early in the day."

A lot of people are very shaken by Howell Raines. Should they be shaken? They should not be, he said. "But it's one thing to know something intellectually, and another to feel it. . . . It is true: I feel a need to get their energy level up. I don't apologize for that." However, he is not family unfriendly. He was a correspondent with two small children. For those who for family reasons need to be in one place, "We're trying to match up positions and assignments." Assignments in Washington and New York require little travel. Assignments to bureaus demand travel. Without mentioning Kevin Sack by name, he said one bureau chief asked to remain another ten years in the same place, and he refused. Although he wants to be sensitive, he also wants to be realistic. To cover the world and wars requires travel and hardship. He quoted Hyman Roth's advice to Michael Corleone in *The Godfather,* "'Don't complain. This is the business we've chosen.'"

After the questions were exhausted, he thanked them for their candor, and ended lunch with a Bear Bryant story, followed by this: Serious, great journalism was being played at the *New York Times,* and "I want to thank you for committing so many serial acts of journalism."

Early that evening, in the small room behind his office, Raines settled into an armchair. Since the tape recorder was on, Raines would not pour himself a glass of bourbon. I asked him if he had softened his message in the past few weeks. He conceded that he had. "I always thought that if you covered politics twenty or thirty years, you ought to learn something," he said. "I thought one day I would get a job where I didn't make any rookie mistakes, and, since I figured this was my last job, I guessed that I was safe. One mistake I made is that I have an intensity, and . . . in my enthusiasm for this work my passion sometimes comes across as a harshness, or my intensity gets mistaken for an adversarial or aggressive instinct that I don't have." He admitted that his "metabolism" message had been misconstrued and left "people feeling stressed or agitated."

Three days later, Raines's charm-and-humility offensive continued when he presided over a two-day newsroom retreat for about eighty senior editors in White Plains, New York. He opened the proceedings by reading a speech that began, "I thank you from the bottom of my heart for your patience and good humor and professional support during my on-the-job training as executive editor. . . . I do hereby declare that, as far as I'm concerned, our competitive metabolism has been raised!" He talked about the future. "We're on a journey," he said. "Twenty-four years ago when I joined the *Times* it was a great New York newspaper with national aspirations. Now it is a great New York newspaper, a great national newspaper, and turning towards international aspirations."

At the *Times,* the question of continued profitability is a constant one. Company revenues, compared with those of such media giants as AOL Time Warner and News Corp., appear puny: $3 billion in 2001. Yet the *Times* does have one of the largest documentary television production companies in the United States, and its Web site, nytimes.com, is the number-one newspaper site in the world. The *Times,* in a joint venture with Holt, has relaunched Times Books, which had been a Random House imprint. The paper's correspondents will soon be told of a new policy that discourages staff members from submitting book proposals to other publishers. "We are putting more emphasis on *New York Times* writers giving Times Books a first crack at efforts growing from their work for the *Times,*" Raines told me. "The guts of it is that we want first refusal."

Yet the principal focus of the *Times* remains what Sulzberger calls the "fine art of slathering ink on dead trees." In mid-March, Sulzberger devoted most of his weekly Wednesday lunch to newspaper growth. At the beginning of the year, the *Times* had learned that the *Wall Street Journal* planned to introduce, on April ninth, a thrice-weekly section, Personal

Journal, aimed at broadening the paper's appeal to both readers and advertisers. To counter this move, the five executives who regularly attend the Wednesday lunch—Sulzberger, Raines, Robinson, Boyd, and Collins—decided to hurry what were still vague plans for a new section offering stories on second homes, real estate, and travel and lifestyle for upscale readers. They wanted it to appear before the *Journal*'s.

Escapes, as the section was called, had an inauspicious debut; it seemed rushed, geared more to advertisers than to readers—not quite a real section. When Paul D. Colford, of the *News,* asked whether the new section was related to the *Journal*'s, Gerald Boyd insisted, straight-faced, that it was not. It was "related to the *Times*," he said, which had desired "for a long time to present readers with a smart way of packaging some of the things you now see in the *Times* in different places."

At an earlier March retreat, for desk editors and their business-side counterparts, Raines said that he hoped to find "a marquee national columnist, on the model of Red Smith or Jimmy Cannon," to write about college sports. (He didn't say it, but he also hopes to expand the *Times*'s daily sports coverage, which is only about half what *USA Today* offers.) He added that he wanted to increase the *Times*'s coverage of the immigrant communities and the New York City school system.

There are other changes that Raines didn't talk about at this retreat. In April, he appointed Patrick Tyler chief correspondent in Washington, and he has told people he trusts that in a year or so he plans to promote Jill Abramson to a masthead or major department post, and then to name Tyler bureau chief. In coming days, he expects to appoint Adam Nagourney the national political correspondent, replacing Richard L. Berke, who was recently made deputy Washington bureau chief. He wants to return to the "Walter Kerr model" and have a separate Sunday theater critic. At first, he believed that three movie reviewers were too many, and worried that none had the authority of the late Vincent Canby; he does not want all three to appear on the same day and wants them writing on broader subjects as well. He is impressed with the *Times Magazine* and is pleased with the three full-time book critics. As a rule of thumb, if a critic doesn't command attention—as he feels that the book reviewer Michiko Kakutani does, or as the former drama critic Frank Rich did—he will step in. He expects to soon hire a new Weekend editor from inside the paper, and is looking inside as well as outside for a new Arts & Leisure editor. He plans to shift Alessandra Stanley, who has reported from Moscow and Rome, to a highly visible role writing about television. He says that he plans no major changes before the summer, when a few editors might be rotated, but it is inevitable that bigger changes will come.

THE
CELEBRATION

Except for a few technicians setting up the microphone, the newsroom was unusually quiet at 2:30 P.M. on April eighth. *Times* personnel were waiting to gather for the announcement of the 2002 Pulitzer prizes, although the outcome was no surprise: Sulzberger and Raines had learned the previous week that the paper had won an unprecedented seven. Now Joe Lelyveld appeared in a blazer and dark gray slacks; he went over to his former office and tapped on the narrow window. Raines hurried out and they embraced. Soon, Raines was hugging Max Frankel, Abe Rosenthal, Bill Keller, Arthur Sulzberger, Sr., and Arthur Sulzberger, Jr. By 2:55 P.M., hundreds of staff members had surged into the newsroom, leaning against desks and file cabinets, crowding the DMZ staircase, and pressing toward the microphone to create an air of intimacy in what is, essentially, a fluorescent-lit factory room whose ceiling pipes are painted over in eggshell white. This was the first time that all living former executive editors and the current and former publisher had attended a newsroom event together. Abe Rosenthal, who hadn't been in the newsroom since the paper dropped his column in November of 1999, stood beside Raines, wearing a bright red bow tie. Then everyone waited for Columbia University to make its Pulitzer announcement, at 3:00 P.M.

Minutes later, Raines went to the microphone and hopped onto a small platform. He wore a white shirt and a red striped tie and was smiling broadly. As if he had willed it, for the next hour few phones beeped, no major news erupted. Raines didn't look at the notes he had scrawled on yellow paper as he said, "I was reminded today of the words of Mississippi's greatest moral philosopher, Dizzy Dean, who said, 'It ain't braggin' if you really done it!' Ladies and gentlemen of the *New York Times,* you've really done it!" Raines spoke about his predecessors in the newsroom—"We are living links in an unbroken chain of commitment"—and singled out Joe Lelyveld and Bill Keller. Applause filled the room as Lelyveld, who was leaning against a file cabinet next to Sulzberger Sr., smiled demurely. Raines called Sulzberger Jr. "a great publisher," and gave him a bear hug as the room applauded again.

Sulzberger asked the room to fall silent out of respect for the victims of September eleventh and its aftermath, including journalists like Daniel Pearl of the *Wall Street Journal,* who was murdered by Islamic terrorists. When he spoke again, he said, "Howell mentioned a lot of the folks on whose shoulders we stand, but he forgot one"—deliberately, Raines later said— "and I'm grateful that he did, and that is my father." The applause reached its peak, and the older Sulzberger had no place to hide, which is clearly what he wanted to do; the gray, slightly stooped patriarch, who had a bright red ribbon looped around his neck holding an ID badge, blushed and engaged in nervous chatter with another painfully shy man, Lelyveld. At most newspapers, publishers are the ones responsible for cutbacks that boost profit margins. At the *Times,* the Sulzbergers are royalty.

Roger Cohen, who had recently been promoted to foreign editor, introduced Barry Bearak, whose stories from Afghanistan won a Pulitzer for International Reporting. After thanking Celia Dugger, his wife and the cochief of the New Delhi bureau, Bearak said, "I've read a great many wonderful stories that didn't make the Pulitzer prizes; many of them were written by people who are in this room; many of them were written by my colleagues who were in Afghanistan this year."

C. J. Chivers was one of those colleagues in Afghanistan, but he had never met Bearak because they traveled separate roads. But as he stood listening to him he was moved. "I'll remember this as long as I have a memory," he said. "After everything he had been through and has done for the newspaper and the risks he's taken, he was talking about the larger institution, and not himself."

Jon Landman stood to accept the Public Service Prize awarded to the section A Nation Challenged, which included its daily "Portraits of Grief." He spoke briefly, then raised a plastic champagne cup and said, "Make a toast to whoever is standing next to you, and to yourself."

All the nervousness about the executive editor took a vacation on that afternoon. "What a day. I'm so proud of you all. I'm so proud of us," Raines said when he returned to the platform. He recalled the advice that Landman had offered about what he should say. "Whatever you do, ban all sports metaphors!" Landman told him. Raines ignored the advice. "Whenever anyone congratulated Coach Bryant"—he was interrupted by laughter, and paused for effect—"on winning a game, he always said the same thing: 'I didn't play a single down. The team won the game.'" Raines lifted his glass.

Raines knew that the difference between a great coach and a good coach was often a matter of inches. That day, morale soared at the *Times*, but he knew that it might plunge again—as it did a few weeks later when the newsroom learned that the investigative editor, Stephen Engelberg, who won his third Pulitzer this year, was leaving to become a managing editor at the *Portland Oregonian*. The newsroom blamed Raines for losing Engelberg, as it blamed him for losing Kevin Sack—believing that Raines could have done more to keep them. Engelberg had not been happy with Raines last fall, but the strain between them had eased; he told those he trusted that his move had little to do with the new editor, who had offered him a promotion. It was a "lifestyle decision," Engelberg told friends, explaining that it would be a good situation for his three young daughters; his wife would be working for the *Oregonian* herself; and they would be closer to his wife's family. In an odd way, the seven Pulitzers also worried newsroom veterans. Would Raines become more cocksure?

Raines wasn't happy about these doubts, but he insisted that his focus was on improving his newspaper. He felt free enough to pour himself a glass of bourbon and water as he settled on a couch in his small back room. "Change always takes people out of their comfort zone," Raines said one evening. "I'm not rattled by the friction of the moment. You have to set your sights on a beacon that is a journalistic ideal, and it's important not to get knocked off course by those winds of criticism. The caricature of me that I see in some of these accounts is completely unrecognizable to me. And therefore not particularly disturbing. I know who I am and I know where I will come out."

POSTSCRIPT

For the first nine months he was executive editor, the criticism of Raines came mostly from inside the paper. This would change. Starting in the late spring and summer of 2002 it was often said that the *Times* was, in effect, leading the opposition to Bush administration efforts to impose a new regime on Iraq. Spurred by Raines's desire to "flood the zone" and to be fearless, the paper ran a series of front-page stories about the pitfalls in Iraq. These included a Patrick Tyler story that erroneously claimed that former Secretary of State Henry Kissinger joined former associates of Bush's father in opposing an invasion. This story, in particular, roused the Republican right to assert that the *Times* was becoming politicized, was following the liberal dictates of its former editorial-page editor. Conservatives were not alone in making this claim. In March and April of the following year one heard complaints that the *Times* coverage of the war in Iraq was too negative—in probing stretched-thin supply lines or the breakdown of civil order in Baghdad—and was not appreciative enough of the speed of America's victory. This lament—that the press dwells too much on negative news—is of course familiar. Sometimes the complaint is true, and sometimes it comes from people who want to shoot the messenger or who themselves have a political agenda.

Those who believe Raines and the *Times* had an agenda were granted ammunition in late 2002 when the paper flooded the zone and featured on its front page a series of accounts of the Augusta National Golf Club and its refusal to admit women. Augusta is an important story, but the question asked here—as it was when the paper overplayed the confrontation between Harvard's new president and the university's Afro-American Studies Department—was whether the *Times* had lost its balance and was prosecuting a point of view. When it came out that *Times* editors had killed sports columns by Dave Anderson and Harvey Araton that either questioned the World War III nature of the Augusta coverage or dissented from the paper's editorials calling on Tiger Woods to muster the courage to protest, this criticism grew more intense. The *Times* was now accused of censorship. The resulting furor harmed the world's best newspaper.

There are several competing theories to explain what occurred. The first claims that one consequence of a strong editor like Raines is that junior editors will cravenly vie to anticipate his whims. The result is anticipatory censorship, as underlings scuttle work that might anger the boss. A second, more benign, theory notes that the *Times* has traditionally opposed airing its own dirty laundry, a reason it has never hired an ombudsman. The paper has always believed it unseemly to display intramural squabbling. A third theory asserts that Raines was the censor. After spending years freely shouting his own liberal views on the editorial page, people worried that he was now fiercely imposing his own ideology on the news page.

In one sense, it doesn't matter which theory you embrace: The *Times* was clearly damaged in each. My own view is that conspiracy theorists were wrong. Raines and the *Times* are not consciously imposing an agenda on reporters. But I do believe that both Raines and The *Times* have some blind spots or unconscious biases, as was shown when editors delayed and then downgraded the New Jersey trooper story. Too often, they also lacked humility. In the Augusta case, they waited too long to apologize for a series of colossal blunders.

The over-the-top coverage of Augusta reflected something else: a desire to broaden the traditional definition of sports news, as the *Times* sought to broaden itself as a national paper. Similarly, to broaden cultural news, Raines in the fall of 2002 replaced John Darnton as cultural editor with Steven Erlanger. Subsequently, he appointed Frank Rich associate editor for cultural news. Rich's task is to help Erlanger; and by giving Rich a column each Sunday anchored on page one of the Arts & Leisure section, Raines hoped to inject more "authority" into cultural coverage. These moves were aimed, in part, at a wider national audience. To reach an international audience, in the late fall of 2002 the *Times* strong-armed the *Washington Post* into selling its half ownership in the *International Herald Tribune*. The aim was to leave the *Times* as sole owner of a paper that would give it an international distribution arm. To borrow a phrase, they were "extending the brand." The new *Tribune* would report to Raines.

Then, in the spring of 2003, Raines and the *Times* were rocked by perhaps the most serious journalistic scandal in the paper's history. After protests from other newspapers and an internal investigation, the *Times* set five reporters on the task of exposing how reporter Jayson Blair, twenty-eight, had repeatedly fictionalized and plagiarized his stories—not just once, as seemed to have been the case with the *Washington Post*'s Janet Cook in 1981, but dozens of times. The *Times*'s 7,200-word May 11, 2003 piece convincingly documented Blair's fraud, as did the accompanying 7,000-word excerpts from Blair's fictionalized stories. But unlike the *Post*'s account of Janet Cook's fraud, or the David Shaw account in the *Los Angeles Times* in 1999 of how the newspaper made a secret deal with Staples to run a special issue of its Sunday magazine without telling readers it was really an advertising supplement, the *New York Times* account did not clearly identify the editors who were responsible. It did not tell readers which editors received the April 2002 e-mail warning from Metropolitan Editor Jon Landman to get rid of Blair, and why they ignored it. It did not confront editors to find out why, when Blair was subsequently promoted to the National desk, they did not communicate their concerns. It did not confront editors on the National desk or elsewhere to find out why, after the U.S. attorney in Maryland and other law enforcement officials attacked Blair's exclusively reported facts in the Washington sniper case, not one editor asked him to privately identify his sources, as is customary. And it did not confront in any serious way the question of whether Blair got a pass because he was a flatterer or because he is black and every editor knew the publisher and the executive and managing editors were passionately committed to newsroom diversity.

Or as Raines would admit when irate *Times* reporters pressed him at an open meeting of the staff on May fourteenth, "I believe in aggressively providing hiring and career opportunities for minorities." A moment later he added, "Does that mean I personally favored Jayson? Not consciously. But you have a right to ask if I, as a white man from Alabama, with those convictions, gave him one chance too many by not stopping his appointment to the sniper team. When I look into my heart for the truth of that, the answer is yes."

This moment of candor did not stop what became an open staff revolt. Because he was a strong editor, Raines succeeded in imposing his will on a great institution. By flooding the zone after 9/11, Raines elevated the *Times*. But his strength was also his flaw.

After the *Times* account of Jayson Blair's journalistic felonies appeared, I was on the *Today* show and discussed two glaring holes in the *Times* account: Which editors were responsible? And what, if any, role did affirmative action or favoritism play? Raines did not challenge this interpretation. He said that he had deliberately—and appropriately—recused himself from editing the account.

A friend outside the paper asked him, *Is it possible that your editors are so fearful of Howell Raines that they were afraid to insist on asking these two basic questions?*

Raines thanked this friend for his candor and said he wished to be equally candid: *I sometimes think you listen but don't hear what I say.* He wanted this friend to hear that he was committed to unearthing the full truth.

The friend repeated the question, and Raines said he hoped his staff was not fearful. Sadly, it was Howell Raines who didn't hear. He hadn't heard what his staff had told me about his autocratic management a year before; he hadn't heard, or comprehended, the full depth of rage loose in his newsroom. Nor had his managing editor, Gerald Boyd. Boyd is a solid journalist and an honorable man. He has neither Raines's intellectual range nor leadership skills that shout *follow me*—a reason Joe Lelyveld had decided he did not see Boyd as a future executive editor. It did not help that Boyd could be as brusque as Raines, and just as intimidating. Those who couldn't get in to see Raines rarely dared visit Boyd. Boyd could not compensate for Raines's management weaknesses because he shared them. He could not tell Raines that he lacked a constituency or was dead wrong, because Boyd was equally isolated and because he did not stand up to Raines, as a deputy must. At a Raines bachelor party in the winter of 2003 in the wine cellar of a Village restaurant, each of the twenty or so men in attendance tipped a glass to roast Raines—except for Boyd, who offered a lugubrious but heartfelt tribute to "my boss."

Back in the spring of 2002, Raines had vowed he could change. He began holding Tuesday lunches with the department editors—business, metropolitan, foreign, national, sports, etc.—insisting that he wanted a dialogue. He neither listened nor heard. "The lunches became a mono-logue for Howell," complained one editor who was considered a Howell person. Finally and most important, Raines didn't hear what the staff screamed in May of 2003. The publisher, Arthur Sulzberger, Jr., did hear—that the staff was mutinous over what they thought of as his autocratic, top-down management style, fed up with fear and favoritism and Bear Bryant stories. So three weeks after assuring the staff he would not accept Raines's or Boyd's resignation if offered, on June 5, 2003, Sulzberger announced that he had. In truth, he had fired them. In July, Sulzberger implicitly conceded his own mistake when he appointed Bill Keller to replace Raines.

Howell Raines blazed a remarkable journalistic career, and now it seemed to end, ignominiously. Like Jayson Blair—or Kenneth Lay—he made mistakes and paid for these. Unlike them, he did not lie or cheat. Raines and Boyd are men of talent, and no doubt they will rebound.

Howell Raines, for one, continues to arouse enormous curiosity. When this profile of him first appeared, and since, people asked me: *Is Howell Raines insecure?* They presumed that a short guy who went to Birming-ham-Southern and wrote in-your-face editorials and broke china in the newsroom must be a candidate for a psychiatrist's couch. I was more sure of the answer a year ago than I am today. An insecure man, I think, would not have allowed me to roam his newsroom almost at will, or to attend dozens of unscripted meetings over a period of four months; he would have tried to micromanage me, would have constantly and annoy-ingly asked, "Am I going to like this piece?" "What won't I like?" "What are people saying about me?" As he had said of Bear Bryant, "There was no whining." Yet Raines bridled at criticism, took it personally, and sur-rounded himself with an ay-men corner, which is not the mark of a se-cure man.

In June, Raines exited gracefully, without whining, as Bear Bryant might say. Sadly, in July 2003, he eradicated much of the goodwill his graceful exit had engendered with a hubristic hourlong interview on the *Charlie Rose Show*. No doubt, Raines was eager to have a last word on the weekend before his successor was chosen. But instead he demonstrated that he had heard little. He described the *Times* as "lethargic" and "complacent" and resistant to the reforms he had sought to impose. A man who a year before had apologized to his staff for suggesting that their "metabolism" was inadequate, and who just months before had apologized for his autocratic management style, now portrayed himself as a victim.

THE *Times,* to its lasting credit, displayed another quality under Raines and his predecessors, a trait increasingly rare in journalism: It deems its newsroom more important than its business side. Few editors could make the decision to jettison ads—as Raines did on 9/11—without consulting the publisher. By contrast, the *Los Angeles Times* was singed when it danced too close to the flame of the business totem of the nineties: synergy.

DEMOLITION MAN

WHEN DEBORA VRANA, a business reporter for the *Los Angeles Times,* arrived at her office on October fifteenth, she found a press release from an advertiser along with a note from an advertising-sales executive asking, "Could this run on page two or three?" The note arrived just days after the *Times*'s new publisher, Mark H. Willes, announced a major reorganization—one meant to tear down the traditional wall separating the business and editorial sides of the newspaper—and the resignation of the editor, Shelby Coffey III. Vrana raced to the office of William Sing, the business editor, who hurried to talk to Leo Wolinsky, the managing editor, who got in touch with Michael Parks, Coffey's replacement.

As it turned out, Parks recalled last week, "It appears to have been a naïve mistake by someone who heard, 'There are no walls.'" Janis Heaphy, the senior vice president for sales and marketing, concurs, saying, "It was human error." The newsroom, though, feared that barbarians were already at the door. After all, Willes, a former executive with General Mills, had revealed his plan to elevate managers from the business side to work alongside Parks and the editors of the newspaper's many sections. By doing so, Willes said, he hoped to reduce bureaucracy and ventilate the often inbred culture of journalism, and, by aligning the paper with civic causes—one definition of *civic journalism*—make it more a part of Southern California's sprawling communities while "simultaneously continuing to protect our editorial integrity and journalistic quality."

Outside the paper, Willes, who is also the chairman and CEO of the paper's parent company, Times Mirror, was pummeled. The headline in *Time* magazine's account of the changes referred to Willes as CAP'N CRUNCH. The *New York Times* headline announced A GROWING CLASH OF VISIONS AT THE LOS ANGELES TIMES. Benjamin Bradlee, the former executive editor of the *Washington Post,* says of Willes, "He alarms me because in his vision of civic journalism, what's good for the community and what's good for the advertiser are an inch apart. He has no commitment to the pursuit of the truth. I say this when I never met the man, but he worries me. He doesn't feel like he's trespassing if he gets into a newsroom."

The man at the center of this seemed slightly bruised when we met in his office. Willes, who is fifty-six, has a full head of perfectly combed gray hair, and he wore rimless, oversized eyeglasses that reflected the light from a floor-to-ceiling window that yields a vista of downtown L.A. and the San Gabriel Mountains. "One of the things that have struck me as a little odd about the coverage that we've had is that people are rushing to judgment," he said. "All of the things we're changing are on the business side, yet everybody thinks that somehow it's the editorial side that we are going to mess up. There must be a way to have truly great journalism and a great business enterprise."

What Willes is trying to do has huge implications both for the nation's second largest metropolitan newspaper and for journalism itself. Willes and his allies think that their critics are armchair generals, but it may be Willes who turns out to be the naïf. Willes, after all, is doing more than rearranging his newsroom; he is assuming that his restructuring won't erode the editorial independence of his newspaper. At the same time, he is betting his $3 billion company that newspapers can grow when circulation in the United States has fallen by 10 percent in the last dozen years. While Willes has proclaimed a new newsroom structure for the twenty-first century, he may ignore the lessons of the eighteenth century, particularly James Madison's admonition: "If men were angels, no government would be necessary."

WHEN MARK WILLES was appointed chairman and CEO of Times Mirror, in May of 1995, few noticed that he had a Ph.D. in economics from Columbia University, or that for two years he had been a professor at the Wharton School and for eleven years a member of the Federal Reserve Bank of Minneapolis, including three years as the bank's president. What stood out was that for fifteen years at General Mills, Willes had served as the company's chief number cruncher, and that he was born in Utah and had been reared a Mormon. (His uncle, Gordon B. Hinckley, is the president of the Mormon Church.) Willes immediately announced that at Times Mirror he expected to double operating profit margins and "grow our earnings per share by fifty percent in 1996," and that each of the company's businesses—seven newspapers, magazines, and specialty publications; book publishing; cable television programming; professional information services; and consumer multimedia—"must earn at least a twelve percent return on capital." He was quickly typed as a dollars-and-cents character right out of Sinclair Lewis. "Below his eyes were semicircular hollows, as though silver dollars had been pressed against them and had left an imprint," Lewis wrote in *Babbitt.*

Within months of his arrival, Willes had fired more than two thousand employees and closed the New York City edition of *Newsday* and the evening edition of the *Baltimore Sun,* both money-losers; in his first full year, he cut costs by $232 million. He killed the national edition of the *Los Angeles Times,* and sold Harry N. Abrams, a publisher of quality art books, because its profit margins were too slim. The *New York Post* dubbed him "the cereal killer," an epithet that pleased Wall Street and helped boost Times Mirror stock from $23 a share when Willes arrived to about $55 a share. "This is how you sell Cheerios," the former General Mills executive kept telling his newspaper executives, to the growing alarm of newsrooms everywhere.

But Willes did achieve his financial goals—brilliantly so—and within the company he began to shift his message. He curbed a tendency to make analogies between newspapers and consumer-product companies. "People reacted strongly and focused on that rather than on the point I was trying to make," he says. "I tried to find other analogies—power tools! Anything that would work." He began to talk more about rebuilding "trust" within the company, about the Pulitzer prizes his papers had won, about the obligations a newspaper has. He restored the national edition. He captured the attention of journalists by insisting that he would transform the newspaper business into a growth industry, one that would hire more reporters. Newspapers were vital, he declared in speeches; they offered "one-stop shopping," perspective, and portability.

Willes did more than preach; in mid-1996, he supported a drop in the price of the *Times* from fifty to twenty-five cents, after which daily circulation began to inch up. He went further, audaciously announcing an "aspiration" to boost the million fifty thousand copies that the *Times* sells daily by five hundred thousand, seeking "dramatic" rather than "incremental" change—thus the reorganization. He insisted that this was a realistic goal, although during the last six years of Coffey's nine-year tenure, the *Times* had lost daily sales of two hundred thousand newspapers. "If we can grow by fifteen thousand, that would be a great year's work," an executive who knows the company intimately says.

Tonnie Katz, the editor of the *Orange County Register,* which enjoys twice the circulation of the *Times* in the vast region south of Los Angeles, says that the *Times* is perceived as "a paper from outside the county," and, pointing to figures published last week, she notes that "the gap between the *Times* and the *Register* continues to widen." Indeed, in seven of eleven counties where other newspapers compete against the *Times,* the L.A. paper is number two. Willes, though, remains messianically optimistic: If only the paper could increase its low, 28 percent penetration in the Los Angeles market, and particularly its small Latino reader base of 19 percent. Or if it could change the minds of the eight out of ten new daily subscribers who choose not to renew each year. But something else was driving him, Willes told me, a cause that sounded larger than all his arguments about penetration, market share, and renewals: An increasingly segmented marketplace for information means that "we have a responsibility to be the thing that people have in common"—a common database, the glue that provides "a sense of community."

Even as Willes, the chief executive, was making people in the newsroom nervous, he was exciting them by saying that he wanted more and better coverage of downtown Los Angeles. (When Willes tried to create an advertiser-driven section aimed at Latinos, however, many in the newsroom complained that it would "ghettoize" them.) Often, he could be found chatting with reporters and editors. It galled him, as it did Coffey and other top editors, that the launch of a second weekend Calendar section was stalled for more than a year by internal bureaucratic snags. Willes pushed Richard T. Schlosberg III, the publisher, and the editors "to see if we could learn anything from the workout sessions General Electric"—the parent company of NBC—"has gone through," Janis Heaphy recalls. Schlosberg decided to invite the business seer Peter Drucker to spend a day with him, Willes, Coffey, and half a dozen or so senior editors and business executives.

They met on May 16, 1996, at a Marriott Hotel in Ontario, California, about thirty miles from downtown L.A. Drucker, who was paid a handsome consultant's fee, talked about the history of Western civilization and about American culture and how it was changing; about the evolving role of newspapers; and about the power of marketing. At one point, Michael Parks recalls, Drucker, who is eighty-seven, talked about his grandson, saying that he subscribed to a niche magazine about how to play the trumpet. What the *Times* should do, Drucker said, is think of its various sections—such as sports or calendar—as niche-magazine products within an overall brand; the niche targets particular readers, while the paper maintains its broad appeal. Willes perked up at that: "I thought: That's a world I understand." Why not put together teams, not just with one person from the business side but with people from ad sales and circulation and marketing working alongside an editor? "It was a peak day for all of us in how Drucker helped us think differently about our business," Schlosberg recalls.

"Let's get a Drucker process going" became a refrain, and it led to new niches like Monday's Health section. Because Willes had streamlined the company, he was around the flagship paper more. Schlosberg, a former air force pilot who served two tours of duty in Vietnam and had been in contention for the CEO job when Willes was picked, was beginning to feel crowded, several of his colleagues say. "Dick was used to his own command," a senior executive observes. Besides, he adds, with the California economy robust again, and with circulation and advertising inching up, Schlosberg felt that he had served his "tour." In September of 1997, the fifty-three-year-old Schlosberg startled the *Times* by announcing his retirement. Schlosberg insists that he admires Willes and enjoyed working with him, but, he says, with his kids grown, "I wanted to have time to have a life."

Willes, as he has done more than once in public, choked back tears when making the announcement. He stunned Schlosberg by taking the publisher's title himself rather than awarding it to someone else. Perhaps no one was more surprised than Shelby Coffey, a neighbor, friend, and fellow marathon runner of Schlosberg's, who told a friend that he had lost "a buffer."

Having worked for three publishers in nine years, Coffey, who is fifty-one, began to question whether he should continue. The black hair that once flopped on his forehead had turned gray; he was gaunt, and his skin had chalky pallor. Coffey does not allow a single negative word about Willes to escape his lips, and presents himself as the good team player. But friends of Coffey's say that he was made uneasy by Willes's fervor; for example, at a Christmas party where Willes invited a choir to sing carols and said that though he knew it was not P.C. to invoke Christ, he would anyway. Coffey was startled in September when Willes asked: Why don't our journalists, in an effort to get closer to the community, join more community and charitable boards? Coffey took the traditional view that for journalists to get involved risked a real or apparent conflict of interest, since their paper was expected to write impartially. At a regular meeting with editors, Coffey recalls asking, "Am I being too old-fashioned about this?" They chimed that he was not, and Willes accepted their answer.

But the question dovetailed with concerns friends say Coffey had with Willes's willingness not only to embrace a cause like educational reform but also to pour the paper's resources into it and to enthusiastically insert the *Los Angeles Times* into the debate. Coffey was uneasy, a close California friend says, with the fact that "part of Mark's agenda is that he has an agenda. Mark wants to change the world." Indeed, Willes, while not an ideologue, seems to be passionate when it comes to "experimentation." Most newspapers say that they seek the truth and try to help readers "understand the world around them," Willes told me. "We reaffirm those two. But we're also going one step further and saying that the reason for doing those things is to help improve the performance of society. It's not enough to just stand on the side and observe. It's not enough to have your ace reporter say, 'My goodness, look how effectively they're rearranging the chairs on the *Titanic*,' and write a stimulating series on deck chairs. We think that we've got a responsibility, within appropriate bounds, to help the place work better." To traditionalists, this sounds suspiciously like the reporter as participant rather than as observer.

The proposed reorganization of the newspaper was a concept that Willes and others had been pushing since the session with Peter Drucker. Coffey and Parks helped draw up the plan, yet it became clear, as David Laventhol, Times Mirror's editor at large, told me, that Coffey "felt it was not going to work out" with Willes. Laventhol has been a mentor of Coffey's and once served as the president of the parent company.

On October third, Coffey recalls, he lingered after a meeting and told Willes, "I want to give you a gift you might not appreciate immediately but will in time. Every new publisher deserves a chance to choose a new editor."

"OK, I choose you," Willes replied. They talked back and forth, Coffey saying that he felt it was time to move on and Willes demurring. "I tried very hard to get him to stay," Willes says.

The reorganization announcement came the same day—October ninth—that Coffey's resignation was announced, and in retrospect, Willes says, "the timing turned out to be unfortunate. It raised a question in people's minds: Did he disagree?" A five-page press release heralded "a top-level reorganization" designed "to help the *Times* grow and connect more effectively with readers." Henceforth each editor would have a business partner—a brand manager—working alongside, responsible for galvanizing the entire business side of the team. In response to the frequently asked question of whether or not he was traducing the traditional wall between church and state, Willes says, "I've tried to make a distinction between walls and standards. Walls get in the way of ideas, flexibility, experimentation. If we were ever to lower our journalistic standards, then all these people who criticize us ought to have us shot."

It rankles Willes that his integrity is being questioned. Even if people won't take his word when he talks about his "public trust" obligations, they should believe him, he says, because as a practical businessman he knows that "if we did anything to break that trust" the *Times* would lose its credibility, and thus would lose both readers and advertisers. Willes is backed by the new editor, Michael Parks, a Pulitzer Prize winner who served the *Times* for fifteen years abroad. "There are now fewer questions on this floor than there are in the East Coast media," Parks says.

As economists like Willes often say, it's important to disaggregate: An editor would be foolish to design a new section without consulting business counterparts to learn if advertisers will support it, or what timing would be most attractive to advertisers, who provide 90 percent of the *Times*'s billion dollars in revenues. Magazines like *BusinessWeek* and *The New Yorker* have editorial retreats to which they invite select advertisers. The *New York Times* publishes an automobile section that barely disguises its commercial intent. At the annual meeting of the Magazine Publishers Association, in Scottsdale, Arizona, in early November, publishers were beseeched to form "partnerships" with their advertisers, whatever that means.

Yet there is much ambiguity about how Mark Willes's new structure will work: about how conflicts between the section editors and the section general managers will actually be resolved, about how the teamwork culture of business can mesh with the adversarial culture of a newsroom. The *Times* has sold this as a radical restructuring, yet to allay fears it insists that the changes affect only the business side. But even on its face this cannot be so. Donald F. Wright, the president and CEO of the *Times*, for example, thinks that it would be terrific—as does Willes—if reporters recommended to their editors or business "partners" certain advertisers that should be in the paper. There was also confusion about the title— general manager, news—that was given to Jeffrey Klein, who is Parks's business-side counterpart. Why use "news" in his new title, I asked Klein, if he was to be divorced from news? "Interesting question," Klein, a Columbia School of Journalism graduate and formerly the paper's First Amendment attorney, replied. "If the title was simply general manager, without *news*, it would suggest that I have oversight over every area of the paper. There would be more confusion."

Max Frankel, the former executive editor of the *New York Times,* says that the L.A. paper's restructuring plan dreamily ignores the likelihood of what Janis Heaphy called "human error." Frankel says, "My attitude is always simple: The very top of the hierarchy should talk across the wall to our counterparts. But none of the editors down below, the day-to-day editors, should ever be burdened by commercial considerations." He fears that reporters could come to share the burdens of a money-losing section and begin to think not of readers but of advertisers. "It can't work," Frankel says. "Human beings are human beings, and they respond to pressures. And the temptations are nothing compared to when people know they can get at our people. There will be exponential increases in pressures." Benjamin D. Taylor, the publisher of the *Boston Globe,* worries that by lowering the wall the *Times* may create as much confusion on the business side: "If an advertiser has a complaint for our ad-sales person, our ad-sales person has the protection of saying, 'Look, we have a wall. You'll have to complain to the editor.'" Without the wall, ad sales is more vulnerable to pressure.

Editors and reporters are confident that Michael Parks is their fire wall, and that their fine newspaper, despite its faults, will remain a publication of record. They want Mark Willes to succeed. They like the fact that he champions growth and the virtues of newspapers, that he professed shock and chagrin when he was told of the note the advertising salesperson had sent to the reporter Debora Vrana. Willes tells his reporters that as a former professor he, like them, is used to asking questions. And he, as a former Federal Reserve Bank official, has also, like them, exercised a public trust. "While this is not newspaper experience, it is relevant experience," he told a meeting of his national and overseas staff on September seventeenth. At the same time, Willes makes colleagues uneasy when, in promoting his thoughts, he seems to cross a line from CEO to evangelist.

Last week, a Times Mirror executive described Willes as "a big believer in data"—a reliance that suggests another flaw in his approach. "It's easy to say that we should not fashion our news coverage to make advertisers feel better or to promote advertisers," Doyle McManus, the *Times*'s Washington bureau chief, says. "That one is not hard. Mark Willes understands that. The more extreme issue is that it is both a business necessity and a civic imperative for a great newspaper to increase its circulation. Clearly, an editor must think about marketing. . . . The more difficult, and much more subtle, question when you move to a market-based model of journalism is this: Is there a point where we are eroding, damaging our core journalistic mission?" In the age of Mark Willes, that remains the question in the anxious newsroom of the *Times*. And for this question there is no data, only beliefs, judgment.

POSTSCRIPT

I had a sense, listening to Mark Willes zealously describe how he was confident the *Times*'s circulation would soar, that he was not speaking as a hardheaded businessman who relied on data. He could point to no comparable newspaper circulation gains. He believed circulation would grow, and therefore it must. End of discussion. (In fact, daily circulation at the nation's fourth largest daily continued to decline through the spring of 2003.)

Similarly, he believed his own good intentions would protect the editorial integrity of the paper. They didn't. There are those who believe people like Willes are malevolent. I think they are ignorant. Like the wasp's, it is their nature as business executives to search for synergies. They appreciate James Madison's admonition about the need for checks and balances within governments, but not within business.

And so it was that two years after reporting this story, in October 1999, the *Times* was rocked by "scandal." Willes and Kathryn Downing, forty-six, whom he had selected to follow him as publisher earlier in 1999, had succeeded in breaking down the wall between business and editorial—only to have it collapse on them. Eager to boost ad revenues, Downing helped steer a record 164 pages of advertising to a single issue of the paper's Sunday magazine. The entire issue was devoted to the opening of the Staples Center, the new downtown arena. Like other newspapers eager to "extend their brand," the *Times* was one of ten founding partners of the arena, paying the Center $3 million a year for the right to advertise within the arena and, in return, requiring the paper to print once each year either a special section of the newspaper or a yearbook. What Downing—and Willes, who made the decision—neglected to tell the staff was that this issue of the magazine was really the special section of the newspaper required by their Staples partnership, and that Staples would share half the advertising revenues. In other words, the magazine was, in the ill-chosen words of the paper's advertising director, John McKeon, "a promotional vehicle." He viewed the arrangement as synergistic, and it was. But for the independent journalistic name of the *Times,* it was negative synergy.

Within hours of this revelation, the press was all over the story; three hundred journalists signed a petition questioning their paper's integrity and demanding an apology from management. Downing quickly apologized, and told a room full of irate reporters and editors, "The question is, How do I come up the learning curve faster?"

Downing's contrition was fake. For just two months earlier, she had joined a couple dozen editors, journalists, publishers, and CEOs at an Aspen Institute retreat designed to narrow the cultural gap between business and editorial. After two days of intense, free-floating conversation moderated by Jim Lehrer, with the journalists in attendance speaking up about why the church/state wall was so vital and why editorial integrity and quality were menaced by profit marginalism, Downing finally spoke for the first time near the end of the second and final day. She said she came from a business background, but that listening to the discussion she had come to appreciate that "editorial integrity" was not the mumbo jumbo she once thought it was. She confessed that she had learned much from this encounter, and she would return to the *Times* with a new attitude. Afterward, several of us were so heartened by her remarks that we thought these retreats a success.

Months after the Staples incident, Willes lost control of his company when the founding Chandler family and the board of Times Mirror engineered a sale to the Chicago Tribune Company. With eleven daily newspapers, overnight the Tribune became the nation's third largest newspaper company. Within weeks, Willes was gone, as were Downing and editor Michael Parks.

I knew a bit about the Tribune, for I had reported on that company. Gene Roberts, who had just stepped down as managing editor of the *New York Times,* after earlier serving as the distinguished executive editor of the *Philadelphia Inquirer,* approached me about a series on the state of American newspapers that would be funded by foundations and Columbia University. Roberts would assign twenty-two pieces on newspaper companies, and each would run in the *American Journalism Review,* and then be collected into a book. He asked if I would write the inaugural piece. As we kicked around the various newspaper chains, I said that I thought the Chicago Tribune Company might be paradigmatic. It was a company that embraced synergy and lowering the wall between business and news, that was heavily investing in Internet ventures, and that—unlike Willes, Knight Ridder, or Gannett—was being relatively quiet about its moves.

SYNERGY CITY

I T WAS A LONG DAY at the annual PaineWebber Media Conference in New York City in December 1997—a mind-numbing procession of men in dark suits, with wall charts, overhead projections, spreadsheets, and supplement materials. But it was a big occasion, nonetheless: a chance for America's newspaper companies to show off to Wall Street. One after another they trotted by, like thoroughbreds emerging from the paddock.

For the New York Times Company and its young chairman, Arthur Sulzberger, Jr., there was a prime slot to tell assembled analysts and managers that his company meant to "enhance society" with journalism of the highest order. Other entries preened for the buyers: Gannett, Times Mirror, Knight Ridder—strong runners all.

And there in the middle of the pack came four men from Chicago's Tribune Company. They wore dark suits that might have come from the same rack. None of them bore a well-known name. There was the chairman and CEO, John Madigan; the publishing president, Jack Fuller; the broadcasting president, Dennis Fitzsimmons; and the chief financial officer, Donald Grenesko. Their company was among the oldest—150 years—but certainly wasn't the largest, and their newspapers weren't the best read. But that didn't matter because Tribune had a story to tell, and it was just the story Wall Street wanted to hear.

In charts and appendices, they showed a company that owned four newspapers—and sixteen TV stations (with shared ownership of two others); four radio stations; three local cable news channels; a lucrative educational book division; a producer and syndicator of TV programming, including Geraldo Rivera's daytime talk show; a partnership in the new WB television network; the Chicago Cubs; and new-media investments worth more than $600 million, including a $10 million investment in Baring Communications Equity Fund, with dozens of Asian offices hunting for media investments. Tribune's annual profits were sailing past $600 million, and its stock price, as of that December morning, had soared to 58¾.

Since this was a performance, one they had carefully rehearsed, most of the numbers these four executives offered the Wall Street analysts and reporters who attend this weeklong annual review of various media companies were upbeat. Even when they offered a bleak number, as when they noted that the *Chicago Tribune*'s circulation was down 4 percent, it was coupled with a bright number (ad revenues up 5 percent). The Tribune, the four men said, was "a content company" with a powerful "brand." Among and between its divisions, they said, there was "synergy." Unlike *New York Times* chairman and publisher, Arthur Sulzberger, Jr., who earlier this day had said the "core purpose" of the *Times* was "to enhance society" through its "journalism," the Tribune executives stressed their commitment to maximizing shareholder value. Unlike the *Times,* Knight Ridder, or Times Mirror, who preceded them at this conference, the Tribune no doubt pleased investors by showing how much less reliant on print they were. Last year the publishing division brought in more than $430 million, they said. And CEO Madigan said that broadcasting and education revenues would grow roughly twice as fast as newspaper revenues. The year 1997, said finance chief Grenesko, had been "a truly great year—a fitting way to celebrate our 150th anniversary. . . .

We expect to set several new records this year in revenues, earnings, and cash flow. . . ."

It was a well-scripted, well-rehearsed performance, thorough and thoroughly upbeat. And the word "journalism" was never uttered, once.

The Tribune Company cannot match the sheer size of Gannett, with its eighty-seven newspapers, or Knight Ridder, with its thirty-one. It lacks the stature of the *New York Times*. It hasn't the cachet of the *Washington Post* or the visibility of Times Mirror. But Tribune has become a prototype for the cutting-edge newspaper company of the future. Tribune's profit margins, not Gannett's, lap the industry. Unlike most newspaper companies, which are reliant on print, its nonnewspaper revenues account for more than half its profits. Its newsrooms are multimedia models with robotic cameras, digital audio and video equipment, and a central command desk shared by editors from its TV stations, its twenty-four-hour local cable news channel, its radio stations, and its Internet publications. Without the bombast of Mark H. Willes, the CEO of Times Mirror and the publisher at the *Los Angeles Times,* Tribune has already done, quietly, what Willes loudly vowed: lowered the wall between news and business. Tribune's journalism is called *content*. And its editors and executives alike blather endlessly about *synergy, brand, brand extension, content, branded content, information provider, partnering*.

On the surface, this is a quiet, established company with stolid executives who take no chances. For all the outward magnificence of the Tribune Tower on Chicago's Michigan Avenue, with its carved inscriptions from Abraham Lincoln and encrusted stones from the Parthenon and Coliseum, the carpets inside look industrial; the spare furniture could have come from a Holiday Inn. The extremely unfamous executives upstairs don't swashbuckle.

But the dull gray uniform is a deception. The Tribune Company swings from the trees.

Its four newspapers—the flagship *Chicago Tribune,* the *Orlando Sentinel,* the *Sun-Sentinel* of Fort Lauderdale, and the *Daily Press* in Newport News/ Hampton Roads, Virginia—enjoy 27 percent operating profit margins. State-of-the-art color printing plants have allowed the newspapers to shave costs, eliminate composing rooms, and target dozens of sections for news and ads. Its newsrooms were the first to blur the lines separating print, TV, radio, and Web sites. Its sixteen stations put the company in second place among TV group owners, with operations in eight of the top eleven markets. In partnership with Warner Bros., Tribune owns one-quarter of the expanding WB Network, which boosts the ratings of Trib stations and reduces their programming costs, and one-third of the cable TV Food Network. Tribune Entertainment has become a major producer and syndicator of television shows. And don't forget the Cubs, who don't win much but do provide free *content* for Tribune TV, radio, and cable.

In Tribune's diversification, perhaps most startling—and telling—is its embrace of the new media that many newspaper executives still regard with fear and bewilderment. (When the Tribune readied a front-page exclusive on the Chicago police superintendent's friendship with a felon, the news appeared first in its online edition, a publication with a staff of fifteen reporters.) Tribune is miles ahead of other companies that moved early into the electronic realm, including Knight Ridder and Cox. An initial investor in America Online, Tribune now owns 1 percent of this eleven-million-customer behemoth. Together they created Digital City, which vies with Microsoft's Sidewalk to offer online guides to restaurants and entertainment in cities across America. Again with an eye on Microsoft, Tribune started CareerPath, the largest online classified effort, in partnership with various other publishers. Another arm of the company, Tribune Ventures, has invested millions in an astonishing array of start-ups, including Excite, the Internet navigation network; StarSight, an electronic TV program guide; Peapod, an online grocery shopping service; and CheckFree, the leading electronic payment processing system. And it won't stop there. "We are spending forty million dollars on new Internet-related stuff in 1998," says Grenesko, up from thirty million last year.

Overall, the company generates annual revenues of nearly $3 billion, and profits of nearly $800 million. And the cost of new online investments was more than offset by a 1997 pretax gain of $188 million when Tribune sold stock from its Internet investments. Many publishers insist they're in the information—not the newspaper—business. But Tribune has moved money, not just its mouth. "This is a strong company that looks to the future, not the past," says Robert Pittman, the president of AOL.

At Tribune, synergy is the mantra. "It's all over the company," says Madigan, the tall, silver-haired, and bespectacled chairman and CEO. "It's just gotten to be a way of life." Synergy, Tribune-style, occurs in the Washington office, when James Warren, bureau chief for the *Chicago Tribune,* and Cissy Baker, bureau chief for Tribune Broadcasting, attend one another's story conferences. Synergy occurs when Baker feeds the same TV story to her sixteen stations; when a TV or radio station, or a twenty-four-hour cable news channel, or one of the online publications uses a story from the Tribune newspapers; when Tribune reporters "extend the brand" by appearing in different media; when the Cubs help transform WGN-TV into Chicago's sports mecca; when the WB Network saves Tribune TV stations $8 million a year in movie expenses; when the Florida papers share sports or legislative coverage; or when Digital City on AOL advertises beachfront real estate from the *Sun-Sentinel*'s classified ads.

Synergy has its limits, but at Tribune they're not business limits. They're often matters of taste. Most stories that Jim Warren's fourteen-person D.C. bureau produces are deemed too long, complicated, and verbal—too *serious*—for Tribune TV, whose stations tend to favor all the news that bleeds. "If all the TV stations want is live shots from the Marv Albert trial and I'm not even covering it, there's no middle ground," says Warren. Though each of Tribune's three non-Chicago papers has at least one correspondent in the D.C. bureau, they normally pursue stories with local angles. The papers get almost all their national and international news from wires.

For the study of the problems that bedevil American newspapers at the close of the century, Tribune is a lab-perfect culture. All the great questions of the business are asked inside Colonel Robert R. McCormick's splendid old tower: Can newspaper circulation grow dramatically, as Times Mirror's Mark Willes asserts? (No, say the Tribune people: Growth must be found in other venues.) If Tribune papers get 38 percent of revenues from classified ads—and an even larger share of profits, says Grenesko—can this precious franchise be saved? (They're working on it—online.) Is old media dead media? (Old media is "flat," they say.) Does the future of news lie around the world, or around the corner? This battle, too, has been fought in Chicago, and a winner crowned. The colorful old colonel, who ruled the paper from 1911 to 1955, affixed this phrase to its masthead: "The world's greatest newspaper." He thought its domestic and foreign bureaus eclipsed those of the *New York Times* (which, in the colonel's view, was a pinko paper anyway.) Although Madigan professes great respect for those who risk harm to pursue stories overseas, his business heart lies elsewhere. "The emphasis on local news has been increased tremendously," he says. "The effort is to drive the paper down as much as we can and to get as much local news as we can."

The company has also fought the battle between Wall Street and Main Street, the latent conflict between shareholders and subscribers. Tribune executives focus unapologetically on their stock price. Grenesko says that every August each business unit is asked to sketch proposed revenues and expenditures for the next year. In September, an eleven-person operating committee reviews these figures. The committee usually bounces them back, insisting that spending be held down and numbers be presented again in November, before seeking Tribune board approval in December. What criteria do committee members employ to determine that the first sketch is unrealistic? They do it, says Grenesko, by carefully talking to Wall Street and gauging its response. "The operating committee decides the goal—say $2.40 a share." Then, he says, they tell the divisions, "This is what Wall Street is expecting from you."

What if Wall Street is unrealistic?

"They have not been unrealistic," says Grenesko.

Even apart from TV and new media—at the Tribune papers themselves—the editor in chief rarely presides at the daily page-one meeting. The editor's gaze is fixed on the future, on new zoned sections, multimedia desks, meetings with the business side, focus group research on extending the brand, or opening new beachheads in affluent suburbs. "I am not the editor of a newspaper," says Howard Tyner, fifty-four, whose official resume identifies him as vice president/editor of the *Chicago Tribune*.

"I am the manager of a content company. That's what I do. I don't do newspapers alone. We gather content."

Perhaps, as Tribune's financial success suggests, the newspaper company of the future will not *be* a newspaper company. Or as Executive Vice President James C. Dowdle has told Wall Street analysts, "We believe that content alone will not be enough as the Web develops. It will be more than words and pictures. It will be audio and most importantly, video. Customers want the whole package. And pretty soon they're going to want it on demand. Tribune is the best positioned media company to do this." Boasts David D. Hiller, senior vice president for development, "We believe we are building the media network of the twenty-first century—the next NBC."

But at what cost to its newspaper franchise? The *Chicago Tribune's* circulation, like that of most metro papers, has been slipping for years—down 30,000 in the second half of 1997 alone to 654,000. More ominous to some is a perceived decline in that venerable paper's editorial quality. Last fall, *Time* magazine wrote about the most compelling newspapers in America—a subjective exercise, to be sure, that even *Time* hadn't tried for thirteen years. Still, it should be noted: In 1984, the *Chicago Tribune* ranked solidly on the magazine's ten-best list. In September 1997, the *Trib* wasn't even mentioned in the discussion.

ENTERING THE NEWSROOM of the *Chicago Tribune,* your eye is drawn to a massive multimedia desk, around which are arrayed editors from WGN-TV, WGN Radio, ChicagoLand TV (or CLTV, the twenty-four-hour local cable news channel), the *Tribune's* Internet edition, and the Chicago Digital City affiliate—all working together to disseminate news around the clock. Behind them looms a 26-by-24-foot TV studio, with an elevated set for an anchor and three cameras. In most companies, a Berlin Wall separates the different media; at the *Tribune,* all media units report to David L. Underhill, vice president for video and audio publishing. "The goal of our unit," says Underhill, a former engineer and broadcast executive, "is to be a synergy group. I love the word. It implies working across group lines."

This breach of group lines was first achieved at the *Tribune*'s Washington bureau, housed on the second floor of an office building at 1325 G Street, N.W. The 16,000-square-foot newsroom was converted in 1995 to a joint facility for print, TV, radio, and online. "We are the first bureau to combine newspapers and broadcasting into one newsroom without a wall," says Cissy Baker, a former CNN producer. "Everyone knows each other. Every day Jim Warren knows what we're covering."

Warren, the *Chicago Tribune* bureau chief, is a thin, intense, thoughtful man who joined the paper in 1984. He's best known in Washington for his campaign against Cokie Roberts and celebrity journalists who accept pay for giving speeches to organizations they cover. But on this December morning, he's talking synergy. Shortly before my visit, the *Tribune* ran a joint-byline piece by reporter Frank James and TV reporter Shirley Brice about a three-day conference on Web pornography. "There's an example of added value," Warren says. "We turned out a newspaper piece and a TV magazine piece."

From his cramped glassed office in the newsroom, Warren ticks off other bureau synergies. Every Sunday night he and national correspondent Michael Tackett air a one-hour radio show for WGN. Warren orchestrates a weekly *D.C. Journal* for CLTV. National columnist Clarence Page, who has an office in the bureau, is a commentator for WGN. When Warren's thirteen reporters break stories, the *Tribune*'s TV stations interview them in the newsroom. Stations also use reporters as commentators. And in concert with A. H. Belo, a medium-sized media conglomerate with a similar newsroom in the same building to serve their sixteen TV stations, the two companies have no trouble luring the secretary of state and other notables to G Street, where they get a one-stop opportunity to talk to thirty-two TV stations and papers like the *Tribune* and the *Dallas Morning News*.

TV exposure provides subtle synergy. For Washington reporters who aren't from the *New York Times, Washington Post,* or *Wall Street Journal,* the most common frustration is not getting noticed. "One of the big problems for a paper like us is getting your calls returned," says Page, whose political and social commentaries won a Pulitzer Prize in 1989. "That's one of the reasons I came down here." It's also one of the reasons he appears on TV shows like *The NewsHour with Jim Lehrer* and *The McLaughlin Group*. Page's calls get returned. "I attribute that to my tireless propensity for self-promotion," he says with a smile. "I'm kind of Mr. Synergy."

Warren has often ridiculed the food fights on Washington talk shows, but he himself became a regular panelist on *The Capital Gang,* a former CNN shout fest. "You have no illusions about the frustrations of not being read here," he says. "But to me that's been a challenge. To us it's a reason to try and take a more combative stance toward Washington and the culture." He says he was recently invited to a private party whose host was Washington insider Robert Strauss. "I'd never met him. Why was I invited? It had to be TV."

But even in the *Tribune*'s multimedia newsroom, synergy has its downside. For all the fanfare, Baker has only three full-time reporters, and each averages a single story a day. She concedes that on most subjects they "don't have an opportunity to become well versed." A subject about which Baker is well versed—U.S. laxity toward the threat of a terrorist chemical attack and how easily a terrorist could "destroy the District's water system"—is one she'd love to run with. "If I was at CNN, I'd be jumping all over that story," she says. "But Tribune stations are dedicated to local news." The Denver station's 10:00 P.M. newscast, Baker says, is typical—three minutes a night for national and international news. New York, Chicago, and Los Angeles might use "a bit more," she says. Today, the big story she'll pitch to her stations is, again, smut on the Web. "The Internet story is an instant local story," she explains. "Viewers have children and they have computers."

The grim synergy/exigency calculus is much the same at CLTV. The local cable news effort began in January 1993 and now employs 146 souls in a squat, glass-walled office building in suburban DuPage County. What viewers get is news lite: seven live thirty-minute segments a day, with regular weather and traffic spots. Reporters can update stories seamlessly because studios are digitalized. But the seven segments are repeated continually to fill twenty-four hours. "I'm just proud of the fact that we are not sensational," says Barbara Weeks, the general manager. "We try to present straight news." But there are only five to seven reporters on an average day. By 5:00 A.M., when the first newscast airs, there is one working reporter; by 8:00 A.M., there are two. "We can only spend an hour or two on a story," admits Bill Moller, a reporter and anchor who is troubled by this superficiality. Once again, synergy is a goal. WGN Radio contributes traffic reports. The *Trib* provides Alicia Tessling, who prepares cooking recipes for cable as well as the paper. The *Trib*, in turn, plugs her cable appearances.

Although 1.7 million cable viewers can get CLTV, it reaches an average of only 31,000 homes each hour. The channel has yet to earn a profit. Nevertheless, advertising sales have more than tripled in the past four years. And, says Weeks, by bundling the only local cable news channel with the number-one newspaper in Chicago—not to mention the number-one radio station, the number-one independent TV station (which doubles as a cable superstation), the Chicago Cubs, and their various online offerings—"any of the Tribune business units can get together and offer a supersynergistic effort. It's very compelling to an advertiser."

Executive Vice President Dowdle says CLTV should turn profitable in 1998 and will blast off within a few years when technology enables cable to "multiplex"—that is, to multiply ads, just as the newspaper does, by selling zones. For an advertiser, TV becomes an efficient purchase when it can aim a rifle at a specific audience rather than hitting everyone with a shotgun. In "addressable advertising," the size of the audience often matters less than the ability to target it. "If we can regionalize the signals," Dowdle says, "and divide Chicagoland into five or six different regions, which could possibly correspond with our newspaper sections—Northwest, Southwest—we could then have information that would be relevant to the Northwest section. We could sell ads to the Northwest sections. That's the upside of it."

For the moment, in all areas of the Tribune Company, synergy seems to herald "fill-in-ergy." Executives see synergy as a way to reduce costs. If reporters help out on TV or radio, they enjoy the exposure—and the company benefits from their extra work, with no extra pay. If Jim Warren works harder, he really doesn't need a secretary, so he goes without. The bureau operates without its own copy editor. Warren says he has lost a handful of positions in recent years to expanded suburban coverage in Chicago. So now no one in the bureau covers the Pentagon; they fill in.

Page says the bureau has shrunk from "twenty-four people, at one point," to twenty.

Tackett, who became a national correspondent in 1986, says he was told only once that he "couldn't go somewhere because it cost money." Still, he feels the squeeze: "I'd like to see more people hired here." Ernie Cox, Jr., a top *Tribune* photographer for four decades, told me just before his recent retirement, "I'm not able to travel as often as I used to. . . . I travel nowhere unless I can get in a car and cover it. I used to get on a plane and cover anything up and down the West Coast. Now they just use the AP." When President Clinton came to Akron, Ohio, last December for a town hall meeting on race relations, the *Tribune* wasn't there. It published a front-page account by James Bennet—of the *New York Times*.

Cost cutting has trimmed the *Tribune*'s once-vaunted network of bureaus. The paper has gone from eleven domestic bureaus and thirty-two correspondents in 1987 to six bureaus (Washington, New York, Los Angeles, Atlanta, and Springfield and Bloomington, Illinois) and twenty-seven correspondents today. Overseas bureaus have been trimmed from eleven to ten—offices in Toronto and Berlin were shuttered, although Manila was added. And the Moscow office was reduced from two reporters to one. (The *New York Times*, by contrast, maintains twenty-seven overseas bureaus.)

Tackett, for one, sees advantage in a homier *Tribune*. "I don't have to worry about a bureau chief who fought in the last war sitting over my shoulder and telling me what to do," he says. Tackett goes out of his way to praise Warren, as do others, for refusing to "bigfoot" his minions and snatch the best assignments for himself. "I don't have people in Chicago looking over my shoulder. You have fewer layers." Reporters also say they appreciate not being pigeonholed. "I'm the New York bureau chief," says Lisa Anderson, "but I just spent one month in Africa doing a team report. I've had the luxury of only writing three stories since May. Why? Because I'm part of a team of twelve working on a series." That team traveled throughout Africa, South America, and Asia inspecting child sponsorship agencies.

In fact, raw figures reveal the *Tribune* staff hasn't shrunk at all. In the last decade, the number of full-time editorial employees has risen from 613 to 662. And it's no mystery where the troops are headed. For example, there's that glass-walled office amid the parking lots in DuPage County . . .

WITH FEWER THAN 200,000 customers in the city proper, the *Trib* doesn't have the largest circulation in Chicago—the *Sun-Times* does. But the *Tribune* has been the paper of choice for Chicago's vast Republican suburbs since the days when Colonel McCormick branded Herbert Hoover a closet leftist and raged against the "crackpot socialism" of the New Deal. Those suburbs are still the heart of the *Trib*'s 654,000 daily and 1 million Sunday circulation—and the place where affluent readers entice advertisers.

Last year, to shore up a circulation slide in the western suburbs of DuPage, the former fox-hunting country where the colonel used to reside, bureau chief Terry Brown was dispatched to direct a platoon of 10 reporters and 3 photographers who bivouacked in the CLTV newsroom. The office also got a beefed-up sales and circulation staff of about 160. In Shaumburg, another wealthy western suburb, another circulation drop drew another new *Trib* army—40 correspondents.

"One of our goals is to get more involved in the community," says Brown, a former editorial-page writer and *Wall Street Journal* reporter. In his office overlooking the CLTV parking lot, Brown is newsroom casual— no tie. He's one of four lieutenants who help command this suburban outpost, along with one executive for advertising, one for distribution, and one for promotion. They all report to the DuPage general manager, or "minipublisher." Brown says the team has undertaken extensive market research, primarily focus groups, to find out what readers want. What he has learned, he says, is this: "They don't think of us as their local paper. The *Tribune* has the reputation of being aloof and arrogant." Brown talks about how the *Trib* must become "more visible" and "more friendly." The DuPage executives are even discussing sponsoring Little League teams.

But isn't there a conflict between being "more friendly" and the demands of independent journalism?

"I think you can be both," Brown says. "You can be aggressive and yet not be aloof."

It's in the suburbs where some *Trib* reporters fear a breach of the wall between church and state. In fact, the wall has been chipped at everywhere. The *Trib*'s managing editor, forty-two-year-old Ann Marie Lipinski, along with corporate marketing executive David Murphy, head the paper's "branding committee." Together, they attend reader focus groups to determine, in the words of *Tribune* publisher Scott C. Smith, "what they should be writing about." Smith quickly adds, "Now, we don't substitute a popularity contest for journalistic judgment." But he insists on "a balance." And Lipinski, who won a Pulitzer in 1988 for investigative reporting and is widely thought to have the inside track to succeed Tyner, doesn't camouflage her business intent: "I'd like more people buying the newspaper. Certainly increased circulation is either one-A or one-B of this project." She sees her forays into marketing as learning experiences, ways to escape the confines of the newsroom. "I don't think research, a priori, is a bad thing—that's what you do when you do interviews," she says. "The objective is not to conduct a poll on which five stories should be on page one tomorrow. Readers expect us to make those decisions." But she adds, "I put some stories in the paper that readers suggested." In a focus group last fall, for example, as the crisis with Iraq was building, she heard a reader blurt, "No one's explained to me what this son of a bitch has. Can he bomb me?" Lipinski promptly ordered up a story on the actual military and terrorist threat posed by Saddam Hussein.

Mark Willes magnetized considerable attention in the fall of 1997 when he vowed to use a bazooka, if necessary, to lower the wall between business and news at the *Los Angeles Times,* yet the *Tribune* has accomplished this by stealth. While insisting that there are certain church/state principles that are inviolable—"You don't want editors or reporters thinking of the business implications of news judgments," says *Tribune* publisher Smith—he nevertheless agrees with Willes that the wall is too high and, "You've got to coordinate efforts across the newsroom." Where he differs is in style. "There's no need to make pronouncements," he says.

The danger is that when the editor operates as part of a team with the business side and they all take it as their mission to become part of the community, to remove their reputation for aloof arrogance, they may sacrifice the paper's keep-your-distance watchdog role. DuPage bureau chief Brown, now in his early fifties, brings to his task the credentials of a traditional journalist. "One reason the editor of the newspaper asked me to come out here," he says, "is that I am an old-timer and I can stand up to advertising people and say, 'Look, we are not going to print what the advertiser wants.' Yet I'm softening up here. This is going on in the industry. You see it at the *Los Angeles Times.* The editorial department of the *Chicago Tribune* was the least understood part of the paper. We wanted it that way. We wanted to protect our turf." But thumb-in-your-eye defiance has to change, he says, because newspapers are fighting for their lives and need better communication between business and editorial, not to mention the community. "I have a better understanding, or at least empathy," for the business side, he says. "If we do a special dining guide that our advertising people sell a lot of ads against, they'll say, 'We're not trying to control content. We just want to know if you're going to be writing about a certain restaurant.' I don't see anything wrong with their wanting to know about the product—God, I'm talking like this, talking about *product!* But I have no problem as long as they don't make requests about what I write or when."

Isn't there danger of pressure to assure a friendly review?

"I would be very troubled if I saw advertising guys talking to my reporters," Brown answers. "That's where I draw the line." But Brown is operating in an environment that values teamwork and cooperation. If the old newsroom culture was too cynical, too macho, the fear is that it will be replaced by an environment whose imperative—from the business side, from market research, from the community—is to be friendly.

The church/state issue intensified at the *Tribune* as its focus grew increasingly local. The paper publishes eight zoned editions, and the number will likely rise dramatically within the next few years. There is widespread concern in Chicago that the *Trib* has become a suburban paper. U.S. Representative Jesse Jackson, Jr. (D-Ill.), who praises the paper for "being very fair to me," nonetheless observes, "I didn't realize until I went to suburbia that oftentimes they don't read the same paper I do." What they're missing, he says, is news from another planet—from the heart of his district on the South Side of Chicago, for instance, where eighteen shopping malls have closed and the sagging economy stands in grim contrast to the robust growth in affluent suburbs. "I wish the *Tribune* wasn't just catering to those who are doing well."

Hank DeZutter, a Malcolm X College journalism teacher and co-founder of the Community Media Workshop, says this about today's *Trib:* "Now it's like a baseball team. It can move. It doesn't have the passion for Chicago that it had, as bad as it was. . . . I don't think it cares about the city." Clarence Page doesn't share that assessment, but he still worries. "What bothers me is that we have a Northwest section story and we keep it only in the Northwest section of the paper. What troubles me is when we ghettoize. . . . It happens all the time."

This criticism is sired by a perception, shared by many *Tribune* reporters, that editors are fixated on local news. "It is more difficult to get national and international stories on page one," grouses a Washington correspondent. This is not unique to the *Chicago Tribune.* "If the death and funeral of Princess Diana were the appropriate indicator, there is no dearth of foreign news in American media," James F. Hoge, Jr., editor of *Foreign Affairs* wrote mockingly in the *Columbia Journalism Review* last fall, before cataloguing the dearth of overseas news.

Another concern is expressed by Deputy Managing Editor James E. O'Shea: "One school of thought thinks we ought to be intensely local. My view is that we ought to be more regional. By that I mean a broader newspaper." He reached this conclusion after watching his former paper, Gannett's *Des Moines Register,* constrict its focus from statewide to central Iowa and lose nearly two hundred thousand subscribers from historic circulation highs. "The people in Iowa bought the *Des Moines Register* not to get intensely local news," O'Shea says, adding that readers were proud of the paper's scope and reputation. They took pride that the *Register* had won more Pulitzers than any paper save the *New York Times.* "The lesson I learned is that people buy you if you differentiate yourself." He fears Illinois consumers will turn to the *New York Times* for national and international news, and to the local paper for local news. Thus the *Tribune,* like the *Des Moines Register,* might get squeezed.

The *Tribune* recently lost its foreign editor, Thom Shanker, to the Washington bureau of the *New York Times.* After five years in Moscow and two in Bosnia, Shanker served only one year as foreign editor. He was popular with colleagues, and with executives like John Madigan, who met him on trips to Berlin and Moscow. "John has terrific manners," recalls Shanker. "He wouldn't let me pick him up at the airport. He wouldn't let me get opera tickets for him. He sent me a thank-you note." Shanker didn't think of the CEO as a bean counter. Yet he was determined to leave, telling associates he saw the writing on the wall: The number of bureaus was shrinking, the church/state barrier in the suburbs had become a picket fence. Although Shanker wrote a farewell letter extolling his editors' commitment to "excellence" and asserting that his move was "less about leaving the *Tribune* than about joining the *Times*," he was, in fact, more depressed than he let on. Like others in the newsroom, he thought the paper had suffered an identity crisis. As a member of the national staff puts it, "The paper is not sure anymore whom it is serving."

Or perhaps it is sure. When I asked the publisher, Scott Smith, to respond to the criticism that the paper is retreating from national and international news, he praises his far-flung staff and says he respects that view. "But the economics are not with that. The *New York Times* has economics that work for them in that regard."

Newsroom critics detect the dreaded voice of a bean counter in Smith's response—a complaint at the core of the 1993 book by former *Tribune* editor James D. Squires, *Read All About It: The Corporate Takeover of American Newspapers*. The "blueprint" for the newspaper company of the future, wrote Squires, was drawn by a former Gannett chairman, Al Neuharth, who gobbled up newspapers and slashed costs, shortened stories and generally operated as if his principal audience was Wall Street. But Lipinski, who joined the paper as a summer intern in 1978 and, save for a Nieman Fellowship, has never left, disputes her former mentor. "I feel like I'm working for a paper that's vastly better than the one I joined," she says. "The paper was relatively mediocre then. What Jim is describing is the fashionable criticism. It's very hard for me to balance that criticism with what I know my tools are. . . . If I thought quality didn't matter here, I wouldn't stay."

It is hard to argue that the *Tribune* is not a better paper than it was when Colonel McCormick, like William Randolph Hearst, whimsically ordered up stories and used the front page to ridicule or punish foes. Yet the paper that the colonel called the World's Greatest is clearly not that. It is not the same paper that in 1947 was the first to have at least one reporter on duty every minute the Senate or House was in session. It hasn't covered the White House with the same intensity as it did under Squires. The Sunday magazine and book review are painfully thin. The vaunted international coverage is sometimes thin, as well. Although the October 4, 1997, paper contained a page-one story from Moscow on the joint space mission, the few inside pages of overseas news were filled with wire copy, with the exception of one *Tribune* short from Havana. Arts and entertainment reviews almost always run a day late (for example, a Monday opening will be covered on Wednesday). These specific nits, however, are subsumed by the larger criticism that the *Tribune* is, well, weaker.

"In some ways you're seeing a newspaper not quite as good as it was five years ago," says Jon Margolis, the *Tribune*'s national political writer for twenty-two years. He left the paper in 1995 to write books. "When the bean counters took over," he says, "they hired people who had no memory." The absence of memory became so acute that the paper called back Margolis as a consultant for the 1996 presidential election. He and other alumni can point to a series of changes in service of the bottom line. There has been a delayering of editors; the paper no longer hires reporters after a three-month tryout, but employs "associates" who remain on probation a full year; the paper lost many experienced reporters, all hired in the seventies—Margolis, Eleanor Randolph, Harry Kelly, Dick Ciccone, Bill Neikerik, Charlie Madigan, Jim Jackson—that it didn't replace. "In the last seven to eight years," Margolis says, "you could count on the fingers of your hand the number of established reporters they've hired. There's not much bench strength." As a consequence, he says, the worst effects are yet to come. "To the extent that Squires is right, it's more prospective. You can see a slight weakening. Not because people are not good, but because there are not enough good people."

The *Tribune* has many strengths, including a seriousness of purpose that prompted it to pour enormous resources into investigating the tragic rash of deaths among Chicago children in 1993. In December 1995 the *Trib* published an eleven-part series exploring the ordeal of modern

Africa. In June 1996 it exposed inadequate medical supplies aboard the nation's airliners, a shortcoming more lethal than crashes. The paper often carries snap-to-attention writing, such as Charles Leroux's profile of eighty-two-year-old Bernard O'Halloran, whose debilitating strokes separated him from Agnes, his wife of sixty years. The sports section is readable and feisty, the TV criticism pungent and apt. Its editorial page, under former *New York Times* editorial writer N. Don Wycliff, doesn't have the bite of Wycliff's former page. But he says proudly that the *Trib*'s page is "contrarian." It opposed the independent counsel law that now bedevils the Clinton White House, pushed for elimination of Illinois's teacher tenure laws, and lashed Israeli Prime Minister Benjamin Netanyahu, "whose reckless and provocative behavior has jeopardized the chances for peace"—a blunt stance that could not be found in the *Times* or *Post*. In elections, Wycliff ruefully concedes, the *Trib* is still plagued by knee-jerk Republican instincts. In the 1996 U.S. Senate race, he says, the *Tribune* couldn't turn fast enough and wound up supporting Al Salvi, a Republican who was "way far out there." Tradition, he believes, triumphed over judgment.

The *Trib* is rightly proud of John Kass, who took over the late Mike Royko's page-three column. The son of a Greek grocer from Chicago's South Side, Kass is a college dropout who joined the merchant marine and worked as a butcher before becoming a newspaperman. For ten years he covered city hall for the *Trib*. The competition to fill Royko's slot was ferocious, and the choice of native Chicagoan Kass, says Thom Shanker, "spoke a lot for the paper and how it didn't forget its roots." Here's the beginning of a column Kass wrote about an alderman who was forced to resign last year because he enriched himself and friends of Chicago's mayor:

Ald. Patrick Huels spent a lifetime as a loyal appendage—and only a week as an infected liability. So on Tuesday night, with the political health of Mayor Richard Daley at stake, Huels finally was removed after several painful days of sawing.

The Bridgeport alderman is not the first to be amputated, and he won't be the last. It's the way of politics. But despite the operation, the bleeding won't stop.

Something happened between Daley and his city this week that simple damage control and public relations spinning won't fix. . . . There's money being made at City Hall for the mayor's close circle of fat-cat friends who eat no-bid contracts and sweetheart deals.

There's a freshness to Kass—the kind of freshness sorely missing these days from Bob Greene's columns. (Come the third week in November, Greene is in Dallas, so he fills his space with rumination on the death of JFK. . . .) In time, Kass's name, like Royko's and Studs Terkel's, may become identified with Chicago.

But what about the *news*—the hard information that Alderman Huels used his public office to benefit his private security firm? That wasn't the *Tribune*'s story. The *Sun-Times* broke it last October. Not only was it first, the feisty tabloid also skinned the culprits with a populist, throw-the-bums-out crusade. When the *Trib* finally weighed in on the story, it was in a manner perhaps symptomatic of why it got beat. Critics called it a simple lack of passion. The *Trib* already had two reporters exploring the mores of the city council, so they used the Huels scandal as a springboard for in-depth, contextual pieces illuminating aldermanic culture—and explaining how it condoned Huels's behavior. More Socrates than Patrick Henry, the *Trib* was so busy telling readers "why" that critics say it almost forgot about "what" or "who."

"The *Tribune* has withdrawn from the investigative journalism business," says Michael Miner, media columnist and senior editor of the *Chicago Reader,* an alternative weekly. "Instead of an investigation designed to nail someone, we get long studies of poverty. Their investigative reports are meant to help us understand, not change, anything. . . . A lot of the fun is drained out of the *Tribune.* . . . The *Tribune* is not in the pelt-bagging business anymore. It would rather commune with the bear." Miner has a theory on why the *Trib* is fixated on "why." He links what he sees as a vice to what others see as the virtues of the man at the top: the president of Tribune Publishing, Jack Fuller.

Fuller has his share of august newspaper credentials—he won a Pulitzer Prize as editor of the *Trib*'s editorial page, and succeeded Jim Squires as editor in 1989. Now he oversees all four Tribune newspapers. But his résumé also features interesting "outside" experience. He got his J.D. from Yale Law School in 1973. He served two years as special assistant to the U.S. attorney general in the Ford administration. He has lived on both sides of the barricade—which no doubt contributes to his tendency to see four sides of every issue.

At the *Trib*, the bearded Fuller is perceived as an intellectual. Books form small mountains on his desk and fill the shelves behind him. He writes his own books, too, including a philosophically challenging entry on newsroom ethics, *News Values: Ideas for an Information Age.* The book roams easily from Greek and Roman philosophers to the Reformation and the Founding Fathers. Along the way, Fuller picks up, examines, doubts, and finally dismisses many of journalism's platitudes. For example, he rejects the totem that journalists are meant to "comfort the afflicted and afflict the comfortable." The statement "makes sense," he writes, if it means journalists should report on the suffering of the poor and "have the courage to tell unpleasant truths about the powerful . . . but it also can be an invitation to bias." Should journalists *always* afflict the comfortable, even when they do no harm? "Should they afflict them simply *because* of their comfort? And what about the afflicted? What if telling the truth to and about them would cause them discomfort?" To critics like Miner, this is Fuller blather: "The man is drenched in his philosophy, which is scrupulous to a fault."

In his office in the Tribune Tower, Fuller is still dismissing easy truths, for example, the charge that the newspaper has turned its back on its hometown. "We still devote more inches to the city of Chicago than anyone else does," he says. But he adds that a newspaper must balance reader interests. "If you're in Lincoln Park," he says, mentioning a pricey Chicago enclave, "are you interested in who the sheriff of Cook County is? Some things are universally important, and some things are not."

Fuller has many allies in the newsroom. The growing interest in suburban news, says two-time Pulitzer winner William C. Gaines, "hasn't detracted from anything that I've seen." Gaines joined the paper as a police reporter in 1963 and is its investigative ace. He says the paper is as good, and hard charging, as it ever was. "We always have large projects going. I see the editorial department expanding." The *Tribune* is not without scoops: It forced Chicago Police Superintendent Matt Rodriquez to resign after revealing his brotherlike friendship with a felon; it spotlighted police abuse on the front page; it revealed how some immigrants were assumed guilty until cleared by drug tests. Likewise, columnist Kass rejects the notion that the *Trib* was somnolent on the Huels scandal. "In other words, let's have some more Gotcha!" he snaps. "We got beat. It was a good story. We've beat them. That's the ball game. You don't need all this intellectualizing about it."

But Miner's critique backs into a broader debate about the role of the press, between cynics and skeptics, between hunters and explainers, between those who tend to see clever conspiracies at the root of political behavior and those, like Fuller, who don't think people are that smart and thus tend to blame human accident. This is a debate Fuller is happy to join. "If I got to be *too* something, I guess I'd rather be *too* thoughtful," he says when told of Miner's critique. "I'm not sure this newspaper can justly be accused of being too polite. If anything, the journalism of today is too often fixed on finding the culprit. I believe there are culprits and we should find them and get them out of office. I believe we were spoiled by Watergate to believe every ill of society can be explained by one man. It's jejune. But I don't think the real purpose of journalism is jejune. The influence I'd love to have is to say our job is to get as close as we can every day to an accurate depiction of how the world works without being afraid to point fingers, and yet not feel we have to." Fuller says he's troubled by journalists—he cites the talented Maureen Dowd of the *New York Times*—whose columns eschew ideology but, he believes, succumb to an equivalent ideology of cynicism, equating all actions with a cynical intent.

Some at the paper would trade Fuller's cool musing for some old-fashioned heat. There would have been hell to pay under Squires, they say, if the *Trib* got beat on a corruption story. Columnist Page praises the paper's explanatory journalism but says, "That place is like an aircraft carrier. It's a very large operation. It needs strong leadership at the top—a go-for-the-jugular instinct. I haven't seen that instinct since Jim Squires and Bill Jones." Jones was a young Pulitzer-winning investigative reporter who became managing editor. He died of cancer in 1982.

When Squires was editor, through much of the eighties, shouting in the newsroom was common. People who made mistakes feared for their jobs. "The *Tribune* is a place where there is lots of excellence, but no one yells at you if you don't achieve excellence," says a former *Trib* reporter who asked not to be identified. "The *Tribune* is putting so much of its effort into 'synergy' and 'brand.'" When Squires left, says a veteran *Trib* reporter who also requested anonymity, "passion walked out the door." Squires may have been explosive and even tyrannical, "but so was Colonel McCormick. It sure helps to have a strong personality at the helm."

In his newsroom, Jim Squires often managed by fear, not unlike former Chicago Bears coach Mike Ditka. Joseph Andrew Hays, the former Tribune Company vice president for corporate relations, recalls the time he dropped Squires what he thought was a friendly note asking: "How come the paper no longer reports the bulk prices of milk, as it once did?" He still winces when recalling Squires's withering reply: "You stay off of my turf and I'll stay off of yours." Lipinski makes a point of saying that there was a "dressing-down—but not in the center of the newsroom," when the *Sun-Times* beat them. Her boss, Tyner, concurs. "There's not been a lot of screaming since Squires left," he says. Tyner's arm sweeps toward the newsroom, just outside the bay window of his office. "If you went around here and talked to folks," he says, "what you'd get is, 'We don't want to be flashy.'" National correspondent Michael Tackett says he never understood why Squires yelled at grown-ups, but he says the role of editor has changed. "Today it's much more of a corporate officer," overseeing a joint newsroom and exploring new technology and trying to figure out how to grow. Ask Tyner, for example, what he hopes his legacy will be, and before he mentions "maintaining the quality and integrity of the paper," he first chooses to emphasize his efforts to "pull all this stuff off," to digitalize and repaginate and to make the *Tribune*'s multimedia newsroom work.

For his part, Squires is unrepentant. He sticks to the critique in his passionate and acerbic book. Now raising horses at his farm outside Lexington, Kentucky, he praises Fuller and Tyner as good men who deserve credit for not tarting up the news. But today's *Tribune,* he insists, lacks "energy and passion." He links this failing to his book's larger theme, the corporatization of news: "The newspaper has always been relevant to the lives of people when it had passion," he says. "What it's trying to do now is keep up its profit margins. That's different. You're looking at a good newspaper, a newspaper with talent and serious people at the top like Jack Fuller and Howard Tyner. But they are existing in a different world. I'm not as concerned about the survival of the newspaper as I am about the survival of journalism. What the *Tribune* is today is what every big newspaper is to its owner—a franchise. It's viewed differently than newspapers used to be viewed. We used to think of it as a quasi-public service to inform people about what they needed to know. Who's cheating whom? . . . What disease is lurking? . . . What government is wasting their tax money? . . . Journalism's job has always been to educate people. Today the owners view it as an information franchise whose job it is to make money."

Squires's critique echoed in the eloquent speech ABC's Ted Koppel gave to the Committee to Protect Journalists' International Press Freedom Awards dinner in December. Rising to speak after several brave journalists from around the world had been introduced and after the audience had heard of their torture and imprisonment, Koppel said:

> It is not death or torture or imprisonment that threatens us as American journalists, it is the trivialization of our industry. We are free to write and report whatever we believe is important. But if what is important does not appeal to the reading or viewing appetites of our consumers, we'll give them something that does. No one is holding a gun to our heads. No one lies awake at night, dreading a knock on the door. We believe it to be sufficient excuse that "we are giving the public what it wants." We have the responsibility to do more: to focus on foreign events and explain to the American public how and why those events have an impact on us. To resist and reject the comfortable illusion that Americans don't care about what's happening overseas. They don't care only because they've been lulled into believing that what happens overseas

will have no real impact on their own lives. . . . The most important events of the past couple of years have not been the O. J. Simpson trial and the death of Princess Diana.

We have more tools at our disposal and we are more skillful at applying them than any previous generation of journalists. But we're afraid of the competition, afraid of earning less money, afraid of losing our audience. They face death and torture and imprisonment; and we are afraid.

FOR SEVERAL MONTHS I subscribed to the *Chicago Tribune* and the other three newspapers that fly the Tribune Company flag. A few impressions hit me immediately. First, the three sister papers get their national and international stories from the wire services and other newspapers, though rarely from the *Chicago Tribune*. This frustrates *Trib* reporters, who wonder what became of synergy. Alas, Chicago is an hour behind its colleagues. "Usually they don't get us stories on time," says the *Sun-Sentinel* managing editor, Ellen Soeteber, who came from the *Trib* three years ago and is widely credited with bringing new energy with her.

A second impression is that these are essentially local newspapers, probably better than most in their midrange circulation categories. (The *Sun-Sentinel* daily circulation is nearly 257,000; the *Orlando Sentinel,* 251,000; and the *Daily Press* in Virginia, 100,000.) Tribune acquired the Florida papers in the midsixties, the *Daily Press* in 1986. When comparing the *Trib*'s acquisitions with Gannett's, Fuller pointedly says, "Our signature is running good newspapers, and when we buy a newspaper we make it better." Although the smaller papers don't publish as much investigative or enterprise reporting as the *Tribune,* you can still find exemplary work. The Orlando paper undertook a months-long investigation of Central Florida's overcrowded schools, a series that helped provoke a special session of the state legislature. Nor did Orlando editors censor TV critic Hal Boedeker when he eviscerated the monotonous news coverage by Central Florida News 13—the *Sentinel* and Time Warner's jointly owned twenty-four-hour cable news channel. The Fort Lauderdale paper exposed Florida's sex entertainment business. The reporter on that six-part series, thirty-four-year-old Jose Lambiet, who arrived two years ago from the *New York Daily News,* marvels, "They left me alone for six months!" Nor did editors flinch when he wrote a sidebar on the paper's practice of taking ads from sex services. Lambiet wishes the *Sun-Sentinel* did as many whistle-blowing stories as the rival *Miami Herald;* he says the *New York Daily News* was more dynamic to read and adds, "We're kind of boring." But he's proud of his new paper. "We think more about what we do. The *News* just slaps things in the paper. They did a sex series in the *News*—it took them a week to do. An editorial meeting at the *News* was like a gang meeting. Whoever yells the loudest gets the story. Here they think things through a bit more."

In Virginia, the *Daily Press* has run tough editorials blasting Pat Robertson and the National Rifle Association. And when Oliver North ran for the Senate in 1994, it published weekly editorials headlined, OLLIE'S LIES. Publisher Jack Davis sounds like the *Chicago Tribune* editor he once was, citing these editorials as among his proudest achievements. "We lost maybe hundreds of subscribers who were mad at us for our weekly insistence that Oliver North was not a trustworthy person," he says.

A third impression is that there are notable weaknesses in the Tribune papers. At each of the papers, half the front page is locally generated, but their A sections invariably brim with bylines from other sources. For example, Fort Lauderdale's November eighteenth edition ran forty stories in its twenty-eight-page main section. Only two came from the *Sun-Sentinel* itself; thirty-eight were from other newspapers or wire services, and that was not unusual. All five columns on the op-ed page were syndicated. Rather than do its own profile of a southern writer, the Orlando paper skimped by running a *New York Times* profile of best-selling author Charles Frazier, because the Virginia paper saves money by reprinting *New York Times* book reviews. Each paper has a correspondent in the Washington bureau of the *Tribune,* yet their Washington stories tend to be provincial, seeing national events through a Floridian or Virginian prism. Janet Reno, the U.S. attorney general, is a continuing story because she is from Florida. ("If I don't have this job, I go home to Miami," Reno declared, a quote that was boxed on the October sixteenth front page of the *Sun-Sentinel.*) In Orlando, with a market heavy on young service workers (courtesy of

Disney World, Universal Studios, and others), the *Sentinel* seems light on government reporting. Publisher John Puerner says his audience wants mostly sports, classifieds, and entertainment listings.

Fort Lauderdale's editor is Earl R. Maucker, a neat, mustachioed man of fifty who tends to speak in clichés ("Nothing succeeds like success!") But he is thoroughly up-to-date on Tribune Company philosophy: "This is, in all honesty, a reader-driven newspaper." Maucker says he wants readers to be "comfortable." And they won't be if the "newspaper breaks on the doorstep" because it is "heavy" with government and investigative news. The result of this ethic can be seen across the company: All three sister papers feel light, at least by metro standards.

It doesn't take a Wall Street whiz to notice another characteristic of Tribune papers: financial health. Unlike many city newspapers, they are located in vibrant economic enclaves. The Orlando paper monopolizes the region. Only 15 percent of its readers, says Editor John Haile, read a second newspaper. The *Sentinel* reaches 37 percent of all potential households, 55 percent on Sunday, according to Puerner's figures, and offers advertisers 140 zones—one reason he cites for revenues growing 25 percent over the past four years. Haile prides himself on the fact that he thinks like a publisher as well as an editor, and he frets about inroads Cox might make into this market. Cox already owns nearly half the *Daytona Beach News-Journal,* plus Orlando's top TV station and a cluster of radio stations. But the *Sentinel,* he knows, has a sizable head start.

In Fort Lauderdale, the *Sun-Sentinel* owns fast-growing Broward County. No longer the mecca for college students on spring break, this has become an affluent residential area, more like Beverly Hills than Coney Island. The *Sun-Sentinel* has more competition than its brethren in Orlando—from Cox Newspapers' *Palm Beach Post* to the north and Knight Ridder's *Miami Herald* to the south—but it has better penetration numbers. Reflecting more affluent, more news-conscious readers, 44 percent of potential subscribers receive the paper daily, and 62 percent on Sunday, says Publisher Robert J. Gremillion. Adds editor Maucker, "People would die for the kind of problems I've got!"

In Virginia, the *Daily Press* lost circulation when it raised its price a few years ago (a mistake publisher Davis says he would not repeat). He says circulation has stayed flat for the past ten years, but revenue has increased "dramatically." The *Press,* like its sister papers, has state-of-the-art printing presses that allow later deadlines and zoned editions. Plus, all three papers operate without unions, enjoying more freedom to manage costs. And, like the *Chicago Tribune,* they have redefined how they do business.

Indeed, this is yet another characteristic of Tribune papers: a business culture that permeates every edition. Across the company, editors and publishers express a common devotion to editorial independence, to maintaining a wall between business and editorial. No doubt Fort Lauderdale's Ellen Soeteber is correct: "In some ways these pressures were worse in the old days. It was more small town, and the newspaper was part of the local power structure." She concedes there's always a risk when the wall between business and journalism is lowered. "But less of a risk than before the corporatization of newspapers—which has allowed them to be more independent of the local power structure."

A financially strong corporate owner offers protection, adds Jane Healy, managing editor of the *Orlando Sentinel.* She won a Pulitzer in 1988 for a series exposing the downside of unchecked development. "Developers pulled advertising, and the publisher didn't flinch," she remembers. "I never even heard about it. That's a benefit of a healthy newspaper."

On the other hand, corporatization brings a new, and sometimes, too-cozy culture. As happens regularly on the television networks, where the morning shows or local newscasts often shill for the entertainment shows and stars of its corporate parent, Tribune papers sometimes shill for their business partners. In October, the *Sentinel* stripped a story about the start of its twenty-four-hour cable news operation across the top of the front page: LOCAL NEWS CHANNEL DEBUTS TONIGHT. The *Daily Press,* on election day, plastered its front page with a notice to VISIT DIGITAL CITY HAMPTON ROADS TONIGHT FOR UPDATES ON THE GOVERNOR'S RACE and to watch columnist Jim Spencer on WAVY-TV.

With passion, Orlando's Haile speaks of the need to preserve the wall between business and news because "the newspaper trades on its credibility." But Haile is a reasonable man—someone who loves his job, sees himself as an entrepreneur, and takes pride in being open to change. So he adds, "Too many journalists seem afraid to confront the future. It's almost as if . . . somehow journalists will make the wrong decision about where you draw the line. I think you ought to have more confidence in yourself." The *Sun-Sentinel*'s Maucker goes further. "It's all attitude," he says. "You don't have to declare there are no walls. We've had project teams since I got here. There's always been a belief here in a team approach. . . . There are no walls. There shouldn't be any walls."

Does this mean, I asked, that someone from ad sales could call his editors?

Well, it's OK to call them, Maucker says, which is what most editors would say. But then he goes further: It's OK for an ad manager to call his bureau chiefs, too.

At Tribune papers, the lingo of market research fills the air. People talk of setting up "joint task forces," of "listening to readers." Says Haile, "We have to rethink how we define news. My newsroom may not be in sync with what readers think. For example, if no one in my newsroom is interested in Puerto Rico and my readers are, we are in trouble." The editor, like the publisher, must bring a business sensibility to his mission. Haile welcomes the paper's cumbrous research into what readers want. "You've just got to try and keep ahead of them. We have to have some relevance to them. If they have no interest in government and politics, we have to find out what they are interested in." Ask publisher Davis to cite the strengths of his Virginia paper, and he immediately answers, "It knows its market." Fort Lauderdale's Soeteber says, "We're oriented to our readers."

To help track readers' desires, editors attend two monthly focus group sessions, a common practice at the four papers. Giving readers more of what they want, Soeteber insists, "is not dumbing down the news. It means what issues are most meaningful to their lives." Maybe. Or it might also be true, as James O'Shea, the *Chicago Tribune*'s deputy managing editor, tartly observes, that most readers don't know what they want. "If I go to buy a suit," he says, "I don't go and say, 'I want a brown suit.' A newspaper is the same. You don't know what you want when you pick it up."

Finally, one notices that each Tribune property sees itself as an information company, not just a newspaper. Each has an online newspaper and a Digital City guide on AOL. (Orlando also offers a Black Voices site.) Each has a TV broadcast partner or a twenty-four-hour cable news partner. And, except for Orlando, each has a radio partner. Indeed, the *Sentinel,* says publisher Puerner, is "a regional media holding company." He sees his newspaper in the pivot, with a variety of businesses rotating about it: three magazines, including *Magic Magazine,* a joint publication with the Orlando Magic basketball team; a direct-marketing company, Sentinel Direct, which sells the newspaper's database to advertisers and direct-mail firms; a sign company, Sentinel Signs, which manufactures banners and storefront signs; a market research firm, Sentinel Tele-Services; Sentinel Classifieds, a company that bundles newspaper, online, and magazine classified ads; and Sentinel Printing, which prints sections for noncompeting newspapers and produces TV books and other publications. The mission is to provide one-stop services for customers, be they readers or advertisers. "It's like mountain climbing, as you go up you have to secure yourself and keep moving up the rock," Haile says. "We know about technological change. But as you go up you have to find someplace to secure yourself."

This climbing entrepreneurship is touted in every newsroom. Davis of the *Daily Press* says, "The whole energy level of the newspaper has picked up. You feel you are reaching a bigger audience, having more input, with hardly any more work." Reporters at the four papers sometimes express annoyance that they're not paid for these extra appearances. But they welcome the occasionally larger audiences and the sense of riding the wave of the future. "I feel we're in the process of carving out our place with technology in the marketplace," says Doreen Christensen, who has worked at the *Sun-Sentinel* for eighteen years and currently edits its TV section. "I view it as my job to assure that the newspaper has a place in that new marketplace, and I am making sure that I am not left behind when the train leaves the station."

There is less mention of the downside: resources and attention being siphoned from the papers. In Fort Lauderdale, publisher Gremillion says that this year some money for multimedia will come from the newsroom. "Anything we do in 1998 is going to come out of shifting resources around," he says. But there is an advantage, he insists, when other media provide "a promotional vehicle to brand" the newspaper. These promotional platforms reach nonreaders. They also, he says, save marketing dollars with "free" advertising. It all dovetails neatly with the mission of the Tribune Company, which corporate literature describes as "an information company" seeking "to create leading branded content."

OVER THE TRIBUNE COMPANY'S 151-year history, three men loom largest: pioneering editor and Lincoln champion Joseph Medill; his grandson, Robert McCormick, who reigned—the only word for it—for more than four decades; and Charles Brumback, who was CEO just from 1990 to 1995, but whose passions dominated the company throughout the eighties and, to a large extent, still do. The vituperative, jingoistic, FDR-bashing *Tribune* of Colonel McCormick was both biased and lively—troglodyte and risk taker, abuser of free speech and champion of it. In his engrossing biography, *The Colonel: The Life and Legend of Robert R. McCormick,* Richard Norton Smith dissects and celebrates the "complexities of this life-long maverick cum pillar of the establishment, whose *Tribune* reflected America as in a funhouse mirror. 'I contain multitudes,' Walt Whitman had written. So did Colonel McCormick." The colonel's *Tribune* branched out into radio in the twenties (WGN, for World's Greatest Newspaper) and television in the forties, before either was popular. It was the first to initiate color printing, and among the first to build a paper mill and introduce a Sunday newspaper.

McCormick's *Chicago Tribune* was a family-owned enterprise that reflected the boss's every whim. It wasn't until years later, under the tenure of editor Clayton Kirkpatrick that the paper gained respect for its rising independence—the summit being in 1974 when it published a forty-four-page supplement containing the Watergate tape transcripts and called for Richard Nixon's resignation. In the seventies, under CEO Stanton R. Cook, management was centralized and professionalized. In 1983, Cook steered the company to Wall Street and its first public stock offering, just at the start of the Reagan-era boom market. But the regal Cook—who looked like a CEO from central casting, with flowing gray hair, dark suits, and wing tips—may be remembered most for spotting Brumback, a short, bald, pear-shaped, penny-pinching accountant who wore oversized baggy sports jackets and short-sleeved shirts, and who busied himself shutting off lights at the *Orlando Sentinel* to lower the electric bill.

Brumback was Orlando's business manager when Cook anointed him the paper's acting general manager in 1976. Sensing his own limitations, Brumback enrolled in a one-week crash course run by the American Management Association. "I knew enough to know I really didn't know what professional management was all about," recalls Brumback, who still has three of the textbooks from the course. Taught by management consultants, as well as current and retired CEOs, the retreat gave him a framework and showed him how to plan, how to decentralize management without yielding control, how to seek synergies, and most of all, how to create a climate of professionalism and risk taking.

Brumback dispatched his own managers to the same management boot camp. He got rid of Orlando's creaky letterpresses and invested in an automated offset plant that produced zoned editions. He poured money into marketing, sliced costs, and generally set everyone around him on edge. Brumback adopted a crude refrain: "Look to your right. Look to your left. One of you will be gone next year." An early computer buff, Brumback owned one of the first Apple computers. He became convinced that the microprocessor would transform business. On the subject of technology he was an evangelist. In interviews with business-side job candidates, he'd ask if they could type without looking at the keyboard. He encouraged his managers to take computer tutorials. "You got to get your hands on it," he'd beseech, warning that those who feared or ignored technology did so at their peril. He sought out new businesses, new technologies, that could multiply his assets. John Puerner recalls joining Tribune as a financial analyst in 1979, and as part of his initiation being dispatched to Orlando. "I was inspired that Charlie had created a new-media test bed. He was exploring how newspaper content could be redistributed in many forms."

The same year Brumback became general manager, James Squires, then thirty-six, was sent to Orlando to edit the paper. The two men forged a close union. Squires toughened news coverage; Brumback stiffened the bottom line. Both attracted Chicago's notice. "By 1981," says Squires, "the *Chicago Sun-Times* was still the best-read newspaper in Chicago. Ruth

Clark and her pollsters were still telling the *Tribune* that their readers were dying. It seemed that the *Sun-Times* was growing in the suburbs, where the *Tribune*'s strength had always been." The publisher of the *Sun-Times,* James Hoge, was "running a hell of a show," Squires says. In 1981, CEO Cook chose Brumback to become president of the *Chicago Tribune,* but kept the publisher title for himself. Brumback joined the board of directors of the parent company, and in 1982 he would lure Squires to Chicago to edit the flagship paper.

Brumback was scared. "Orlando," he recalls, "is one of those magical markets where our mistakes don't show." In Chicago, there was no room for error. And he fretted that he had no experience dealing with unions— a gap that, indeed, would haunt him later.

But Brumback did not act scared. He knew there was growing competition from television and computers for readers' leisure time, as well as competition for ad dollars from TV and direct mail. So he moved quickly to control costs, the way he could first address the "appallingly low" single-digit profits. His initial target was the costly hodgepodge of 250 distributors who had muscled agreements to deliver the paper. "We didn't know who our customers were," Brumback says. "I couldn't advertise a price for the *Chicago Tribune* on television because I didn't know what the distributors were charging." He agreed to pay $45 million "to buy back something we never sold." With the help of computers, Brumback collected the names of subscribers, allowing him to bill electronically and to use direct mail.

Meanwhile, *Tribune* trucks were fighting daily with tunnels to the Tower, narrow loading bays, and Michigan Avenue traffic jams. Brumback supervised completion of a $250 million, twenty-one-acre, modern printing plant complex—called Freedom Center—with water, rail, and expressway access. "Cook's strategy was to improve the productivity of the organization," says Brumback, who recalls finding the equivalent of 4,700 full-time employees when he arrived at the *Tribune*. With a term that butchers use for rich, fatty meat, Brumback explains, "We had a lot of 'marbling.'" With Cook's concurrence, Brumback took up his knives.

In all, he would slice 1,000 slots from production areas, and about 700 more from editorial and other departments. He attacked the church/ state divisions by installing staircases connecting the newsroom, on the fourth floor, to the ad and business departments on the second and third floors. He consolidated back-office functions, such as payroll and human resources, for all divisions. Cuts rarely occurred all at once, or exclusively, through layoffs. Newsroom cutbacks were less glaring because he relied on attrition. Brumback demarbled midlevel editors, researchers, receptionists, secretaries. And when in 1985 the paper's typographers went on strike, Brumback broke the union by hiring temporary replacements who became permanent, and trimmed 250 more jobs.

Brumback was hugely unpopular. Many reporters thought he cared more about technology than journalism. Clarence Page remembers that when Brumback visited the Washington bureau, he was only mildly interested in news. "But when I told him I'd just bought a new computer, he was really excited by that, and asked lots of questions." A *Trib* editor recalls, "He was mean to people. He didn't care much about people and their hurt. He would say things that were cruel." Yet that same editor, who asked to remain unidentified, marvels at Brumback's prescience: Those surgical cuts in the early eighties spared the *Trib* the turmoil and anxiety—perhaps the even more traumatic cost cutting—that occurred at Knight Ridder or Times Mirror in the nineties.

From Orlando, Brumback brought another insight to Chicago: Profit margins were determined not just by cutting costs, but by revenue growth. By offering color and thirty-two zones, he reached new advertisers who wanted inserts aimed at specific neighborhoods. By building a computerized database and starting a direct-mail company, he could advertise to *Trib* readers and nonreaders. Years later, says Timothy J. Landon, vice president for strategy and development for Tribune Publishing, the company would generate ten million dollars in revenue (and 25 percent profit margins) just on niche magazines that carry information about cars or real estate, as well as classified ads. The *Tribune* also makes money printing the *New York Times's* Midwest edition and distributing it in Chicago. Today the paper's operating profit margin stands at 28 percent—and more than half that growth comes from revenue rather than cost reductions. Says *Trib* publisher Scott Smith, "The key is the total revenue per subscriber, which is the highest in the industry" at about a thousand dollars a year.

Brumback brought a third insight, says Landon, who joined the paper as a twenty-one-year-old intern in 1985: "If you've got the cash flow, you can afford to take chances. That came from Charlie." The same year Cook brought Brumback to Chicago, he lured James Dowdle from Hubbard Broadcasting to lead the *Tribune*'s diversification into electronic media. At the time, Tribune owned TV stations in Chicago (WGN), New York City (WPIX), and Denver (KWGN). Under Dowdle, the company would expand from three to sixteen stations, reaching a third of the national audience. Dowdle and Brumback were soul mates their first six months in Chicago, sharing an apartment in the John Hancock Tower. Dowdle remembers coming home late and watching the rumpled Brumback bang away at something called a personal computer, a machine that at the time was still a novelty.

Brumback banged away at work, too. As Tribune president, he told executives that if they learned to use a computer, the company would buy them one. John Madigan, who was then the chief financial officer, recalls, "Charlie was tightfisted. But on computers he was very liberal. That created a comfortability and familiarity. . . . A lot of Luddites saw the light quickly."

When Cook took Tribune public in 1983, there was new capital for investment, and new discipline. Up to this point, the company's stakeholders were comprised of family members. It was a way, says Brumback, to impose on the company the scrutiny of shareholders, who could reward, or punish, its performance—to a point. Like other family-owned newspaper companies that sold stock (the New York Times, the Washington Post, Dow Jones), Tribune protected itself by ensuring that control stayed in friendly hands. Today, the not-for-profit Robert R. McCormick Tribune Foundation, whose shares are voted by current and retired company executives, controls 18 percent of the common stock; employees, who enjoy a generous stock benefit plan, hold all the preferred stock.

Brumback, whose influence had long since eclipsed his titles, was named chief operating officer of the parent company in January 1989.

He was promoted (over John Madigan) to president and CEO in August 1990, succeeding Cook. Brumback immediately set out to change Tribune's traditional corporate culture. In 1991 he initiated quarterly management retreats for about fifty top executives. "He said, 'I want this to be a more entrepreneurial culture,'" recalls Orlando's Haile. "I said, 'Charlie, no one believes you. We've been a cautious newspaper company.' But it started a cultural process that really changed the Tribune." (At the most recent management forum last November, one hundred Tribune executives spent a day at the company's education publishing subsidiary in Washington State, and another day at Microsoft.)

And Brumback initiated something else: a year and a half of intense weekly strategy sessions among the top five executives, a group he called the development committee. Its twofold mission would have fateful consequences. The committee sought ways to grow, which would prompt a focus on new-media investments. It also meant they would rethink investments that showed slow growth.

Tribune was already trotting on the electronic track. In 1989, while other companies clamored to invest in Prodigy and Compuserve, Tribune was the first outside investor in Steve Case's fledgling Quantum Computer Services, exchanging $5 million for 10 percent ownership of what would become America Online. As Brumback gathered the reins of the company, electronic investment was spurred to a gallop. These investments were very much aimed at Tribune's new audience: Wall Street, which punishes anyone who's said to be in "yesterday's business." That threw a baleful light on two of the Tribune's grandest old investments. Even before Cook and the board chose him as heir apparent, Brumback had warned that the future of the company's Canadian paper mills and the *New York Daily News* would have to be resolved.

The Canadian plants were the best in the business, but paper mills need almost constant upgrading at huge cost. Newsprint was becoming a more competitive commodity, reducing its profitability at the same time that the Tribune could buy paper cheaply elsewhere. Brumback and his committee decided to sell the Canadian mills. As for the tabloid *Daily News*—well, that was more complex.

Another grandson of Joseph Medill, Joseph M. Patterson, founded the *Daily News* in 1919. The feisty "picture newspaper" grew steadily until, by 1949, it was selling 2.5 million copies a day, more than any other paper in America. But by the eighties, after decades of inefficient management and union corruption, the *News* was losing readers and ads, and was saddled with featherbedding contracts and an antique printing plant. The *News* was sucking cash from the parent company. In 1981, under Cook, Tribune made a deal to sell the *News* to Joe L. Allbritton. But at the eleventh hour, Allbritton claimed he hadn't been told of the financial liabilities imposed by union contracts he would inherit. When the Tribune refused to indemnify him against those potential costs, the deal fell apart.

But Brumback and the development committee wanted resolution. They would, in Brumback's words, "fix it or get out." "Charlie was determined to be bold," recalls Smith, who was then senior vice president for finance. To fix the *News,* Tribune managers imposed new work rules and had the *News* hire the same law firm that advised them during the 1985 Chicago strike, King & Ballow, led by attorney Robert Ballow. Brumback thought they were hiring a "labor expert" to calibrate a careful strategy. But the strategy turned out to be short on care. Instead of isolating a mob-linked or racially gerrymandered blue-collar union—and walling off the white-collar Newspaper Guild from the strife—Tribune lumped all ten unions together. *News* workers became convinced that the company wanted to rid the paper of unions, and in 1990 they went on strike. With Brumback's sanction, the *News* hired replacement workers. There was violence. The mayor, the governor, New York business leaders—even Cardinal John O'Connor—supported the unions.

Unlike Chicago, where the Tribune was powerful enough to bust a strike—or England, where Prime Minister Margaret Thatcher's government in 1986 helped Rupert Murdoch when he attacked wasteful work practices by protecting those who crossed the picket line—in New York the police sided with strikers. They did not arrest those who broke the law to impede replacement workers. Trucks were vandalized, scabs beaten up. The *News* was struggling to publish every day, but no one seemed to care. Most newsstand dealers wouldn't sell the replacement *News,* and those who would found few buyers. This went on for months. New Yorkers sneered at the rubes from Chicago—*The Gang That Couldn't Shoot Straight.*

"No question we underestimated the control of the streets of New York," says Dowdle, who attended daily strategy sessions. Looking back, Smith says, "Did we miscalculate things? . . . Sure." But he insists that failure stemmed from a Tribune virtue: Company managers were simply "eternal optimists. We really did believe we could do better in New York."

They did worse . . . and worse. The Tribune pegged *News* operating losses at $114 million for 1990. By the time they sold the *News* to the fly-by-night British baron Robert Maxwell in March 1991, the red ink was a flood. "Over the decade," says Smith, "we lost something over $500 million."

Brumback, for his part, says today, "I don't know what we could have done differently." He rejects the notion that his strategy failed. "It did work," he insists. "Our strategy was to fix it, or get out." They got out.

By the end of 1991, even though the Tribune owned six TV stations, four radio stations, and the Chicago Cubs, and even though it had made a handful of new-media investments, two-thirds of its revenues still derived from newspapers. Brumback was determined to reduce this reliance.

In 1992 the *Chicago Tribune* became one of the first newspapers to put an edition online. In early 1993 it was among the first to establish a local twenty-four-hour cable news outlet, CLTV. Both efforts would be replicated in other cities where it owned newspapers. Starting with the investment in AOL, the company staked a series of new-media ventures, often joining with the powerhouse Silicon venture capital firm Kleiner Perkins to bankroll start-ups like Excite, a navigation system to roam the Internet.

Brumback stepped down as CEO in May 1995, and was succeeded by John Madigan. By contrast with the short, bald, gruff Brumback, Madigan was Wall Street smooth, with silver hair and a ready smile. If Brumback was the former infantry lieutenant who led the charge up a hill, Madigan, a former investment banker at Salomon Brothers, was more the stylish general staff man. But like his predecessor, Madigan was determined to change the business mix. He was preoccupied with the Tribune's stock price. "This is a company with a lot of momentum," Madigan told shareholders at the annual meeting in May 1996. "But we're not satisfied with our stock price performance over the last several years." The price was then 70⅜ a share. (The stock would split two for one the following January.) Wall Street still perceived the Tribune as too dependent on print.

So Madigan accelerated Tribune's investment in other media, expanding into software, education publishing, and multimedia. He bought into the start-up WB television network. Then in July 1996, soon after the federal government relaxed restrictions on the number of broadcast stations a company could own, Madigan announced a blockbuster acquisition: For $1.1 billion, Tribune would buy Renaissance Communications' six TV stations. With one stroke, Tribune now reached into one-third of all broadcast homes in the nation, and 70 percent of cable homes, courtesy of superstation WGN. By winter, Madigan finally could boast that half of Tribune's revenues came from sources other than newspapers.

WHAT DO YOU LIKE, I asked John Madigan, about the *Chicago Tribune?*

Seated at a tiny wooden conference table in his modestly furnished office, Madigan answers slowly, with evident care. "The overall coverage is very good," he tells me.

What did he admire about his other three papers?

"I don't read them regularly," he says. "I do when I go there."

It's hard to know whether Madigan is being coy or polite; as CEO, perhaps he doesn't want to criticize by omission those he neglects to praise. Or is he someone who pays more attention to numbers than the journalistic product that generates those numbers? When I ask about the police-blotter news so prominent on his TV stations, he says, "I can't regularly watch those stations," though he surmises that "our newscasts are a better quality than that."

Tribune has maintained profit margins because the company has inventively found ways to generate new revenues. But if newspaper profits can't keep pace with those of broadcasting, entertainment, educational publishing, and new media, won't Wall Street thump the laggard papers?

That's when journalists want to hear that the CEO loves his papers— and is willing to sacrifice a few margin points to maintain their luster. Although Madigan, when asked, will answer that the media business holds a special trust because it provides information and helps shape public attitudes, he's not much for speeches about the World's Greatest Newspaper. "I like the blend of local, international, and national factors," he says of the *Trib.* "It's packaged well. There is an effective use of color and formatting. I think it's the best-looking paper there is."

This prompts another question that can be heard in *Tribune* newsrooms: Does the company *believe* in newspapers? Within management ranks, from Madigan on down, the question is dismissed as ludicrous because it assumes that newspapers are static. Tribune regards papers as vessels to carry the company wherever it seeks to go. "The newspaper is at the center of what we do," says Orlando publisher John Puerner. "And it will remain at the center. And everything else we do is complementary." The rub is that this strategy is crimped by the fact that Tribune owns only four newspapers. The proclaimed synergies with local broadcasting, cable, and online seem to require more papers at their center. "You'd love to have a footprint in more of the top thirty markets," admits Landon, the strategic vice president. "If we could have held on to the *Daily News* in New York, it would have been a great thing."

The flip side, Jack Fuller points out, is that national papers like the *New York Times* and *Wall Street Journal* would love to have the local franchise and multimedia arms of Tribune. "Our problem is that we don't have enough of the top thirty cities. No one does. The national brands' problem is that they don't have the local clout we do. The *Times* has been successful at taking a fairly shallow cut of people all across the country." Each of the big newspaper chains, Fuller says, have vulnerabilities: Gannett, the biggest, has only one metro, the *Detroit News,* in the top thirty markets; Knight Ridder is excluded from the nation's three largest markets, as is Cox. Tribune has tried to acquire more papers, bidding in 1997 for Disney's newspapers and Minneapolis's *Star Tribune,* among others. But in every case Tribune was too "disciplined" to pay top dollar. The company has simply put its money elsewhere. "There are also other ways to be involved in newspapers," says Don M. Davis, president of Tribune Ventures. "We can be in Digital Cities without owning newspapers. Or we can own iVillage and other interactive forms."

Tribune's strategy may bump into other obstacles. Under the cross-ownership rules of the federal government, a company may not own both a newspaper and a broadcast outlet in the same market—unless the company did so before the rule came into force (as is the case with WGN in Chicago), or unless the government finds a public interest in waiving the rule (as it did when Rupert Murdoch's News Corp. was allowed to rescue the *New York Post*). The Federal Communications Commission, so far backed by the courts, has ordered Tribune to choose between its Fort Lauderdale paper and TV station WDZL. (The FCC let a March 1998 deadline lapse so it could review the cross-ownership rules.) The FCC's argument claims that in a democracy no corporation should dominate the means of communication, and without the rule there would be less diversity of voices. The Tribune's argument, advanced by its broadcasting president, Dennis Fitzsimmons, is that the rule is antiquated. When we see the consolidation that occurs in the cable industry or radio, he says, "the idea that we should set aside newspapers and television is crazy." Cable giant Tele-Communications, Inc., has a lock on 80 percent of all cable boxes in Chicago, he says, while CBS owns eighty-eight radio stations. "This dwarfs our market share." If the company means to prosper from multimedia synergies between newspapers and TV and radio stations, the rulebook will have to change.

All newspapers confront another obstacle: Fragmented information choices are robbing papers of circulation. In the past decade, overall newspaper circulation has dropped 10 percent, a trend most analysts expect to continue. A few publishers believe they can defy gravity and grow circulation: Mark Willes has set a goal of boosting the *Los Angeles Times* circulation by 500,000, or 50 percent; few of his own executives believe this is possible. Willes can point to the *Times* of London, whose circulation jumped from 350,000 copies in 1993 to more than 800,000 in 1997. But to accomplish this feat, owner Rupert Murdoch slashed the price of the paper and introduced more tabloid features to the once august *Times*. England, however, isn't analogous to the United States, since three out of four people in the United Kingdom read a daily paper, while only one in two do in the United States. John Madigan considers himself a realist. He says he'd be satisfied to "hold circulation" flat. But he frets, "We know young people are less inclined to read than their parents."

And what effects will newspapers feel from the Internet? Merrill

Brown, the editor in chief of MSNBC online, a joint effort of NBC and Microsoft, claims to have data "starting to show" that people who get most of their news from the Internet are canceling their newspaper subscriptions. "We are being reached by three hundred thousand different machines each day," he says; lumping together all news Web sites, Brown estimates that "a couple of million people a day get their news this way." Unlike with a newspaper, online users can "customize" their news, get it instantly, and get it free. What they don't get—certainly not from MSNBC, as Brown concedes—is much local news.

The other electronic menace to newspapers—Brumback recognized this early on—is the efficient way classified ads can be presented online. Buying a home? An online classified can show you color pictures, offer endless details, and link you to the right Realtor. Want a new job? Online listings can link you to desirable openings in other states. Nationally, classifieds are a $15 billion market. Chief Financial Officer Grenesko says they represent 46 percent of Tribune's newspaper advertising revenues. Ask *Tribune* publisher Scott Smith to describe his biggest worry, and his answer is succinct: "Our classified business collapsing." Classifieds are the single most profitable section of a newspaper, he says, and because newspapers monopolized these, they could "charge more." If electronic competitors reduce newspaper market share from 80 to, say, 50 percent, he fears, ad rates and profit margins would collapse.

That's why Tribune has put so much effort into Internet classifieds. With the Washington Post and Times Mirror, it has started CarPoint, which is platformed on AOL. And Tribune has a connection, CareerPath, with seven other publishers (representing seventy papers) to target employment ads. In their worst nightmares, Tribune executives see Microsoft, with its deep pockets and technological prowess, extracting chunks of the classified market. But as is true with online news, Microsoft is thin locally. Landon sounds like a combat commander when he declares, "Our whole bet is to neutralize Microsoft's positioning, and then force it down to local ground wars."

Technology is compelling newspapers to fight these multifront wars. The Internet is likely to siphon off more customers, as will interactive television. With greater bandwidth, TVs or computers will be able to summon not just text, but audio news and full-motion video. Tribune sees not only challenges here but opportunities. Because electronic links will allow companies to collect data on the interests of each customer, says Jeff R. Scherb, Tribune's senior vice president for technology, "you may get to the point where zones can be your house." Scherb believes the role of newspapers and journalists will change when consumers can interact and retrieve more information than papers provide. "I don't think ink on paper will ever be replaced," he says. "It's hard to surf the Web and find things you don't expect. You have to go looking for things." Still, he considers a decline in the printed page inevitable.

In his office at the McCormick Tribune Foundation, in the Tribune Tower, Charles Brumback looks up phone numbers, checks his schedule, and exchanges e-mail—all from a wireless PalmPilot. At his desk, he's equipped with the computer equivalent of a souped-up car: a three-gigabyte hard disk with an Iomega Zip drive that stores a hundred megabytes on a single disk. He subscribes to technical publications and changes his equipment frequently. But he has not changed his view that Tribune must flourish as a multimedia company. In the future, Brumback says, "the successful company is going to be the table of contents to the Internet."

I ask Brumback to describe his proudest achievement. "We really are today recognized as a successful information and entertainment company," he says. "I think we've applied technology to our products, to news, in a way that makes the end product much more interesting. We have people who are not afraid of the future. We have some middle-aged editorial types who just came to life."

One of those middle-aged types is the raspy-voiced columnist John Kass, forty-one years old and the father of twin boys. He is comforted by the *Tribune*'s extraordinary efforts to probe and prepare for a different future. Kass recounts the time he worked on a small daily, when the steel company in town announced sudden and massive layoffs. "People were saying, 'They should have understood the steel business had changed.' It was a good lesson for me. I know everything changes. I try and put aside for changes. Those guys weren't prepared. The company wasn't prepared. What we're trying to do is prepare for the future so that the company can continue."

In preparing for that future, it may be that the greatest obstacles will not be technical but cultural. There is an inherent clash between the culture of business, which wants to maximize profits, and the culture of journalism, which wants to maximize coverage. If circulation doesn't grow, business pressures will push money out of newspapers to somewhere else. At the same time, the tools to measure what readers want become more refined. "One of the great, and terrifying, things about the Web is that everything is measurable," says Hiller, the *Tribune*'s chief strategist. Whether readers prefer horoscopes to international news, sports to science, gossip to government—all this can be quantified, he says.

So what happens when an editor's judgment collides, as it will, with market research? If readers say they prefer horoscopes to foreign news, I ask Hiller, won't there be pressure to drop foreign news?

"People really do want a quality editorial experience," he says. "On the open Web is chaos and madness. What we do as a newspaper is bring some coherence." Pressed, however, he responds, "I think, ultimately, the market works."

Meaning what?

"I think, long-term, you get in trouble not giving the public what it wants."

And if it wants horoscopes?

"Then I'd give it to them."

As it happens, it's in Chicago's western suburbs where you find perhaps today's most extreme experiment in marketing-generated news. Here Copley has augmented its daily newspapers with a free weekly whose "community" is a zip code—indeed, its *name* is a zip code, *60504*. Its news content owes less to what journalists think than to what careful market surveys say the public and advertisers want. The result seems less a newspaper than an electrocardiogram.

At a well-run company like Tribune, where managers and editors alike speak of "quality," "credibility," and all the other heartfelt words that suggest they understand they have no product without good journalism, the problem is not executives who intend to do harm. The danger is inadvertent harm. Journalism is an act of faith. It is not concrete, like a balance sheet. Readers spend their money and time on the faith that journalists strive to learn the truth and don't cut corners. Journalists place their faith in the words of Abraham Lincoln—words etched into marble at the Tribune Tower's splendid entrance: "Let the people know the facts and the country will be safe."

POSTSCRIPT

When the Tribune Company acquired Times Mirror in early 2000, it added seven newspapers to its fold, including *Newsday* in New York. Since Tribune already owned WPIX-TV in that city, visions of synergy danced in the heads of executives. However, as good a newspaper as *Newsday* is, it was essentially a suburban paper vying to supplant two familiar tabloids, the *New York Daily News* and the *Post*.

And this wasn't a familiar fight for the Tribune Company. It was in competition with two tabloids who did not keep score by either profits or synergy. The following piece was prepared for *The New Yorker* in the winter of 2002. It never appeared. There was a miscommunication; my editors wanted more of a colorful inside-the-tabloids piece, and I had produced more of a business story. As a noted philosopher once said, "Shit happens."

NEW YORK'S
TABLOID WARS

T HE NEWSPAPER WAR in New York merits one of those *National Enquirer* headlines announcing another Elvis sighting. In this peculiar battle, the *New York Daily News,* the first tabloid newspaper in America, is pitted against the *New York Post,* the nation's oldest continuously published newspaper. Unlike the media world at large, where corporations obsess over their profit margins and share price, in this tabloid war the rules of modern capitalism are suspended. Profitability is not the sole measure of success, for each newspaper has suffered enormous losses over the years; the *News* is marginally profitable, at best, and the *Post* hasn't made a nickel in more than thirty years. The synergy sought by the owner of each paper has less to do with business opportunities than with gaining a political or power platform.

The principal combatants—Mortimer B. Zuckerman, the real estate developer who owns the *News,* and *Post* owner Rupert Murdoch, CEO of the fourth largest media company in the world—don't have deep roots in

New York. Zuckerman was born in Canada, Murdoch in Australia. Unlike other cities where newspaper choices shrink, in this war readers are offered a choice of four—soon five—New York dailies. These include a newspaper, the *New York Times,* that strives to escape its New York base; a suburban daily, *Newsday,* that wishes to claim it; and soon a *New York Sun* that insists no one adequately covers the city. The battles between these three other papers remain sideshows to the barroom brawl between the *News* and the *Post,* which is as much about power, pride, and politics as profit. It is not likely to end soon.

What isn't different about the *News* versus *Post* battle is the grumbling. The *News* is located on the windy, western end of Thirty-third Street, where reporters grouse that the bleak office tower was chosen because the rent was cheap. Journalists did, of course, complain as well about their old low-ceilinged newsroom in the former Daily News Building on East Forty-second Street, but they loved the hublike location that was within walking distance of restaurants and subways. In their new remote location, staffers enter a vast newsroom with dungeonlike windows so high off the floor that they sometimes phone outside to learn if it's raining. They whisper about the lack of teamwork at the top. No one had to remind them that Zuckerman has raced through editors like a kid with a deck of cards—picking five in eight years. This time, he says, he's picked right.

The editor, Edward Kosner, does not appear to be someone who would relate to the *News*'s working-class readers, for he is a punctilious, dapper man of sixty-four who wears black-framed eyeglasses and white shirts. A veteran of many editorial battles, Kosner started as a reporter and then became an editor at the *Post,* moved on to eventually become the editor of *Newsweek,* and the editor of *New York* magazine (when Murdoch owned it) and of *Esquire* magazine. After being replaced at *Esquire,* he joined the *News* as Sunday editor in 1998, and in 2000 became the fifth editor Zuckerman would appoint. He is often credited for bringing a mature, calming editorial hand to the paper.

His counterpart at the *Post,* Col Allan, has a different pedigree. He has spent forty-five of his forty-eight years in Australia. Allan has worked for Murdoch's News Corp. for nearly three decades, most recently as editor of the *Daily Telegraph/Sunday Telegraph,* that nation's largest. When he was appointed, there was grumbling that Allan was too much of a stranger to New York, too formal in his cuffed white shirts, and too volatile. While Murdoch praises the highly visible changes that Col Allan has made at the *Post* since he arrived in May 2000, his critics long ago affixed him with the unfriendly moniker Col Pot. There was grumbling, as well, that the *Post,* which hasn't made money since Murdoch acquired it in 1975, might close if Allan failed.

There was less grumbling about the paper's location, which used to be cramped offices on South Street straddling the East River, which could barely be seen, since the windows were caked with dirt; now the paper has an uptown newsroom on the spacious tenth floor of the News Corp. skyscraper on Forty-eighth Street and Sixth Avenue. Although they work for a behemoth media company, employees feel like they work for Rupert, as many have for much of their adult lives. While the *News* attracts more advertising dollars, and twice as many readers, the *Post* is often described as more fun to read. Of course, *fun*—as opposed to *accurate*—is an odd way to characterize a newspaper.

The business strategies of the two papers are odder still. The usually tough-minded Murdoch seems to embrace a faith-based business plan. He believes the *Post*'s circulation will dramatically climb and advertising will magically follow, although he can cite no other American newspaper as a model for such growth. Murdoch has pared the price of the paper from fifty to twenty-five cents, lavished one-quarter of a billion dollars on a new state-of-the-art South Bronx printing plant that produces color pictures that look like paintings and whose location just north of the Triborough Bridge allows *Post* trucks to zip in and out of the city. The *Post*'s circulation has jumped 22 percent in the past year, but its losses have also jumped. Zuckerman, meanwhile, has lost more money than he's made on the *News.* To save more, he purchased a second-tier Jersey City printing plant, which often results in somewhat fuzzy pictures for "New York's Picture Newspaper."

At each paper, employees are happy to explain what the other is doing wrong. *News* editor Kosner dismisses the *Post* as "a supplemental read," while saying the *News* is a "primary" or must-read. His executive editor, Michael Goodwin, likens the *Post* under Allan to "a British paper" or a supermarket tabloid, usually featuring an oversized color photograph of a nonlocal event. Goodwin, fifty-two, is a silver-haired former *New York Times* reporter who became the editorial-page editor of the *News* and who was at the helm when the page won its first Pulitzer in fifty-eight years; when Kosner was appointed the editor, Goodwin became his deputy. He compares the two papers this way: "Pete Hamill once said, 'The *News* is a paper you bring home and the *Post* is a paper you leave at the OTB parlor.'" Emerging recently from a page-one meeting, Goodwin sounded more like a thoughtful Timesman than a tabloid warrior. Asked if he worried about what the *Post* might put on its front page, he said, "Not really. The papers are so different. I worried more about the *Post* pre-Col Allan."

Allan, in turn, calls the *News* too "serious," too dull, for him to lose sleep over. And his city editor, Jesse Angelo, who at twenty-eight is already a veteran of Murdoch's tabloids in England and Australia, places the two papers on his cluttered desk and points to what he calls "the stripper story" in the *Post* that morning. It recounts how a nineteen-year-old stripper lured a fifty-five-year-old lawyer away from his wife, was showered with a thirty-carat diamond ring and—his voice now rising with excitement— "then plotted with her ex-boyfriend, allegedly, to have him offed. Just a remarkable story!" He pauses to savor the flavor, and continues, "Just pure tabloid gold! Which, by the way, in an act of just pure cowardice—we beat the pants off the *Daily News* on the first day and they haven't touched it since—which is just inexcusable! You get beat on a story, you come back gangbusters the next day and make sure you beat them." He points to a somewhat blurry photo on page one of the *News* and mischievously sneers, "Is that an artist's rendition or a photograph?"

While affecting unconcern, in truth these competitors fret about each other all the time. "The *Post* makes the *News* better," says *News* columnist Pete Hamill, sixty-six, who grew up as a *Post* columnist, has served as the editor of each paper, and though he now writes novels, can't stay away from the fray. Hamill is proud to work for a tabloid, and aside from shorter stories and more pictures, he says "people working for tabloids don't go out on a story with lower ambitions than reporters for the broadsheets. Or with some Hildy Johnson roguery in mind. That's bullshit out of old movies." A press card, he says, is a ticket to explore and have a few laughs and, maybe, make the world a little better place. *News* editors still swell with pride over their classic 1975 page-one headline: FORD TO CITY: DROP DEAD. And everyone still smiles when recounting this *Post* page one: HEADLESS BODY IN TOPLESS BAR.

What a field day headline writers could have if their wit were turned on themselves. The *Post,* for example, is consistently right-wing and prides itself on being antielite, yet the heart of its readership is drawn from Manhattan's elite. And editor Allan derides what he imagines to be Chardonnay-drinking West Side swells, but he nevertheless resides among them. At the *News,* Zuckerman and his copublisher and longtime partner, Fred Drasner, who was once featured playing stickball in *News* TV ads, have in recent years been like an estranged couple who can't divorce because their finances are so entangled, and so they live together but barely speak. And Zuckerman's mania for control is such that his press spokesman wasn't permitted to pass along his official biography without permission.

At the *Post,* family rules: Rupert Murdoch, who is seventy, has made his son Lachlan the cochairman of the paper (with his father) and the deputy chief operating officer of News Corp.; he has said that he would like Lachlan to one day replace him as CEO. Since the *Post* has already lost more than $500 million since Murdoch assumed command twenty-seven years ago, this leads to very different predictions: that Rupert will fold the paper because he won't allow his son to fail, or that he will keep it going because he will find a way for his son to win. Zuckerman, the sole owner of the *News,* may be a billionaire, but he doesn't have Murdoch's deep pockets. James Hoge, who was publisher of the *News* from 1984 to 1991, and is today the editor of *Foreign Affairs,* remembers once chatting with Murdoch and mentioning that the *Post* must be losing an alarming $20 million per year. With an edge to his voice, Murdoch responded, "'That's one week's interest to me.'"

Lachlan Murdoch is only two decades removed from the framed picture above his desk of an eight-year-old in a cap standing in front of a *Post* delivery truck hawking papers. He is a handsome baby-faced man with slightly spiked short brown hair, big earlobes that protrude sideways, and modish rimless eyeglasses. Seated beneath a ficus tree on a pure white,

L-shaped couch in a black pinstripe suit, white shirt, and tie, he seems to be impersonating an older person.

"We are engaged in the most exciting newspaper battle in America and maybe the world," Lachlan Murdoch told me. He is not as active as his father was—he does not come in and dictate front-page headlines. But he did intercede last spring and replace the editor. He estimates that he spends about three-quarters of his time in his ninth-floor office in the News Corp. midtown building, with the rest spent in Australia, where he oversees ten daily and two hundred suburban newspapers. The four national British newspapers still report to his father. Although he is only thirty, like his father he has strong opinions about journalism. "I don't have a high regard for the quality of American newspapers," he says, looking across the room at a display of News Corp.'s newspapers, which sell seven million daily copies and are delivered to his office, just as they are to his father's. "The journalism is excellent. The words. But if you pick up almost any newspaper in America, they are poorly designed and messy. . . ."

Despite a daily *Post* circulation that is 200,000 below the *News*'s 730,000, he predicts, "We will catch up to the *Daily News* in the next eighteen months." He believes both papers can coexist, especially since they appeal to different audiences (80 percent of *Post* customers supplement the information they get by reading another paper, whereas about two-thirds of *News* customers rely on it alone). Yet he acknowledges, "History suggests that only one paper will be left standing."

Zuckerman is convinced that paper will be the *News*, which he calls "the voice of middle- and working-class people in this city." A trim man who plays a furious game of squash and relentlessly exercises, he walks slowly this day, taking small, careful steps. He recently underwent an emergency operation after he held his four-year-old daughter, Abigail, aloft and his hernia burst through his stomach wall. The hernia gives him pain, as does trying to decode the *Post*'s strategy: "I don't understand what they're doing. They are not as competitive as people think. They have a different audience in many ways." He notes that the *Post* is a second read and therefore nonessential for advertisers who can reach readers through other newspapers. Of course, he worries about his competitor more than he lets on.

He knows the *Post* is more "fun" because it is a "second read." Thus the paper was imbued, even before the arrival of Murdoch, with a more care-free attitude in its headlines and even some of its stories. It had been an afternoon paper and carried a sense that it should be a quick, supplemental, and entertaining read. *If we make a mistake, the* Times *will catch it. We're providing a diversion.* This attracts readers, and repels advertisers.

Zuckerman, who is sixty-four, owns no other newspapers, and after selling the *Atlantic* and *Fast Company,* he now owns only one magazine, *U.S. News & World Report.* As a business, the *News* is on much firmer ground than the *Post,* yet Zuckerman concedes he has lost more money than he has made since purchasing the paper in January 1993. Nevertheless, he says it is stupid for competitors to assume that he will give up. They are thinking financially; he is thinking more personally. He has built more than one hundred buildings, he says, but journalism provides much more satisfaction. He gets to travel and talk to opinion makers, gets invited to opine on TV interview shows, gets to write a weekly column. "I really care about what the role of journalism is," he says. "It's my way of having a window to and understanding the world around me. . . . I like the involvement it gives me."

There is no corporate line of succession, so what would happen if he should get hit by a car? Zuckerman smiles and tells of gathering the staff last year to introduce Les Goodstein, the new president of the paper. Accompanied by his then-wife, Marla, and his daughter, Abigail, Zuckerman announced, "I want you all to meet the next publisher of the *Daily News:* Abigail Jane Zuckerman."

HISTORY

The *News* became the nation's first tabloid or picture newspaper in 1919. "It was something no newspaper had done before, which was to go for mass circulation and working-class readers," says *New York Post* editorial writer Eric Fettman, an amateur newspaper historian. Quickly, the *News* became known for its punchy prose and memorable photography. As the nation's oldest newspaper, the *Post* was already in existence, having been founded by Alexander Hamilton in 1802. It was converted into a tabloid format by owner Dorothy Schiff in 1942, and she also turned it into a newspaper with a distinctly liberal voice. The *News* remained king of the tabloids, and by 1949 it was selling nearly 2.5 million daily copies. But the decline had begun. The city had four fewer newspapers after World War II than it had had twenty-five years before. In 1949, A. J. Liebling predicted in one of his well-read Wayward Press pieces in *The New Yorker* that the city was racing toward "a one- or two-paper town by about 1975." Victimized by the popularity of television with its vivid pictures, by the aspirations of the working class to own a patch of grass in the suburbs, by the flight of retail advertisers—and by management's own mistakes, including a crippling 1966 citywide newspaper strike— by 1975 the city was left with just three papers, the *News,* the *Post,* and the *Times.*

The *News* remained a thriving business for its owners, the Tribune Company of Chicago. The *Post* had one-tenth the *News*'s circulation, and among the reasons was the *News*'s grab-readers-by-the-throat headlines. Editors there even created staff incentives by offering cash prizes for the best headlines. The *News* also reported from the boroughs in ways other papers did not. "We had a staff of twelve in Brooklyn and of thirteen in Queens covering neighborhoods," recalls Michael O'Neill, who was the managing editor from 1968 to 1975, and the editor from 1975 to 1982. Readers, recalls O'Neill, were treated respectfully. During the fifties, when Eisenhower was president, O'Neill says, "We printed excerpts from press conference transcripts. . . . That was our policy, even though we were doing fun and games."

Nevertheless, the *News*'s circulation decline accelerated in the seventies, as did the *Post*'s, and in her eighth decade Dorothy Schiff decided to sell. Only a buyer preoccupied with establishing a beachhead in America's premier city would overlook the red ink. Rupert Murdoch acquired the *Post* in 1975, and soon thereafter converted it into a newspaper with a strong conservative agenda. But federal cross-ownership rules that a company may not own both a TV and a radio station in the same city in which it owns a newspaper forced Murdoch to sell the *Post* in 1988. He had just started the Fox network and needed his flagship New York TV station.

The *News* also changed owners. The Tribune Company, influenced by the Gannett-inspired notion that newspaper profit margins must exceed single digits, sold the *News* in 1991. Over the next few years, the *Post* had three owners, one of whom went bankrupt and two of whom went to jail. The *News,* meanwhile, was purchased by an English swindler, Robert Maxwell, who jumped to his death as investigators circled. The expectation in late 1992 was that neither paper would survive.

The expectations overlooked the vanity, and talents, of two rich men. In early 1993, Zuckerman, who had tapped his real estate fortune to acquire the *Atlantic* magazine in 1980 and *U.S. News & World Report* in 1985, received givebacks from the unions and skillfully rescued the *News* from bankruptcy. Later in 1993, supported by Governor Mario Cuomo and other liberals his paper once eviscerated, Murdoch received a federal cross-ownership waiver to save the *Post*.

Although these were hardly Harvard Business School models, Murdoch and Zuckerman had other ways to compute success. Murdoch's newspapers, and his willingness to employ them to advance his political agenda, awarded him political clout. Sometimes, that clout advanced his business interests. When Murdoch wanted an Export-Import Bank loan in 1979 to finance the purchase of Boeing rather than European Airbus jets for an Australian airline he then owned, he received a $290 million loan soon after lunching with President Jimmy Carter and promising him the *Post*'s endorsement for the New York State Democratic primary. Both he and Carter deny a linkage. More recently, he induced Mayor Rudolph Giuliani to lead a successful campaign to persuade Time Warner Cable systems to carry his new Fox News network. Joined by other network and newspaper owners, he is lobbying a receptive Bush administration to further lift restrictions on the number of stations one owner may control and to terminate cross-ownership restrictions that could force his News Corp. to choose between keeping the *Post* or New York TV stations. Although he has been branded a monopolist in Australia and

England, he now claims that if the Bush administration allows Echo-Star to acquire its only direct satellite competitor, DirecTV, it will violate the nation's antitrust laws. (If Murdoch succeeds in blocking this sale he will reopen the possibility of purchasing DirecTV himself.) And, of course, stories in which the News Corp. was involved usually get bigger play. For example, when Fox News lured Greta Van Susteren from CNN, it was splashed on page three of the *Post;* when Murdoch was warring with Ted Turner over Fox News, Turner was regularly portrayed in the *Post* as loony. "This is not a newspaper but a weapon in the hands of a news-paper owner," says Les Payne, the deputy managing editor of *Newsday,* who is in charge of its city, national, and international coverage. While it is true that Murdoch cannot tell his directors that the *Post* has made money, he can surely confide that it has been good for News Corp. And, more personally, in the words of one close adviser, Murdoch knows that he has gotten "his conservative precepts across in the biggest market in the country."

Zuckerman has seemed less concerned with advancing a set of precepts than with backing winners. He went from embracing Democrat Jimmy Carter in the 1980 election to praising Republican Presidents Reagan and Bush to befriending Bill Clinton; the *News* endorsed liberal Democrat David Dinkins for mayor in 1989 and conservative Republican Rudolph Giuliani against Dinkins in 1993; it endorsed Republicans Alphonse D'Amato for senator and George Pataki for governor in 1998, and then Democrat Hillary Rodham Clinton in 2000. Much less blatantly than Murdoch, Zuckerman's business interests (real estate) have at times been advanced by his ownership of a printing press. To a much greater extent than Murdoch, he cares about getting invited on Air Force One or appearing on NBC's *McLaughlin Group* shout-fest. Zuckerman's most passionate and steadfast commitment is to the state of Israel, which he regularly touts in a weekly column in *U.S. News* (reprinted in the *News*) and as chairman of the Conference of Presidents of Major American Jewish Organizations. This organization makes it possible for him to petition the same governments his journalists cover.

KOSNER VS.
ALLAN

Zuckerman was more fickle in his choice of editors—until he hired Kosner as his fifth editor in March of 2000. At the time, the *News* enjoyed a better than two-to-one circulation lead over the *Post*—730,542 daily papers sold versus 358,545—but the paper had lost focus. Gossip and business news were not anchored on set pages. A top gossip columnist, Richard Johnson, was allowed to move to the *Post*. Investigative reporting went in and out of favor; politics were featured erratically. There were often no verbs and no zip to the headlines. (In a cost-cutting move to please its Tribune Company owners, the *News* had years before eliminated cash bonuses for clever headlines.) Morale among the *News*'s four-hundred-person editorial staff—just under half of whom are reporters—was low.

Kosner came with definite ideas about what he wanted. He redeployed many of the paper's reporters. He invested in breaking news via some first-class investigative reporting. He brought back columnist Pete Hamill, who had served a short, unhappy stint as Zuckerman's third editor. Unlike the *Post*, which under Col Allan got rid of more liberal columnists like Jack Newfield and Sid Zion, *News* columnists don't seem to speak with a single voice. On the same January day Hamill praised Giuliani as "the greatest Mayor in the history of this city," for example, fellow columnist Juan Gonzalez wrote of how "arrogance" had marred his record. Kosner likened himself to former Pittsburgh Steeler coach Chuck Noll, who turned the football team into a Super Bowl winner in three years. "He improved every position every time he had the opportunity," Kosner says. "People don't understand the way publications work. You can't fix it until you fix everything. Newspapers are the result of thousands of decisions made every day by maybe thirty people. I make a lot of those decisions."

Although Zuckerman has left some editors alone—*Atlantic* editor William Whitworth had a twenty-year run—at the *News* he notoriously second-guessed headlines or stories, as he did at *U.S. News & World Report,* where he had eight editors in seventeen years. Zuckerman does little second-guessing of Kosner. "He has excellent news judgment," says the publisher of his editor. "I don't pick up the *Daily News* and look at the front page and say, 'Why did they put that on the front page? . . .' When I made editorial changes, it was because I was trying to improve the product."

Ken Chandler, a former *Post* editor and now publisher, concedes the *News* became more consistent. "No question the *News* has improved," he says. The *News* has its critics. There is restiveness within the paper because management has refused to sign contracts with its newsroom employees, which means it has the freedom to unilaterally reduce employer contributions to employee 401k plans and to impose layoffs without appeal or arbitration, both of which the *News* recently did. "We only get a wage increase when the company decides to give it," says columnist Juan Gonzalez, who acts as the chief shop steward for the journalists. Murdoch's *Post*—unlike the *Times* or *Newsday*—also refuses newsroom contracts and union recognition.

Once, Zuckerman railed about how Murdoch was a mad businessman whose behavior was impossible to predict because he didn't care about losses. By the summer of 2000, the *News* went on the offensive, announcing that it would publish ninety thousand daily copies of a free afternoon paper, the *Daily News Express,* aimed at *Post* business readers. Murdoch was for the first time rattled by the *News.* He thought his paper looked too much like the *News,* was getting too serious, too soft. And he thought that his former employee, Kosner, had made a difference. Murdoch decided to do what he had successfully done in England: start a price war. In September 2000, the *Post* halved its price within New York City; over the next several months, circulation rose by fifty thousand.

But the price cut wasn't enough. By the spring of 2001, the Murdochs were ready to make another change. "What concerned me was that the paper hadn't changed much over several years," Lachlan Murdoch says. Circulation had plateaued. "That's when I realized there was an editorial problem with the paper and we had to take the paper forward," he says.

He believed the editor, Xana Antunes, was crowding the paper with too many soft features, was expanding the paper's female appeal but in the process sacrificing some of its macho swagger. With circulation growth slowed, Lachlan recalls, "We needed to make a change."

Lachlan Murdoch thought of Col Allan. He describes the *Daily Telegraph/Sunday Telegraph,* which Allan edited, as "an in-your-face paper. If anything, it was a little too masculine. But it took a strong stand on local issues." The tabloid splashed bold headlines, its layout was clear. And Allan was not a total novice to New York, having spent three years here in the midseventies as a correspondent for three Murdoch papers.

Arriving in May 2001, Allan sequestered himself in his office, studying the paper. He rarely went out to lunch. His three TVs were set to Fox News, CNN, and the Food Network, which he finds "therapeutic." He inherited a staff that was one-third smaller than the *News*'s, and wanted to get to know their work. Six weeks later, he pounced, firing a top rung of editors, and others. At first he cut back on political coverage. He elevated Jesse Angelo, then twenty-seven, to metro editor.

Allan brought what one *Post* employee calls "a foreign sensibility" to the paper—at first emphasizing crime coverage even though crime is down dramatically in New York. He offered headlines that suggested he was either tone deaf or in heat. BENEDICT JEFFORDS, the *Post* front page screamed when the Vermont senator switched parties, as if switching parties was traitorous and an affront to the newspaper. He purchased a sixty-five-thousand-dollar Mercedes SUV, just like the one Lizzie Grubman backed into Hamptons customers last summer, and had *Post* signs plastered on its sides, christening it the Lizziemobile; he treated Grubman as if she were a member of the royal class. "In England there is true class antagonism that the British tabloids prey on," says *News* editor Kosner, dismissively. "But no one thinks of Lizzie Grubman as an aristocrat!" After September eleventh, Allan had a female *Post* employee pose on the front page with an upright middle finger and the headline, AN-THRAX THIS. On other days, headlines blared ASH-HOLES and TALI-BAM. Allan has "a tin ear," says Pete Hamill. "Sinatra was fond of quoting advice he heard from Milton Berle: 'Don't make jokes to make the band laugh.' There are certain things you do to get a laugh in the newsroom that you don't put in the paper. Some of those jokes now get in the *Post*."

Col Allan in person is a compact man of medium height. His short brown hair is neatly combed, his tie is knotted, his desk is tidy, and his walls are decorated with framed *Post* front pages. The eldest of four children, his father was a real estate broker in Australia, and he says, "We never were able to afford a trip out of the country." He and his wife live on the Upper West Side with their four children, who attend Catholic school. When not working, he watches televised sports. When he thinks of a *Post* reader, he says, "I think of someone like myself, a middle-class person." A moment later he concedes that the *Post*'s readers are more "upscale" than the *News*'s, who "are much stronger with minorities than is the *Post*. Manhattan remains a critical market for the *Post*." Like Rupert Murdoch, Allan disdains most journalists as stern, stuffy members of the establishment. What many journalists call "unfair" in the *Post*, he calls "provocative." The *News*, he says, "is pretty worthy. But they do take themselves seriously."

A favored Allan word is *bullshit*; a favored stance is to generalize. Three things Allan says he's noticed since returning to New York: "The Irish are no longer powerful in New York City, and the Jewish women are no longer shaving under their arms." And even on the Upper West Side, "You have people up there saying and thinking things they never thought." What Allan says he wants in an ideal *Post* story is: "Detail. I want to take our readers into a meeting." He mentions a Bob Hardt account of Miramax chief Harvey Weinstein's eleventh-hour effort to broker a truce between Democratic mayoral candidate Mark Green and Democrats Al Sharpton and Freddie Ferrer. The story "took the reader there," he says. "The detail becomes the narrative."

Metro editor Jesse Angelo, who worked for Allan at the *Daily Telegraph* before joining the *Post*'s Page Six three years ago, looks like a Fleet Street throwback. His black curly hair is unruly, he is comfortable with a cigarette dangling from his mouth, his desk is a mess, and his mind is sharp as he sends his reporters off on assignments. Although he plays tough guy, Angelo attended private Manhattan schools with Murdoch's youngest son, James, went to (and dropped out of) Harvard with him, and was best man at his wedding. Angelo calls the *Post* "the best newspaper in the country." Better than the *Times*? "Oh, please," he instantly says. "Without even blinking." The *Post* is best because it has "verve" and "is so much fun" and "breaks so many stories."

The *Post* does often break business and media stories, and with an assist from Rupert Murdoch, who loves to call in tips, treats business news as hot gossip. While the *News* has had an ambivalence in recent years about gossip—at first flooding the early pages with it, and more recently purging it toward the middle of the paper and getting rid of columnist Mitchell Fink—the *Post*'s first pages are dominated by it. Richard Johnson's Page Six occupies an entire page and is faced off by Neal Travis, followed by Cindy Adams and Liz Smith. With its Mercedes printing plant, the pictures in the *Post* easily best its rivals'. Publisher Ken Chandler says its sixteen-acre South Bronx printing plant "can produce the best color in the United States," which will woo advertisers. "Now we can do eight pages of color. We will have sixty pages of processed color when we're done"—this spring. Joseph B. Vincent left the *New York Times* to become a *Post* vice president and to run this facility, which he says is matched by only three others in the world.

The front page of each paper often reflects their differences. The *News* puts more resources into its own investigative reporting, and often manufactures its own front-page news. Its January eleventh edition, for example, led with a front-page exclusive—THE SHAME OF GROUND ZERO—telling how the six hundred illegal aliens employed to clean up the World Trade Center were not given protective equipment or safety training. A few days earlier, on January seventh, it led with another exclusive—CARD TRICKS—about how hackers were scamming credit cards. A small box at the top of the front page also told of the teenager who flew his plane into a Tampa building in support of Osama bin Laden.

That same day the *Post* had a big picture of a goofy fifteen-year-old with this screaming headline: CRASH KID DID IT FOR OSAMA. *Post* headlines tend, says *Village Voice* editor Don Forst, himself a former tabloid editor, to be more "visceral" and to do what a tabloid headline should: "Always go for the gut." Seeing itself as a more serious paper, the front page of the *News* on the day after Michael Bloomberg was sworn in as mayor carried a washed-out color picture of him being sworn in and wearing a red scarf that looked pink, and listed three of his vows: to keep the city safe, to avoid tax hikes, and to cut spending. The *Post* that day carried a clearer picture of Bloomberg in a bright red scarf and bellowed: MIKE THE KNIFE; a smaller headline said, NEW MAYOR CALLS FOR 20% CUTS.

IS THIS CAPITALISM?

Murdoch has never denied *Post* losses. As a private company, Zuckerman's finances were more hidden—until opened by a federal judge. In a court battle with the newspaper drivers union, which Zuckerman won, U.S. District Court Judge Thomas Griesa declared in 1999 that the *News* lost $23.7 million in 1998, and $1.2 million the previous year. According to Griesa, 1993 would prove to be a year Zuckerman made his largest profit at the *News*—a miserly $8.5 million. Zuckerman refuses to comment on profits since, but after checking, a *News* spokesman says, "The *Daily News* was profitable in 1999 and 2000, but 2001 was a difficult year."

The *News* enjoys some solid business advantages. If the *Post* and *Newsday* are to grow, Brooklyn and Queens are crucial battlegrounds. Yet the *News*'s strength in these boroughs is formidable. The *News* has more reporters (six versus none) assigned to Brooklyn, and more than twice the *Post*'s circulation in Brooklyn, where *Newsday*'s sales are in single digits. The Long Island daily has looked upon Queens as its beachhead in the city, and it has twenty-six reporters assigned to its Kew Gardens office (the *News* has six in Queens, the *Post* none). Despite these expenditures, *Newsday* remains a suburban newspaper to most Queens residents.

The *Post* gained 97,000 daily readers in the six months ending this past September thirtieth, or since the appointment of Allan. Zuckerman attributes the *Post*'s jump in circulation to its twenty-five-cent price. Publisher Chandler demurs, noting that the lower price was instigated on Labor Day, 2000, and that the paper's circulation quickly jumped by 50,000, then stabilized. Other factors pushed the circulation up another 48,000, to

535,000 in August 2001, he says. First, the arrival of Col Allan "and the changes he made. Number two was the phasing out of the printing plant," and the improved look of the paper. Finally, "During the summer we ran with stories ideally suited to the *Post*—Gary Condit and the Lizziemobile. We saw circulation climbing all through the summer." The final circulation boost came from an unforeseen event—September eleventh—which inflated sales of all newspapers.

The *News*'s circulation has held steady, and the *Post*'s circulation growth has been expensive. I asked Lachlan Murdoch if the losses were close to $40 million. "Yeah," he said. "I shouldn't say exactly." Some *News* executives believe this number is still too modest, guessing the losses are probably closer to $60 million. (Do the math, they say: If the *Post* was losing about $20 million before, the price cut would about double that, and 8 percent interest on the printing plant adds another $20 million.) And though the *Post* claims it will generate extra revenues by raising advertising rates for color, Col Allan admits advertising is not up. "Advertising rates always lag," he says, expressing his and Murdoch's faith "that circulation will drive the business."

This belief is vulnerable on several counts. It assumes circulation will continue to grow, even after they restore the price to fifty cents, as Ken Chandler says they probably will. It assumes advertisers will pay more for a second-read newspaper with relatively few female customers. And it assumes that the *Post* will become the first existing newspaper in modern times to sustain dramatic circulation growth. Since 1975, daily newspaper circulation in the U.S. has declined just under 10 percent. Today, only forty-nine cities have more than one daily newspaper, and one-third of these are owned by a single company. *USA Today*'s growth rocketed, but it was a new national newspaper. The national edition of the *New York Times* has grown, but that, too, is like a new newspaper, since the *Times* now only sells 29 percent of its papers in the city. If the *Post* restores its price, and circulation continues to climb, it will become the first existing newspaper in modern times to sustain dramatic growth. The *Post* has experienced growth spurts before—in the eighties, powered by expensive lottery contests, its circulation shot up over nine hundred thousand—only to soon fall back below five hundred thousand. *Los Angeles Times* sales rose several years ago when it cut its price to twenty-five cents, and the CEO of its parent company, Mark Willes, promised that circulation of the *Times* and its other papers would continue to rise. He was wrong. Asked to cite an example of an existing American newspaper that has managed to sustain growth as dramatically as the *Post* hopes to, Laura Rich Fine, Merrill Lynch's respected newspaper analyst, says flatly, "There aren't any."

Nevertheless, Lachlan Murdoch expresses a certitude bordering on religious fervor that circulation will leap another two hundred thousand copies and that advertisers will clamor to be in the *Post*. How, I asked, could his paper defy history?

"It goes to the strength of the *New York Post* as a brand in New York City," he says. "The history of the paper in the city. Everyone knows the paper." He pauses a moment, then reverses course and continues: "Going back: Eighteen months ago we were afraid to play with the paper too much. . . ." He pauses again, and says, "I'm not really answering your question because I don't know why exactly that's the case, other than to say it suggests that you have a potential for the *New York Post* in this city."

I noted that the *Post* disparages companies, like Disney, whose profits are off. Yet his paper hasn't made money in a quarter century, the losses are widening, and the *Post* keeps going. Why?

"I think you have to go back to the history of this company," he says. "We started out with a small newspaper in Adelaide, called the *Adelaide News*." Out of that tiny newspaper, his father forged the largest English-speaking newspaper chain in the world. Over the years, he says, "a culture" formed, a competitive drive, a willingness to take risks, and a belief that they would turn things around, as they have with newspapers or the Fox network or, more recently, with HarperCollins. The *Post* is a "great asset" to have "in the media capital of the world," says Murdoch. "Having said that, we are a public company with shareholders. So you can't have an asset like that that doesn't ultimately break even or make money. And that has to be our goal."

Is there a point where if he's wrong and it doesn't work, they will close the *Post*? "It's not an option for us not to narrow the losses," he says.

THE FUTURE

Gauged by its editorial product, its circulation, its revenues, or its flirta-
tion with profitability, the *News* is winning the battle—ad-tracking firms
report that its ad revenues are nearly four times those of the *Post*. Yet the
two tabloids face other competitors willing to lose money, starting with
the well-financed threat from the east. The Chicago-based Tribune Company, which a decade ago owned the *Daily News* and now kicks itself for
selling it, today owns *Newsday* and spends a small fortune trying to build
what it gave away. Tony Marro, who has been the editor since 1987, still
smolders that his former corporate parent, the Times Mirror Company,
chose to shutter *New York Newsday* when "it was probably breaking even
or close to it." (That is not a view shared by publisher Raymond A.
Jansen because, he says, that paper was predicated "on a lot of wishful
thinking." They were betting the *News* would die. Quickly.)

Newsday has huge obstacles to overcome. In order to expand westward
from its Long Island base, it must compete with the *Daily News*. Yet in its
chosen Queens battleground, *Newsday* sells fewer papers (eighty-two
thousand) than it did in either 1991 or 1996. Publisher Jansen says they are
patient and plan to take Queens, and then Brooklyn, "little by little, block
by block." He predicts that in five years, "We'll be the number-one paper
in Queens." Jansen insists that neither tabloid is his true rival—that the
Times itself is. Too many pictures. Too much gossip and celebrity news,
not enough "intelligent coverage of institutions." (However, *Newsday* editor Tony Marro says, "We see the *News* as our competition.")

Newsday's strategy hinges on a belief that readers want more serious
news than they get in the two tabloids, and on Jansen's calculation that as
the *Times* becomes more of a national newspaper, it leaves "room for
Newsday to cover the metropolitan area much more intensely." *Newsday* is
a broadsheet in the body of a tabloid, and its strategy may be equally
muddled. Today, the *News* outsells the *Times* in the city and sells more

than four times as many copies as *Newsday*'s 102,000. *Newsday*'s essential strategy seems to be to pray—as it did a decade ago—that the *News* will fold, or be sold to them.

Another announced competitor willing to lose money is the *New York Sun*, which is backed by Conrad Black's Hollinger International, among other neoconservatives. In the spring they plan to begin publishing a daily aimed primarily at the *Times*. The *Times*, says editor Seth Lipsky, a former *Wall Street Journal* reporter and editor of the *Forward*, "is a national paper that's marbled with some local news. We will be a broadsheet that covers local news and is marbled with international and national news." The initial staff will be "under forty"; the circulation will be small and targeted at Manhattan. Although the *Sun* sees itself as an alternative to the *Times*, its editorial pages will echo those of the *Journal*'s. The *Sun*, says a January fifteenth press release, will be pro growth, pro lower taxes, pro school choice, and pro smaller government. Its news columns, says Lipsky, will avoid what he believes creep into the *Times*—unconscious liberal assumptions. Might the *Sun* bring its own more conservative assumptions to news coverage? "The answer to that is probably yes," Lipsky says.

WHATEVER THE OUTCOME of this competition, uncertainty hovers over the future of New York's newspapers. Over the past half century, animated television pictures eclipsed the power of tabloid stills; department store advertising, once the backbone of newspaper ad revenues, shrank, as did blue-collar jobs; the suburbs emptied cities of sizable parts of their middle class; weekly newspapers offered more community news and local ads; twenty-four-hour cable news channels, beefed-up local TV newscasts, and the Internet generated a never-ending news cycle, robbing tabloids (and newspapers in general) of the shock value of screaming morning headlines; online classified advertising threatens to rob newspapers of their most significant source of ad dollars.

"The shape of the battlefield will change over time," says *Newsday*'s managing editor for content development, Howard Schneider. "In ten years," he predicts, "we won't be talking about circulation. We'll be talking about audience share"—for information delivered over the Web to a PC or handheld device or over radio or television or print platforms.

If he's right, large diversified companies like News Corp. and the Tribune Company enjoy certain advantages. But to borrow from corporate lingo, so do brands. And so far at least, the *News* brand has survived strikes, bungling owners, bankruptcy, blurry pictures, a tag team of editors and editorial philosophies, morning papers stalled in traffic, and nonspeaking copublishers. We are left where we began, with a bar fight that defies capitalism and is aimed at one overriding goal: to be the last man standing.

POSTSCRIPT

By March 31, 2003, the end of its last six-month audit period, the *Post* still fell short of Lachlan Murdoch's prediction ("We will catch up to the *Daily News* in the next eighteen months"). But it did enjoy the most robust daily circulation growth—up in eighteen months by more than 86,000 readers to 620,080 copies. *News* circulation in that period was flat. But the *News* still sold 116,950 more daily copies than the *Post* at twice the price, with nearly twice as many copies on ad-rich Sunday. At only twenty-five cents per copy, the *Post* was still losing more in circulation revenue than it was gaining in new advertising. The *News* continued to far eclipse the *Post* in advertising. *Newsday*'s city circulation did not appreciably change, and the *New York Sun* sold an estimated 35,000 daily copies. The *News* remained the most potent tabloid brand, and the *Post* continued to hemorrhage money in 2002 and 2003. The *News* hemorrhaged another editor, as Kosner announced in July 2003 that he would retire in March 2004. His counterpart at the *Post,* Col Allan, gave him this send-off: "He's obviously a man who's found it difficult in recent years. Maybe it's time he went fishing."

Of the *News,* Zuckerman told me, "We had a substantially profitable year." He says this was unexpected. Even if he speaks the truth, it is also true that whether he made money or Murdoch lost money is almost beside the point. Mortimer Zuckerman and Rupert Murdoch had their own *synergy* reasons to pursue this battle.

As will be seen in the next piece, synergy and church/state questions are handled somewhat differently at the *New York Times.*

THE *NEW YORK TIMES*'S OUTWARD BOUND ADVENTURE

O N T H E S U R F A C E , the *New York Times,* the world's foremost newspaper, retains its serenity. Its circulation has grown steadily. Its leadership is secure. Beneath the surface, however, the paper is absorbed in a struggle over change and direction, of which the recent purchase of the *Boston Globe,* for $1.1 billion, is merely one indication. Another indication is what Arthur Ochs Sulzberger, Jr., who has been publisher of the *Times* for seventeen months, has been putting his executives through—the equivalent of an Outward Bound adventure. True, they have not been asked to climb rocks or go rafting in white water, and they have not been asked to pitch tents and live in the wild for twenty-eight days—something that Sulzberger did when he was in high school. He recalls that experience as "a defining moment for me," because, he says, "it pushed me to limits in places I just had never been." What the editors and the executives of the *Times* have been asked to endure instead is an intense emotional search for the kind of "self-discovery" and "team-work" that Outward Bound extols.

Last September, in a speech to his advertising-sales force, Sulzberger acknowledged the difficulties he foresaw at the *Times* by announcing, bluntly, "Change sucks." But despite the pain that change entails, he said, the *Times* "must reject the comfort factor"—must stretch itself, as he had done in Outward Bound. Sulzberger is, of course, aware of the multitude of business questions that the *Times* must confront. Will it continue to print on expensive paper, or will it eventually distribute news only electronically? Will it be more of a national and international paper? What will its advertising base be? Will technology be an ally or an enemy?

Sulzberger knows that the immediate question looming largest over the *Times* is the strength of its New York advertising base. While the paper's daily circulation for 1992 was an all-time high of 1,181,500 copies, advertising linage has fallen about 40 percent since 1987. Five years ago, the *Times* ran 123 million lines of advertising; last year's total was only 77 million lines, though the decline has now slowed. Partly because of a weakened local economy, and partly because of special accounting changes and charges, the New York Times Company reported a net loss of $44.7 million in 1992.

Sulzberger is also aware of another potential pitfall: family discord. "The nightmare is that we as a family won't get along," says one cousin, Michael Golden, who runs the Times Company's women's magazine group. "I don't see that happening. We work hard to see that it doesn't happen." Still, the family is certainly mindful of how dissent among the offspring shattered the Bingham newspaper family and the Gallo wine family. Arthur Sulzberger's father, Arthur Ochs Sulzberger, Sr., known as Punch, who is now the chairman and chief executive officer of the company, and Punch Sulzberger's sisters—Marian S. Heiskell, Ruth S. Holmberg, and Judith P. Sulzberger—have a total of thirteen children among them, four of whom have prominent management jobs at the New York Times Company. (A fifth, Susan W. Dryfoos, directs the New York Times History Project.) The family has set up a trust allowing Punch Sulzberger and his three sisters to select trustees to succeed them when they die. The trust controls over 80 percent of Class B stock, in effect assuring the family dominance of the Times Company for at least another century.

There are a lot of additional cousins who have a stake in the company's future: fifty-seven family members attended the last reunion. In addition to Arthur Jr. and Michael Golden, the cousins who have major roles in the company are Stephen Golden, who runs the forest-products group, and Daniel H. Cohen, who is the director of the promotion department at the newspaper. "You can't keep them all feeling enfranchised," one cousin says. "You've just got to keep some of them—the descendant children—involved in the business. If we can keep that core together, we've got a chance of keeping it all together." But to keep the cousins feeling enfranchised may require that one of them get one of the two top jobs at the company, publisher of the *Times* or chairman and CEO. "It seems to me it's got to be that way, unless they reorganize," Michael Golden says. His cousin Arthur, he adds, "has Punch's confidence, as well he should."

At present, Arthur Sulzberger, Jr., prefers to concentrate not on the question of profit or the question of succession at the company but on changing the atmosphere at the paper, and on altering how the *Times* itself is managed. The war that he wants to wage right now is against an authoritarian decision-making process that exists on both the news and the business sides of the *Times*—a process that he believes breeds insularity and saps initiative. He makes this point by recalling, as he did for the sales staff last September, a question that Todd S. Purdum, then the city hall bureau chief, had raised at a staff luncheon in January of 1992. This luncheon was the first of many get-in-touch-with-your-employees gatherings that Sulzberger has initiated, and Purdum brought the proceedings to a hush with his question: "Why is there so much fear at the *New York Times*?"

Although the question made his editors squirm, Sulzberger welcomed it. "The cost of allowing fear to permeate our newspaper is too high a cost for us to bear," he told his sales force in September. "Fear breeds mediocrity. . . . Some argue that fear is an inherent by-product of any structure based on hierarchy. I can't swear that's true, but I suspect it is.

And if it is true, our course is clear. For the *New York Times* to become all it can and for it to flourish in the years ahead, we must reduce our dependency on hierarchy in decision making of every sort."

To counter this hierarchy, Sulzberger has prescribed the management theories of Dr. W. Edwards Deming, a professor emeritus at New York University and a business philosopher whose theories helped revitalize Japanese industry after the Second World War. Sulzberger and a team of *Times* managers studied Deming's theories during four days of seminars in Washington in 1990. Sulzberger first came across Deming when he read David Halberstam's book about the auto industry, *The Reckoning*. Deming says that businesses must strive for "quality," and that they can achieve it by relying on two basic tenets: first, a scientific approach that seeks to quantify the production process mathematically, so that managers rely on data rather than anecdotes in making decisions; and, second, a more humanistic management, which depends on teamwork, not on orders, to get results.

Sulzberger is a man of remarkable self-assurance. Now forty-one years old, he has a full head of curly dark hair and a lean, firm physique. He lives on Central Park West, and works out at a West Side gym five mornings a week, goes on weekend rock-climbing expeditions, and spends an annual "Rambo weekend" braving the elements with three friends— his cousin Dan Cohen; Cohen's brother-in-law, Paul Hanafin; and Steven Rattner, an investment banker and former *Times* reporter. At work, Sulzberger often wanders through the *Times* offices, on West Forty-third Street, in colorful striped shirts and bright suspenders. He knows that his editors are sometimes irritated by his remarks, and he also knows that they have reason to be proud of their accomplishments. Under Max Frankel, as executive editor, they have improved the writing in the *Times*, have provided readers with more analytical stories, have sharpened the Sunday magazine and the sports and metropolitan sections, have hired more women and minorities for the newsroom, and have given individual writers greater freedom in how they write. Still, Sulzberger seems to some editors to prefer to dwell on the paper's weaknesses rather than on its strengths.

Sulzberger is more visible and more direct than any of his predecessors at the *Times*. After his morning workout, he takes a bus or the subway to work, and usually reads the paper between 7:00 and 8:30. He frequently answers his own phone. He takes reporters to lunch or dinner. He insists that every reporter and editor hired by the *Times* have a private introductory audience in his office, on the eleventh floor. On the walls of this office are framed pictures of his great-grandfather, Adolph S. Ochs, who bought the *Times* in 1896 and led it for nearly four decades; his grandfather, Arthur Hays Sulzberger, who served as publisher from 1935 to 1961; and his uncle Orvil E. Dryfoos, who died after just two years as publisher. Arthur Sulzberger, Sr., succeeded Dryfoos, and was publisher for nearly three decades. Things have changed considerably since Arthur Jr. became publisher. In years past, it was rare for a reporter simply to stroll into the publisher's office, but the door to Sulzberger's office is open, and journalists regularly visit him. "I've had conversations with Arthur I never could have had with Arthur Sr.," Brent Staples, a member of the editorial board, says. "Punch is a lovely and a generous man, but Arthur and I are the same age and the same generation. And if I can get to see him and vent my opinions, then a lot of other people are also coming to his office." Not surprisingly, this direct access sometimes discomforts his editors, though none complain.

The signals that Sulzberger is sending through his actions are unmistakable: He is eager to change the *Times,* and is impatient with the resistance he sometimes encounters. He wants more minority employees in executive positions. He wants more women in executive positions. He wants a less authoritarian newsroom and a business side that is more nimble. He wants each member of the staff to feel "empowered" as part of a team. He wants a more joyous newsroom. One reporter who has shared opinions with the publisher says of executive editor Frankel, "When Max leaves at the end of the day, he leaves a man bent by the great weight of the *New York Times.* That lack of joy has filtered into the newsroom."

"One of his missions is to humanize the place," Steven Rattner, who exercises daily with Sulzberger at the West Side gym, says. About all his objectives Sulzberger is fervent. In response to complaints about morale or the slow pace of change in the newsroom or on the business side, he has said of his managers, with a mixture of determination, cunning, and bravado, "I'll outlive the bastards!"

YOUNG ARTHUR, as he's sometimes called, to distinguish him from his father, had prepared to become publisher of the paper from the time he was very young indeed. He dreamed of this job as a boy living with his mother after his parents divorced, when he was four. His cousin Dan Cohen, who has been close to him since boyhood and who attended Tufts with him, recalls that on the occasions when they got together and played soldiers, "Arthur wanted to be the general." When asked what he aspired to be, Arthur would respond, "Publisher of the *New York Times.*" Punch Sulzberger looks back on his son's apprenticeship at the paper—fourteen years spent as, progressively, reporter, assignment editor, advertising manager, corporate-planning analyst, production executive, assistant publisher, and deputy publisher—and says, "He certainly was better trained than I was. . . . He's been a great source of joy and pride to me. I voluntarily handed over the job to him with my eyes wide open. And I haven't regretted it for a day."

Since becoming publisher, on January 16, 1992, the son has imposed a style of management very different from that of his father. The father says, "We are a newspaper that has to come out every day, and it's not a democracy." Conversely, the son champions democracy in the newsroom. The father remained social friends with Sydney Gruson, the company's vice chairman; A. M. Rosenthal, the paper's executive editor; Arthur Gelb, the managing editor; and James L. Greenfield, an assistant managing editor. By contrast, in recent years the son has deliberately formed all his close friendships outside the *Times,* and no longer regularly socializes with such longtime friends as Paul Goldberger, the cultural editor; Steven R. Weisman, a deputy foreign editor; Philip Taubman, a deputy national editor; and Judith Miller, a writer. Unlike his father, who served on the board of trustees of Columbia University and was chairman of the board of the Metropolitan Museum of Art, the son has rejected invitations to serve on the board of Barnard College and other institutions in order to avoid any appearance of conflict with his duties as publisher; the only boards on which he serves are ones that are related to his business (he is on the boards of the Times Square Business Improvement District and the Newspaper Association of America) and two that he says he chose to "grandfather in" when he became publisher (the New York City Outward Bound Center and North Carolina Outward Bound School).

"He's much more hands-on than Punch ever was," says Anna Quindlen, who is an old friend and was the first *Times* columnist chosen by the son. (This was done at his father's invitation, just before young Arthur became publisher.) "Where they're alike is that both have a sense of family trust to keep this paper better than anything else."

"Punch was much more magisterial in personnel decisions," Max Frankel observes. "He was not managing the paper. Arthur set out, and I think rightly so, to steep himself deeply in the affairs of every department."

To promote his vision of change, the younger Sulzberger has invited all employees to Town Hall for a series of question-and-answer sessions with him; he has initiated management retreats; he has installed a new editorial-page editor—Howell Raines, a former chief of the Washington bureau—and has encouraged a less formal, populist voice on a once mostly solemn page; he has recently hired Bob Herbert, formerly of the *News,* as the paper's first black columnist; and he has pressed the editors to consult their staff more than they have done in the past and to adopt a bottom-up, not top-down, approach. "If people in this organization are getting any single message from senior management, it is that we are trying to open up," Sulzberger says. "We are trying to become more egalitarian."

Sulzberger says that his greatest challenge will be to bring more racial diversity and sexual equality to the paper. This effort was under way long before he took over as publisher, since it conforms to what one reporter calls "the implicit assumption" at the *Times,* which is "moderate liberal." Frankel, who became executive editor in 1986, says, "One of the first things I did was stop the hiring of nonblacks and set up an unofficial little quota system." The new publisher applauded Frankel's hiring policies and also the newsroom's more extensive coverage of women and gays, despite grumbling by some members of the staff that the *Times* was becoming politically correct. At the last two annual meetings of the National Association of Black Journalists, Gerald M. Boyd, the metropolitan editor, recalls, Sulzberger gave dinners to recruit black reporters. "When people see a publisher so engaged, as Arthur is engaged, it makes a hell of a difference," Boyd says, and he points out that last year they hired two of four people they had targeted at a Detroit dinner. The reason the paper should advance minorities, says Dean P. Baquet, a *Times* reporter who won a Pulitzer Prize while at the *Chicago Tribune* and is black, has to do less with justice than with good reporting. "It's because the ideal newspaper is made up of as many smart people from as many different backgrounds as possible," he says. "Small newspapers don't have that mix. How often do you see obituaries of Chinese Americans? Why? Because there aren't many Chinese reporters."

Ninety percent of the news executives on the *Times* masthead are male, and not one is black or brown. "When you get to department and section heads, it gets better—forty-two percent women," says Suzanne Daley, the first assistant metropolitan editor, who is active in the women's committee at the *Times*. "But if you study the people on the masthead, you see that they come from the big five areas"—financial, the Washington bureau, and the metropolitan, foreign, and national desks. "If you look at the managers of these desks, it's about eighty percent men at the head and deputy level."

The *Book Review* editor, Rebecca Sinkler, says, "The *Times* is so big and powerful that changing it is like teaching a hippopotamus how to tango. Moving the hippopotamus around is frustratingly slow. You find yourself getting all juiced up with an idea of how to do something," but what with the memos and the meetings and the search for consensus, she said, change is often measured in inches. The slow pace of change has been a constant source of frustration to the new publisher. He was exasperated that it took so long to launch the new Styles of the *Times* and an expanded metropolitan section on Sundays, to get color printing in the works, to induce the news and business sides of the paper to speak more freely.

To speed the pace, Sulzberger instituted a series of five retreats, the first one involving the members of the newspaper's business masthead. (There are eleven of them, including the publisher.) The retreats commenced in October of 1992 and ran through January of this year. Unlike the traditional companywide retreats, including a three-day gathering of managers in Princeton in May, Arthur Jr. would be less polite, for he believes that self-discovery and candor flow from conflict and adversity and that improved teamwork will follow. That's how Outward Bound works. To promote discussion, he drafted a brief statement describing a journalistic and business value system that *Times* employees might embrace. The purpose was to test "our assumptions as to what we were, what we really stand for," he says, and explains, "If you go into any process of recreating an organization, you better damn well have agreement as to what can't change. What is it that above everything else we hold sacred?"

There was probably a hidden purpose in the retreats as well. "I believe it was his ambition to say, 'I'd like to redefine the job of publisher,'" says Jack Rosenthal, who is an assistant managing editor and the editor of the Sunday *Times Magazine,* and who as the editorial-page editor from 1986 until January 1993 worked closely with both Sulzbergers. One headache that a publisher at the *Times* confronts, the elder Sulzberger says, is this: "We don't operate in the form of a triangle, with the publisher at the top. We are more like a forest of trees, with everything growing straight up." There was reluctance in the news department to share information, he says, adding, "If an advertising man was found on the news floor, he'd practically be lynched. We've got a lot better." The son, however, did not accept a basic premise of his father's, which was that the publisher had to mediate all differences between the business and the news sides of the paper. "It seems to me that Arthur's hope was 'We're all grown-ups—can't we find a consensus model?'" Rosenthal says. The publisher didn't want to referee differences; he wanted one team.

That first retreat, for the business side, was held last October sixteenth at the *Times*'s new printing plant, in Edison, New Jersey. Sulzberger brought along Doug Wesley, a management consultant who served as the facilitator, and distributed copies of his draft statement on values. He challenged the managers to welcome change, to be less hierarchical, to be fearless. There were, of course, the usual complaints about how the news department treated the business employees like second-class citizens, but the dialogue livened up after Wesley remarked that one out of every four companies that started a process of change had dropped it. "Those agents of change at lower levels find themselves out on limbs, and often their limbs get cut," he said. A three-hour debate followed, with the business people challenging Sulzberger by asking this basic question: "Arthur, how do we know you won't take us down the road of change and then abandon us?"

The retreat ended inconclusively, and over the next several weeks the publisher summoned the business-side executives to two more such meetings, at which they argued over what change meant and wrestled with the statement of values. Sulzberger was pleased by the dialogue. "These meetings have to become contentious or you're not digging deep enough," he says. "You're testing your fundamental assumptions about what you believe in."

The first retreat for the news side was held at the Hyatt Regency Hotel in Greenwich, Connecticut, on December first and second. All the senior editors then on the masthead—eight white men and one white woman—were invited, along with a sprinkling of others one or two rungs down. All the participants—there were twenty—gathered around a horseshoe-shaped Formica table in a conference room, and Wesley worked from inside the horseshoe, often pacing from an overhead projector to a portable easel, multicolored markers in hand, to jot down the salient discussion points.

Some of the news executives quickly came to feel that Wesley was acting the part of Grand Inquisitor. He started the first morning by discussing the statement of values, and then jarred everyone by changing the subject and encouraging people to speak candidly about their frustrations in the newsroom—about the fear, the authoritarianism. When they resisted, Sulzberger himself weighed in, describing his own unhappiness with communications at the paper. He challenged Max Frankel and his staff to practice bottom-up rather than top-down management, to open themselves to change, to be—well, *nicer.*

MAX FRANKEL tends to bristle at the notion of "nice," and not just because it's a nebulous word. Ever since he replaced Abe Rosenthal as executive editor, he has thought of himself as the man who made the newsroom less authoritarian and lifted the sense of fear felt by many *Times* employees. He doesn't exile people, as Rosenthal was accused of doing. He doesn't personalize. He relies less on instinct than on fact. To Frankel, it was a fact that he inherited a great newspaper and a great staff and made them even greater. Whatever the complaints about Rosenthal, few people deny that he was a brilliant editor with exacting standards who led the paper during a period of historic growth. But Frankel sees himself as a more avuncular figure than Rosenthal, and he looks the part: He has a round face, thinning gray hair, and his ties are usually askew. Jeffrey Schmalz, an assistant national editor who covers gay issues for the *Times,* and who has AIDS and collapsed in the newsroom two and a half years ago, tells of Frankel's walking by his desk this year to wish him a happy New Year: Frankel left the newsroom but then returned, leaned over Schmalz's desk, and said, "I especially thought of you on New Year's Eve, and I'm glad you have another year."

Frankel believes that the newsroom is filled with "tension," not "fear." He does not see himself as an intimidating figure, except in one respect: "I know I can't walk into a huddle in the newsroom without everyone falling silent. . . . I wish I could be closer down in the chatting and gossip range," he said recently. Frankel was born in Gera, Germany, in April of 1930, and came to the United States with his mother in 1940. He graduated Phi Beta Kappa from Columbia in 1952, and went on to earn a graduate degree in government there. Beginning in 1952, he held a variety of jobs at the *Times,* including Washington bureau chief and editorial-page editor. Not surprisingly, Frankel disdains the kind of emotional, get-in-touch-with-your-feelings approach favored in programs like Outward Bound. At work, he is dour. When Frankel is asked if he thinks that the newsroom is joyless, he responds, "Joyless? No. Do I feel overworked and overburdened? Yes. I say sometimes in jest that the only time I enjoy the *New York Times* is when I'm away and reading it, because from the moment I come in the door what I hear about is what's gone wrong." At the December retreat for the news side in Greenwich, Frankel said of the paper's daily page-one meetings, at which the editors discuss how the day's news will be played, "I've got to make an omelet, and to do that I've got to break some eggs."

Frankel breaks eggs at the daily page-one meetings. They are conducted by Frankel, with the editors gathered around an oval table in his conference room. At the time, Frankel and Joseph Lelyveld, the managing editor, would sit at one end of the table, and Frankel, in his own words, had "forty-five minutes to play tutor." When he found that an editor was unprepared to answer his rigorous questions about a story, he might suddenly raise his fists to his temples or roll his eyes or simply erupt.

Joe Lelyveld, who is fifty-six, can be just as severe. In his previous job as foreign editor, he would interrupt editors in midsentence because they were laboring to explain something he already understood. In one sense, Lelyveld is known as a reporters' editor, and not just because he is considered to have been a model correspondent who combined lively writing with assiduous reporting. Three and a half years ago, when he became number two in the newsroom, he sent a memorandum to editors warning that he wanted "to be as tough on overediting as we are on sloppy prose," and suggesting that if a story needed a sharper focus "the first choice . . . should be to have the writer do it." Like Frankel, he is admired for his probity and his intelligence, but both men are widely accused of talking down to the staff. "They've tried hard to open the newsroom up," one reporter has complained, "but rarely is there a vehicle for Max or Joe to sit down and say, 'What about our coverage of the city? Of culture?' There is no basic discussion of coverage. The coverage is all dictated." Editors voice similar complaints. One editor observes, "They're like prime ministers. They're always exhorting."

Neither Frankel nor Lelyveld apologizes for his management style. "At the end of the day, someone has to make up page one," Frankel says. And Lelyveld says, "Choices have to be made by the minute. You have to decide what to lead the paper with, whom to assign to it. . . . This is not simply an institution for the fulfillment of journalists." Because of daily deadline pressures, a newsroom can be a neurotic place.

AT THE DECEMBER RETREAT, Doug Wesley encouraged the editors to speak up. According to several participants, the national editor, Soma Golden Behr, who worked for Frankel as a member of the editorial board when he was the editorial-page editor, said she thought of him as a warm man, and wondered aloud what it was about the job of executive editor and the page-one meeting that made him seem so harsh. She spoke of how intimidating the meetings were, of how brusque Frankel could be, of how women got little attention, of how humiliated and chastised an editor sometimes felt.

"I think of the page-one meeting as a colloquy," Frankel responded.

"I've been in a lot of page-one meetings," Sulzberger said, "and the one thing I can tell you, Max, is that it ain't no colloquy!"

The room fell silent. "I found it extremely unpleasant," Frankel says of the morning session. "It implied that everything was rotten in Denmark and only profound and revolutionary change in everything we did and everything we thought was necessary. . . . That was the premise of the so-called facilitator." Though Frankel doesn't say so, he and others probably feared that it was the assumption of Sulzberger as well.

Wesley stood at his easel and pressed the editors to free-associate. He asked them to describe in a few words the news department, say, or "the rules of the road" in the newsroom.

"When in doubt, dissemble," was a rule that one editor cited.

"Paradox: The best newspaper in the world can't keep its bathrooms clean," was another editor's contribution.

Each remark was written on the board, for a total of about thirty items.

Frankel exploded. "Let's not play these stupid games," he said. "This is intellectually dishonest. This doesn't represent what we think of ourselves." Few disagreed.

Wesley then suggested that they break up into small groups and continue. According to the notes of one participant, Frankel cried out, "Stop all this mindless clamor for change, change, change! Let's get specific. Let's put the problems on the table and work to solve them."

It was a pivotal moment in the meeting. "Everyone felt for Max," Suzanne Daley, the first assistant metropolitan editor, recalls. One participant remembers leaning over to Arthur Sulzberger and whispering, "It isn't fair. Max made the newsroom so much better that to haul him out like this seems unfair and simpleminded."

"Arthur lost control of the meeting," another participant says, and people began to ask him, "Why did you drag us here?"

After lunch, the publisher explained to his news editors that he had not meant for the morning session to turn into a flogging of Frankel or Lelyveld. He said he admired both of them and the job they did, and that is what he says privately as well—except that he does want them to be more democratic.

When Frankel spoke after lunch, he took care to express his fidelity to the Sulzberger family, which he respectfully likens to "a monarchy" that protects news values, and to reaffirm his commitment to the process of change begun by the publisher. He added, however, that the people in the news department didn't need outside business consultants or productivity experts. They would do it themselves. The publisher welcomed this idea, and the group devoted much of the remainder of the afternoon to producing five revisions of the statement of values.

The next morning, the editors returned to tackle a sixth draft; all twenty participants pitched in. By the lunch hour, they thought they were about done, and after two days of this, most of them had had enough. But Howell Raines, the editorial-page editor, was agitated, and his opinion mattered, since he was one of the first top managers the new publisher had appointed. Raines said he found himself troubled by the statement's summons to the news and business sides of the *Times* to "learn new ways of working together." In a soft drawl—Raines is from Alabama—he challenged a basic assumption of the new publisher: Did the *Times* really need a statement calling on news and business to communicate and cooperate more? "Drafting a statement that talked about the relations between the business and the news sides had inherent dangers," he recalls saying. "If it is drafted so that future managers and editors don't understand the historical wall we have had between business and news, they could seize some element of language to harm the paper," he says. "I felt strongly that we had to think not only of the *Times* but of journalism." He adds, "We have a set of values we have to guard, because if we don't guard them they have no protector. Why reinvent the wheel when the *Times* is a great success?"

Some of the editors wondered why Sulzberger was unwilling to arbitrate between the news and the business departments himself. "You're the publisher of the *New York Times*. That's your job," one editor declared.

Sulzberger says that when the meeting finally adjourned, he felt "a little beaten up." Over the two days, though it was Wesley who drew the most flak, the publisher had no illusions. "He was never their target," Sulzberger says. "I was their target. Even when they were aiming at him, they were aiming at me." He came away undeterred. "In the end, this process has to be guided by me," he says. "I want those challenges."

Suzanne Daley came away thinking that the retreat had been tougher than any page-one meeting, and pinpointed an essential contradiction that recurred throughout the retreat: "If you want to be 'nice,' do you lose your edge? Do you lose your edge if the page-one meeting is 'nice'? When I head for a page-one meeting, I want to know everything I possibly can, because if I don't, I'll be humiliated. If I don't worry about being humiliated, will I care less? We got the way we were by being the way we were. If we change it, do we lose it?"

There is a conflict between deadlines and democracy, news standards and niceness, Howell Raines says. "I'm not sure Arthur has fully confronted the collision between two principles—to treat people more gently, and to be honest with them. . . . This is the most demanding professional environment I've ever encountered. . . . The informing idea is 'You're here because you're the best in the business, and the game is on the field. Get on with it.' Our meetings are meant to rip away the details," he says. "This is a talent meritocracy. We're not building cars here."

The clock is always ticking. Decisions have to be made: On what page to place a story? Does it deserve a six-column headline? Is the lead right? Is the story missing something? A woman reporter on the metropolitan staff says that there'll always be a conflict between professional values and personal values: "You cannot cover a breaking story and be home for your baby-sitter, and Arthur hasn't faced that." Reporters have to be edited, placated, rebuked, reassigned, retired. Each day they are graded on a new performance. Today they star, tomorrow someone else takes a bow. They hunch over phones in a vast, nearly windowless room filled with rows of steel desks, deposit stories into computer terminals, and wait. They are rarely consulted or praised, partly because there is so little time, and partly because editors are notoriously brusque. In such a hurried, withholding newsroom environment, a childlike need for parental approval develops. Because the *Times* considers itself the best, anxiety may run higher here.

Still, Sulzberger believes that the anxiety of the newsroom can be relieved—that people can both make quick, authoritative decisions and be more civil. Based in part on his exposure at the *Times* to the often rancorous labor negotiations between management and unionized blue-collar production workers, in part on his reading of management philosophers like W. Edwards Deming, and in part on his own affable nature, his concept of workplace democracy extends to employee-management cooperation. Such cooperation is essential, he believes, for liberating ideas and energy. It is particularly essential to the *Times,* which in his view is not just a job but a calling.

As Sulzberger and others thought about the two-day retreat after it was over, they sensed that everyone had come away feeling bruised. In discussing the meeting later, Frankel and the publisher decided that to heal the wounds the publisher would invite those who had attended the Greenwich retreat to reassemble, on December fourth, in a penthouse meeting room at the *Times.* The publisher began, one editor recalls, "by acknowledging that it was not a happy occasion and it had got out of control." He then asked the editors to describe their feelings. Out poured their anguish: about how the meeting had conveyed a lack of trust in the news department and its managers; about how they worried that a circulation manager might suggest a story idea to a city editor; about how W. Edwards Deming's production-line ideas were less relevant to a newsroom, which relied on individual performance. Sulzberger took notes on a lined yellow pad. When everyone had spoken, he reviewed the notes and tried to address each objection. But he also made clear that it was his intention to continue as an agent of change. He promised no relief from this. "We'll be at this for ten, maybe twenty years," he says.

Soon after this meeting, Frankel appointed several news-side task forces to improve internal communications and the work environment. Also, he and Lelyveld sent a memo to the senior editors describing a new, more egalitarian seating arrangement for the daily page-one meeting. From now on, it announced, Frankel and Lelyveld would no longer sit at one end of the oval table but would sit among their colleagues around the table. At the first page-one meeting with the new seating chart, Frankel and Lelyveld arranged to serve chilled wine and shrimp, telling colleagues, with a smile, that they hoped to improve the atmosphere. "Strangely enough, the seating arrangement worked," one editor says.

Arthur Sulzberger, Jr., had one more retreat planned, for January eighteenth and nineteenth, which would again be held at the Hyatt Regency Greenwich. This time, both the business and the news sides were invited. The publisher opened the proceedings by expressing some frustrations. The paper had expanded its metropolitan and sports sections and had added a style section on Sundays, and in June it would bring color to the *Book Review,* he said, but all these things took too damned long. "What we discovered was that we were too slow," Sulzberger later explained. A new City Weekly section had stalled, because the business side felt that news didn't want it and the news side felt that business was intruding. Sulzberger said that the traditional wall the newsroom had erected to repel the advertising side was vital. But the wall had become an obstacle that impeded joint planning.

This time, Sulzberger did not rely on Wesley but instead started by reviewing the statement of values himself. It spoke of the *Times*'s twin goals of "editorial excellence" and "profitability." The word *profitability* irked the journalists. They worried that the *Times* might make "a golden calf out of profits," Lelyveld recalls. They didn't decide whether to cover a story on the basis of what it might cost. They wanted to know whether the new City Weekly was being pushed by the business side because it served a journalistic or an advertising purpose. And if it didn't serve a journalistic purpose, they wanted to guard the *Times*'s good name. They felt defensive; they felt a new publisher breathing on them, insisting that they change their ways.

They heard the call for breaking down the wall between the business and the news sides, and sensed the balance of power might be tipping. "This place has been so weighted toward the mission of the paper that traditionally it has not been easy for business managers to make a constructive point without causing fear in the news department," Lelyveld says.

The decibel level rose as the editors continued to talk about excellence, and the business executives stressed the importance of profits. To Frankel, it was a clash of religions. "In the end, how are you judged?" he says. "A writer or an editor is judged by the brilliance of his journalism, even if it costs too much—especially if it costs too much. A business manager is judged by how he cuts costs and makes profits."

Some members of the business side felt they were being condescended to, told they didn't love the *Times* with as much ardor as the news people. "In many cases, journalists view the business side as greedy ogres whose only interest is making a dollar and not a product," observes one important business executive, Dan Cohen. "There are business people who care as much about the product as journalists do."

Despite this skirmish, everyone struggled to be collegial—until the publisher steered the discussion to a part of the values statement that spoke of breaking down the wall between news and business. Howell Raines spoke at length. According to participants, one deputy general manager, John M. O'Brien, was upset at what he took to be Raines's moralizing, claiming it was just another example of the tendency on the news side to relegate business to the back of the bus. The business side was no less committed to an excellent paper than Howell Raines was. Others from the business side jumped in.

At this point, another deputy general manager, Russell T. Lewis, who sat beside Raines, interceded and lent a calming voice. Lewis had some credentials as a peacemaker, for he started his career on the news side, as a copyboy, in 1966, and once won a Publisher's Award for a story he wrote. In effect, Lewis said the business side loved news, too. Love and devotion were not the issue, he said; reality was. And the reality was that if news and business didn't work together, the paper would not come out. They needed each other.

The statement said that news should be protected from "commercial pressure." A business executive made this suggestion: "What if the language read 'outside commercial pressure'?"

No, it applies to inside or outside pressure, the editors insisted. Raines was the fiercest. Some people on both sides complained later that Raines fought too ostentatiously. But knowing the stakes to be high, and knowing the publisher was watching, so did others. In the end, the news and business sides could not resolve their differences among themselves. In this sense, Sulzberger did not succeed. He had hoped to induce both sides to reach agreement without the publisher having to act as referee. When he realized near the end of this retreat that he could not, he announced some decisions.

First, he appointed a committee composed of three members of the news staff and three members of the business staff to draft a final values document. Second, he praised the debate for pinpointing for him where the wall should stand, and announced that no one from the business side should get in touch with anyone from news below the masthead level. No one from circulation or advertising could get in touch with, say, the metropolitan or cultural or business editor. A third decision he made but did not announce was that he would elevate Russell Lewis to president and general manager of the paper, a decision revealed a month later.

In one sense, these retreats were a success for Sulzberger. Many of his managers and editors had been stunned by the vehemence of the debate, but Sulzberger believed that they had been shocked only because they had not previously engaged in an honest dialogue. He came away satisfied. He hoped news and business would now act more like a team—see themselves as one company, not two. "We got rid of a lot of the underbrush," he says. "We uncovered the fundamentals. And we reached agreement." Joe Lelyveld put it another way: "He dragged us into consultations with our business-side colleagues. . . . It had a healthy and cathartic effect."

EVEN IF confrontational techniques help Arthur Sulzberger, Jr., change the atmosphere within the *Times,* he will still face formidable challenges from the outside. First, there is the New York City economy, which lapsed into a recession soon after the stock market crash in October of 1987. The basic question is whether this economic downturn is cyclical or permanent. The Sulzbergers are in the optimists' camp, believing that it is temporary. "I think it's coming to an end," Sulzberger says of the recession. William L. Pollak, who directs the two-hundred-person *Times* ad-sales force, says, "Anyone who says the New York economy won't bounce back hasn't read the history of New York."

Robert M. Johnson, the publisher and CEO of *Newsday* since 1986, is in the pessimists' camp. He thinks history is a poor guide. "This has not been a recession," he says. "This has been a structural change in the New York City economy. The pie has gotten smaller." He mentions the department stores—B. Altman & Company, Alexander's, Bonwit Teller, Gimbel's—that have closed, as well as the shrinking number of classified and financial ads.

A second business question pressing upon Sulzberger is whether, in a period of rapid technological advances, the Times Company's growth strategy has been sufficient. It has been Punch Sulzberger's belief that the Times Company should cautiously stick to the areas it knows best. When he became publisher, in 1963, the *Times* was basically a two-section newspaper, and the company was almost totally reliant on its revenues alone. In 1969, he decided to make a public stock offering—the family retained control through Class B stock—to generate the funds the company needed to diversify. Today, the company owns five network-affiliated TV stations, thirty-one regional newspapers, the *Boston Globe,* an AM and an FM radio station, twenty magazines, two wholesale newspaper distributors, a forest-products division, and an information-services group. The expansion helped cushion the paper and the company from the fluctuations of the business cycle. "One thing we've learned over the years of acquisitions is that we do better when we acquire something we know about," Punch Sulzberger says. "We'll keep looking at new technologies. . . . We have lots of little pieces. We don't see any immediate area where it makes sense to make a massive commitment. So we're watching. A lot of people made a lot of mistakes in the eighties."

When the younger Sulzberger was asked if he shared the view of many that the *Times* had been too cautious in terms of new businesses, he said, "Sure. Now, I'm only speaking about the *New York Times* newspaper. I don't know the company." He knows that telephone and television and computer and newspaper and consumer-electronics companies are all racing toward one another, blurring traditional distinctions. Telephone companies are now in the cable television business. Cable companies offer phone service. Newspapers invest in television, and some produce shows. Studios sell programs to consumer-electronics firms. TV networks become partners with cable companies, cable companies with studios, studios with computer companies. The business is moving fast and, even under the younger Sulzberger and an eight-person strategic-planning group, the newspaper reacts more slowly than some of its executives would like. In its business moves, the *Times* has not been a crucible of change. The publisher has taken a few small steps to reach new readers, including *TimesFax,* a six- to eight-page summary of the day's newspaper that is sent to hotels and cruise ships around the world, and *Critics' Choice,* a weekly magazine on the arts and nightlife designed to reach tourists at their hotels in New York.

Sulzberger Jr. says the *Times* will not make the mistake that the railroads did when they mistakenly believed they were in the railroad rather than the transportation business. Instead of branching out into, say, the trucking business, railroads tried to protect their turf. The *Times,* Sulzberger believes, is in the information, not the newspaper, business. "Time for people's attention is the competition," he says. "It's not just television or news magazines or other newspapers or radio—it's all of that, *plus* the things that people can do with their time that are new and different, whether it's playing Nintendo or calling up movies on their cable boxes. The days when we could write a story about a news event on day one, the reaction to that news event on day two, and the news analysis on day three are gone. You had better have all three of those elements in your first story." He goes on, "Whether we beam it directly into your head or provide it on newsprint—I am agnostic on that. As far as I'm concerned, the day we move away from newsprint is the day we cut some seven hundred million dollars out of our cost structure." He believes that in perhaps twenty years it will be commonplace for newspapers to be delivered electronically as well as by newsprint.

Another problem that Sulzberger faces is that newspapers have become what economists call a mature business; in short, their growth has stalled. The *Times*'s response to this new reality, one Wall Street figure says, is to be a nibbler. "There is a husbanding-of-the-acorns mind-set," he says. "Arthur is much more concerned with what's on the front page than with the price of his stock. He's much more a newspaperman than a businessman." The acquisition of the *Boston Globe* is, in this view, a nibble, not a bold, futuristic thrust. Punch Sulzberger would disagree. After months of negotiations, which foundered more than once over "issues of governance," he says, the sale was concluded on June eleventh. "We're not just buying a newspaper," Sulzberger says. "We're buying a distribution system. We're buying a database. And we're buying a paper that has a much higher penetration in its marketplace than the *Times* has." Sulzberger says the *Times* now has a broader, more attractive database to travel over a future electronic highway. And the purchase was made without sacrificing cash to make future deals. "This is not a cash deal. This is a stock deal," he says. "So our cash is preserved."

The *Times* wants to make friends with potential hardware allies. But if such partnerships are the wave of the future for communications and information companies, that future is still distant, the Sulzbergers believe.

STILL ANOTHER CONCERN at the *Times* is the imminent need to choose the next executive editor. The retirement age for masthead executives at the *Times* is sixty-five, and Frankel just turned sixty-three. Frankel says he has decided that when he leaves, he is not going to write a column, as A. M. Rosenthal does, but instead will write a memoir. "I have a big book in me," he says. "I've been storing it up all my life." First, though, he must sort out when he will retire. "I have to start discussing that with Arthur," Frankel said in April. While Sulzberger acknowledges that "there are differences" between the type of management he advocates and the hierarchical management generally practiced by both Frankel and Lelyveld, he has no desire to see Frankel depart. "I have learned a lot from Max in terms of being a manager," he said.

Punch Sulzberger says he expects to be consulted on the choice. He also says that Joe Lelyveld is the obvious front-runner to succeed Frankel. "I would hope that Max would be there a number of years more, and it would be foolish to name a successor at this point," he says. "There is no reason to. And why lock yourself in? But it is certainly true that Joe has the inside track." Frankel says that "at the moment" he could not imagine another choice but, of course, he says, the decision is the publisher's.

What criteria will Sulzberger rely on in making the decision? "Journalistic integrity and confidence—that's obviously number one," he says, and he cites as other factors "the ability to delegate authority" and a "commitment to diversity" and "making this the kind of place to work that it can be." He adds, "But overriding everything has to be the quality of the news mind." If "the quality of the news mind" determines Sulzberger's decision, Joe Lelyveld will probably be the next executive editor, for many say he has the sharpest mind in the newsroom, a mind that quickly cuts to the heart of a story and can instantly suggest a new lead paragraph or structure.

Lelyveld offers other talents. The publisher knows that he has high standards. He knows that both Lelyveld and Frankel often provoke and nurture the paper's best correspondents. He knows that while many people complain about Lelyveld's intellectual arrogance, the same critics respect him and sometimes refer to him as "a sweet man." He knows that within the *Times* no other contender musters the internal support Lelyveld would, for his appointment is widely viewed as based on merit.

The publisher also knows the debit side of the ledger. He knows that Lelyveld can be abrupt, has problems speaking in public, and is painfully shy. "He has no people skills," one of the paper's star writers says. Lelyveld is aware of his awkwardness. From the time he was a boy through his graduation from the Bronx High School of Science and Harvard, he recalls that his father, a distinguished rabbi, always said to him, "You have to be more outgoing." He knows that some people regard him as aloof, and says, "One reason is that I've always been comfortable in the role of a reporter. I prefer to stand aside, to watch and observe, and not be public. I can be brusque. It's a failing. I don't think it's coldness. It's obsessiveness. I'm very comfortable in small groups. I'm not very comfortable getting up and addressing the staff." When he speaks, there are long, awkward pauses. "I've learned I have to devote time to programming what I'm going to say."

Sulzberger's alternative choice as Frankel's successor is Howell Raines. When Sulzberger is asked to describe Raines and Lelyveld, he says of both men, "wonderful writer" and "first-class intellect." Like Lelyveld, Raines is said to be a demanding taskmaster; he ran the Washington bureau in an autocratic fashion. But Raines has a more vivid personality than does Lelyveld. "He's a very warm and agreeable fellow," says a man who has been at the *Times* for his entire career. Of the younger Sulzberger, this man observes, "I know he's very close to Howell. He picked Howell as his choice. Joe and Max were Punch's appointments." Raines got to know Arthur Jr. in the early eighties, when both worked as reporters in the Washington bureau.

Raines says he would love to write a Washington-based column, but when asked if he would accept the job of executive editor, he paused a long while and then said, "I'm the creature of this newspaper, I suppose. It's not something that I think about, frankly."

While Lelyveld remains the likely choice, the new publisher wants options. He saw his father boxed into a corner with only one obvious choice—Max Frankel—when Abe Rosenthal reached sixty-five. Raines has a strong hand in the card game the publisher will play over the next few years. Like the man who holds the cards, he's an extrovert. Together, they laugh easily at jokes and at Raines's barnyard metaphors. The two men meet every Thursday afternoon to review editorial ideas, and speak frequently. While Raines's support is not nearly as broad as Lelyveld's, Raines did develop a devoted band of followers when he was Washington bureau chief.

And, like Lelyveld, Raines is unafraid to speak his mind. Before Raines took over the editorial page, the publisher had intervened and asked Jack Rosenthal to write an editorial backing away from criticism leveled in a previous editorial at Vernon Jordan, the chairman of the Clinton transition team, over alleged conflicts of interest. Sulzberger says that the earlier editorial "was unfair to a man I did not know" because it "singled him out" as the personification of all the evils of influence peddling in Washington. The members of the editorial board were distressed, and the publisher called a meeting in the editorial offices to explain why, for the first time ever, he had overruled them. He went around the room seeking opinions, and then turned to Raines, who had been invited, even though he had yet to start his editorial-page job. Raines hesitated, torn between the intimacy and the trust he would need with the publisher and the trust he would need with the board members and *Times* readers. According to several people who were there, Raines responded, in his slow, measured drawl, "I don't have a dog in this fight, but I think the first editorial was fine and the second one should not have run. Writing the second editorial inhibited our ability to write on this subject." The publisher says he was not moved to change his position, though several members of the board were impressed. "That was bold—to sit there with a guy who signs his checks," a witness recalls. "In the corporate culture, not many guys would say that."

A few other names are mentioned as potential future executive editors—particularly that of the columnist Anna Quindlen, who is forty. She has told friends that she expects to tire of writing a column in five years or so, and might want to step aside before readers tire of her. Her experience is limited: She has never been a foreign correspondent, and her only editing job at the *Times* was as deputy metropolitan editor. (Abe Rosenthal and Max Frankel both tried to persuade her to become metropolitan editor, but she declined. She wanted to be able to spend more time with her children.) What she would bring, in addition to brains and long-standing ties to Arthur Sulzberger, Jr., and his wife, the artist Gail Gregg, is the bottom-up management approach Sulzberger champions. "I don't think it makes sense for an editor to tell reporters how to cover a story, how long it has to be, or how it should be played," she says. "A reporter ought to tell me. There's too much macho throughout the business—'I know what the story should be!' It's too rare that an editor says to a reporter, 'Is this a page-one story?'" One possibility is to make Quindlen the managing editor under either Lelyveld or Raines, but for

Sulzberger to do that would mean that he would lose her popular column. Worse, from his vantage point, he might have to choose as early as this fall, when one and maybe two assistant managing editor slots open. If he should offer Quindlen such a slot, she would have to decide whether to sacrifice her platform and independence for a climb up the management ladder. Such a maneuver could create a traffic jam, since Sulzberger is eager to promote a black editor to the masthead (Gerald Boyd, the metropolitan editor, would be the choice), and might like a second woman there, too (the national editor, Soma Golden Behr, is now the prime contender).

Sulzberger has more than a few such dilemmas to ponder. Even if Joe Lelyveld—or Howell Raines—is thought of as autocratic, how could he pass on their obvious talent without subverting *Times* traditions? Will the paper, in its zeal to recruit a more diverse workforce, settle for less than the best reporters and editors? In its determination to be more understanding of gay rights, say, or race relations, will the *Times* meekly succumb to political correctness? Will it lower its standards, as many believe it has with its Sunday style section? How does the *Times* stay as good as it is without surrendering to arrogance and insularity? How does it reach younger readers, who grew up watching television and may have attenuated attention spans, without providing quick, easily absorbed information?

Another constraint is his predecessor, who happens to be his father and boss. The son wants to change the institution, yet not suggest that his father, whom he admires, has somehow been derelict. "If I could be as successful as he was, I would consider myself a very successful publisher," the son says of the father. "He saved the paper." But their relationship is more complicated than shared adoration. The father says he tries to resist interfering. "And sometimes I'm not good at it," he adds.

A corollary constraint is that because the elder Sulzberger actively runs the company, the son operates one rung down the corporate ladder. Unlike his father and his three aunts, he's not a member of the *Times*'s board of directors. "He reports to Lance on the business side," Punch Sulzberger says, referring to Lance Primis, the Times Company's president. "When it comes time to get money, he has to wait on line."

Despite the concerns that burden his days, Arthur Jr. says that he truly loves what he does. "For my money, I have the best job in the world right now, publisher of the *New York Times*," he says. "Don Graham warned me in the most friendly way that I have the best job and to hold on to it." Donald Graham, of course, holds two jobs—publisher of the *Washington Post* and president and chief executive officer of its parent company. It is possible that when Punch Sulzberger steps down as chairman, Arthur Jr. will have to choose between the two posts. One family member says that both Michael and Stephen Golden see themselves as the potential chairman. "But I'd put my money on Arthur," he says. "We're a traditional company. He's a Sulzberger. He's the publisher of the company's flagship. And the two others have less knowledge of the newspaper business." It is possible that the family will follow the example of the Hearst Corporation and bring in a nonfamily member as CEO. Many things are possible.

What seems certain at the moment is that Arthur Sulzberger, Jr., like his great-grandfather and his grandfather and his father, will preside over the *Times* for a very long while. Like his predecessors, he will probably decide to invest more money in the paper even during recessions, or when doing so momentarily depresses earnings.

Ironically, while Arthur Sulzberger, Jr., genuinely believes that the vibrancy of the world's best newspaper depends on a more democratic newsroom, he also knows that the *Times* can resist economic slumps and the short-term preoccupations of shareholders only because it is a family-owned monarchy. And despite his genuine affability, like all monarchs the new publisher charts a fairly lonely path. A cousin says, "There are not many people in this company who tell Arthur he's doing a good job whom he can believe." And he will no doubt continue to push for change, cautiously. Although he wants to change the *Times,* he is constrained because he knows he has a tradition and a franchise to protect. "We produce certainly the finest newspaper in this country, and probably in the world," he says. "You don't want to tamper with a system that does that. When I say tamper, I mean experiment—tear it apart without being able to put things back together."

POSTSCRIPT

When his father retired, Arthur Jr. became chairman of the company as well as publisher of the paper. Cousin Michael Golden was elevated to vice chairman. Each joined the board. But unlike his father, Arthur Jr. did not become CEO; for the first time, a nonfamily member, Russell Lewis, became the CEO of the company, reporting to the chairman. Young Arthur quickly established his own priorities; he aggressively steered the Times Company into television production. Eager to expand the reach of the *Times—extending the brand* is the favored phrase—he boosted circulation of the national edition of the *Times;* to extend its reach overseas, he brusquely compelled his friend Donald Graham to sell his half interest in the *International Herald Tribune.*

In some ways, the new chairman mellowed. He sounded less like an Outward Bound instructor. He became less flip, aware that his words carried more weight than he sometimes meant them to. In other ways, he became more self-satisfied. Several years after this piece appeared in 1993, we were on a panel together at the Columbia School of Journalism and, afterward, we shared a subway downtown. As the train rumbled beneath Broadway, I asked what newspapers and magazines he read.

None regularly, Sulzberger replied. He only had time to read the *Times* carefully each day. If an associate or friend mentioned a particular article, he would read it. But he was quite content to rely on the *Times* for his exposure to the world.

The publisher of the *Times* likes to tell his minions they must communicate about everything. He tells a joke about a moose that attended a small dinner party and no one dared mention its presence, prompting Sulzberger to regularly talk about what he calls "moose issues," or things everyone knows but lacks the courage to discuss. It is odd to imagine that a man whose sources of information about the world are limited to his own newspaper is well positioned to be receptive to the openness he encourages in his employees.

The moose got a bit more attention in May 2003 when reporter Jayson

Blair impaled himself—and the *Times*. Sulzberger came to a meeting of agitated *Times* employees carrying a stuffed toy moose in a plastic bag. In an effort to defuse staff rage at Blair and at an authoritarian executive editor and managing editor, Sulzberger held up the moose to assure the six hundred or so staffers in attendance that they were free to say anything.

For the next two hours, and the next three weeks, the *Times* staff rioted against the Raines regime, blaming it not just for Blair and journalistic misdemeanors but for an intimidating top-down management style that made reporters and most editors feel as if they worked for—not with—Executive Editor Howell Raines and Managing Editor Gerald Boyd. When Sulzberger tried to quell the uprising by sacking Raines and Boyd, the newsroom cheered, believing that he had recognized the moose parading in the newsroom.

But had he? Sulzberger has insisted for years that he wanted more open, less fearsome management at the paper—"The cost of allowing fear to permeate our newspaper is too high a cost for us to bear," he said. He even organized embarrassing retreats with professional facilitators to help editors get in touch with their friendlier selves. Yet he chose Raines and the masthead management structure Raines had recommended. He urged Raines to make Boyd the first black managing editor, and although Boyd is respected as a newsman, one could probably count on one hand those in the newsroom who believed his appointment was solely based on merit. When the *Times* ran its 7,200-word account of Jayson Blair's wrongdoing, Sulzberger displayed his injudicious side. "The person who did this is Jayson Blair," he told his own reporters. "Let's not begin to demonize our executives—either the desk editors or the executive editor or, dare I say, the publisher!" After compelling Raines and Boyd to resign, Sulzberger told the *Wall Street Journal* he was stunned to learn of staff unrest. "It caught me by surprise and is in part my failure as a publisher." The staff had been openly restive for at least a year.

At fifty-one, Sulzberger still sometimes made juvenile remarks—telling *Times* employees at their open meeting that the events surrounding Jayson Blair "sucked." He was pleased to see the *Times* rush to describe Blair's perfidities, and at the mass staff meeting he described it as among the finest pieces the *Times* had ever published. Yet if the *Times* had taken more time it might have defanged critics with a definitive account of what happened, as did the *Washington Post* after Janet Cook or the *Los Angeles Times* after it jumped into bed with an advertiser. It was Sulzberger who pushed for the mass meeting of *Times* employees, which probably excited more staff unrest and certainly assured more press coverage. These are said to have been the reservations of his father, Arthur "Punch" Sulzberger, who told friends that Blair should have been a one-column apology to readers and that the mass meeting was a mistake.

No one raised this question at the staff meeting or at subsequent meetings with Sulzberger Jr., but, increasingly, the newsroom whispered: Is the publisher the moose in the room?

WHEN, IN 1994, Max Frankel decided to retire earlier than expected, he announced that he would write the memoir "I've been storing up all my life." When it appeared, colleagues were shocked to discover that Frankel had been storing up a tanker-load of bile, which he deposited on several former Timesmen. As Lelyveld succeeded Frankel and Raines followed Lelyveld, Sulzberger's proclaimed devotion to a friendlier, less hierarchical newsroom couldn't stanch the stream of complaints—which intensified during the Blair affair—that the executive editor was too autocratic. Which begs another question: Is this the price an exacting editor must pay? Or as Suzanne Daley asked, "If you want to be 'nice,' do you lose your edge?"

Fair questions. In the old days, reporters could be both good and nice. Back then—before talk of synergy and brands, before reporters adopted an adversarial pose without the information to actually challenge sources— some legends ruled the newsroom. The subject of this next profile did not become a legend by sticking his tape recorder in people's faces; he didn't even have a tape recorder. He didn't shout rude questions or show off. Instead, as he described an early interview he conducted with a museum director, "I just sidled over to the director and asked him a series of quiet questions, gentleman to gentleman, which he answered readily. I never veered from that in all my reporting experience. It seemed comfortable and decent. And it was by far the most effective way to interview."

THE REPORTER
WHO DISAPPEARED

L AST APRIL TWELFTH, a crowd filled the First Church, in Wenham, Massachusetts, for the funeral of Nathaniel C. Nash, the Frankfurt bureau chief of the *New York Times*. Nash, a much-admired reporter, had been among the thirty-five passengers and crew killed when the airplane carrying Secretary of Commerce Ronald Brown crashed into a Croatian mountain. Seated among the journalist's friends and family were some two dozen newspaper employees, including the *Times*'s publisher, Arthur O. Sulzberger, Jr.

There were three speakers at the service, including the rector of the First Church and the pastor of a neighboring church. The principal speaker was John McCandlish Phillips, Jr., and he caused a stir. Phillips, who is six feet six but weighs only 161 pounds, loomed over Nash's coffin. Wearing a baggy gray striped suit jacket and black pants, and with his long thin neck sticking like a pole through a too-large collar hoop, the sixty-eight-year-old Phillips looked like an overdressed vagrant. When he reached the pulpit, he began to weep. When he spoke, he cited Scripture, scolding those who had sinned and assuring the bereaved that Nash awaited them "in a better place." Nathaniel, he said, "was lovely in life here, a friend of friends, and I expect to see him later there."

Phillips spoke at the behest of the Nash family, who wanted people to understand how devoted Nathaniel had been to Phillips's Pentecostal church group, the New Testament Missionary Fellowship. Nash had joined the group as a Harvard freshman, and after he graduated, in 1973, Phillips helped recruit him to the *Times* as a copyboy. In those days, McCandlish Phillips, as his byline read, was a star reporter at the *Times,* and was the newspaperman whom Nash most admired. And Nash was not the only one who felt that way. Among the outstanding journalists who worked in the newsroom in those days—Gay Talese, Homer Bigart, David Halberstam, Gloria Emerson, J. Anthony Lukas, Richard Reeves—Phillips was widely thought to be the most gifted writer.

Many of those who crowded the spare New England church in Wenham did not know about Nash's spiritual side. "Nash was close to his God," Arthur Sulzberger, Jr., says. "You could have a beer with Nash and not know that." Nor did many at the church know that during the years Nathaniel Nash lived in New York, in the seventies and early eighties, he and Phillips and two dozen or so others met on Tuesday evenings and Sunday mornings to pray and to share their faith that salvation comes only to those who are "born again" as believers in Jesus Christ. Each spring and fall, Fellowship church members trolled the Columbia University campus, reciting Scripture and dispensing literature. Nash played the guitar and Phillips slapped his thigh as the group sang hymns.

Sulzberger, like many others at Nash's funeral, had never met McCandlish Phillips before. Others at the *Times* had known Phillips—in the newsroom he was called John—but had not seen him for decades, although they vividly remembered stories he had written. Gay Talese, who left the paper in 1965 and became a best-selling author, says, "He was the Ted Williams of the young reporters. He was a natural. There was only one guy I thought I was not the equal of, and that was McCandlish Phillips."

Colleagues on the *Times* knew Phillips as an uncommonly polite and generous man who never drank, smoked, cursed, or played cards. He kept a Bible on his desk, and once a week, surrounded by a handful of *Times* employees, he conducted Bible readings in the back of the third-floor newsroom. To competitors like Pete Hamill, then a columnist for the *Post* and now the editor in chief of the *Daily News,* he was "a gentle character" who "seemed miscast as a newsman" among the sharks of what were until the early 1960s seven competing daily newspapers. Or so it appeared, until Hamill read Phillips's copy. He recalls, "He used the senses. He looked. He listened. He smelled. He touched. There was a texture to his writing that was sensual." Phillips's stories often focused on forgotten people: the homeless for whom the Port Authority Bus Terminal became a place not just to keep warm but to socialize; the typesetter who saved a literary treasure from oblivion. Phillips reported fires and murders, he covered Albany and the United Nations, but he was best known as a stylish feature writer. When editors wanted someone to bring a fresh and humorous eye to Abraham Lass, a remarkable Brooklyn high school principal who was also an accomplished ragtime piano player, or to chronicle the last piece of cheesecake sold at Lindy's, Phillips was their man. He could write about Wisconsin that the state "bobs on a sea of curdled milk," or describe a jazz group in which "one player in this noisome pestilence looked something like a blond werewolf, with a veil of hair growing across his face."

It was a brilliant career, but in 1973, after twenty-one years at the *Times,* Phillips startled his colleagues by announcing that he was quitting. He was forty-six. He fell out of touch with his former co-workers, though they would occasionally hear that he had been spotted in Morningside Heights, trying to convert Columbia students. When Phillips left the *Times,* he had had a full head of dark hair, cut short around the temples. At Nash's funeral, former colleagues were startled by the change in his appearance. His ears stood out starkly beneath strands of gray hair at his temples. His complexion was sallow. He looked like an apparition.

What remained unchanged was the ready smile, the somewhat gawky manner, the sweetness. And, for the contingent from the *Times,* memories of a legendary journalist more interested in the truth and texture of a story than in scoring a scoop. And a question: Why did a man with so much talent walk away from it?

————

JOHN MCCANDLISH PHILLIPS graduated from high school in 1947 and went to work at a weekly newspaper in Brookline, Massachusetts. There a colleague introduced him to the Baptist Church, which affected him deeply. But the transforming experience of his life came in Baltimore in 1952, five weeks before he was to be discharged from the army. He had continued to attend Baptist services, and at a service one night, while the congregation was praying, a lay minister bellowed, "Are you willing to go anywhere in the world and do anything Christ asks of you? If you are, stand up!" Phillips did not stand up. "But every word of that went right into me," he recalls.

Four weeks later, those words were still with him. Restlessly, Master Sergeant Phillips rose before the 6:00 A.M. reveille and walked to the small chapel on the army base. "The morning was a low blue," he told me. "It was quiet. I sensed the presence of God with me and I went into that chapel and said yes to God on the basis of that challenge. I told Him I'd go anywhere in the world and do anything He wanted me to do." Phillips expected that he would become either a preacher or a missionary.

First, though, he took the train home to Boston to stay with his father, who was sick. He boarded the train in Baltimore, and as it approached Penn Station, God spoke to him. "Get off the train" is the command he remembers. "I didn't understand it. I simply got off the train." He found a cheap hotel near Times Square, and the next morning he bought copies of the *Herald Tribune* and the *Times.* On a *Times* classified page he spotted an ad for an editorial trainee. He fell to his knees beside the bed and prayed for guidance. Again, he heard the voice of God, telling him, he remembers, that he "had a mission to go to the *New York Times* and get a job."

What did he hear when God spoke? "You don't hear through your outer ear," he explained. "You hear through your inner ear. You are conscious of being talked to, but you don't hear the words."

Wearing his army uniform, Phillips left his dingy hotel room and walked to the *Times,* where the personnel office was crowded with applicants for the editorial-trainee job. Phillips was in the habit of saying "Yes, sir," and

"No, sir," and this made a favorable impression, as did his assurance that he could live on $27.50 a week.

And he did, finding a room at the YMCA on West Twenty-third Street off Seventh Avenue, for $10.50 a week, and eating supper at the nearby Automat, where for 45 cents he could get a plate of three hot vegetables, mashed potatoes, a dish of prunes, and a roll with butter. Most weeks, he managed to save $2.00 to send to his mother, and each week he put 50 cents or so in the collection plate of the Baptist church.

His job was not glamorous. The city room, on the third floor, stretched for an entire block, from Forty-third Street to Forty-fourth Street, and was filled with the sound of telephones, pounding Royal and Underwood typewriters, creaking swivel chairs, blaring microphone summonses for reporters to appear at an editor's desk, shouts of "Copy!" and "Boy!"

There was a lot of gambling in the newsroom. Arthur Gelb, who joined the paper as a copyboy in 1944, rose to managing editor, and is to-day president of the New York Times Company Foundation, recalls that gambling was once so prevalent that the managing editor, Edwin Leland James, "hired two bookies as copyboys. James bet. We all bet on the horses. They paid off with rolls of cash." McCandlish Phillips lugged his Bible everywhere, but he did not try to impose his values on others. He was awed by the newsroom and the eminences who inhabited it—Meyer (Mike) Berger, who wrote the "About New York" column; Peter Khiss, who kept (and generously shared) meticulous files on every subject he ever reported on; Homer Bigart, who, like the TV detective Columbo, was not afraid to ask the childlike question that unlocked the story. It was a room filled with eccentrics, and the copyboy who read a Bible at his desk, addressed editors as "sir," and resembled Ichabod Crane fit right in. When someone called out "Copy!" Phillips was hard to miss, loping like a giraffe across the room.

Early in 1955, Phillips was promoted to reporter and assigned to the "shack" that the *Times* maintained across from Brooklyn police head-quarters. He worked as a legman and learned the tricks of reporting—in particular, the art of the interview. At one press conference, reporters were shouting rude questions at a museum director. As Phillips recalls it, "I just sidled over to the director and asked him a series of quiet questions, gentleman to gentleman, which he answered readily. I never veered from that in all my reporting experience. It seemed comfortable and decent. And it was by far the most effective way to interview."

What made the newsroom take notice of him was not a story for the paper but a satire he wrote that treated life in the Brooklyn shack as if it were a foreign posting. Published in the August 1955 edition of *Times Talk,* the newspaper's house organ, it contained such observations as "Policemen are remarkable linguists. They do their calls in hundreds of languages, none of which owe any debt to English." And this:

> Two weeks ago, a man of about 55 who looked as though he had been made out of scrap iron and old revolver handles dropped in to explain that he had just been sprung from the Tombs; that some old friends had taken the trouble to beat him up his first night out and that he wasn't afraid of nobody, especially cops. He wanted to know why the newspapers suppressed all sorts of important things, like prison conditions and graft among politicians.
>
> "It's a plot," I told him. "But what can I do? I'm just one of the little ones." This cheered him and he left without striking me.

Arthur Gelb remembers the satire—and the new byline, which was then John M. Phillips—vividly. "We all said, 'Who is John Phillips? Who wrote this wonderful piece?' I can't think of any other case where a star was born in the newsroom and overnight everyone in the newsroom knew who he was." Phillips was soon promoted to a desk in the newsroom's next-to-last row.

Professionally, Phillips began to soar; his personal life was not so smooth. His father, a sales representative, who had separated from his mother when their son was three, died in 1958. Now his mother—with whom he'd moved so often that he switched grammar schools thirteen times before the age of twelve—was penniless. He invited her to live with him in an apartment he had rented in Brooklyn. This provoked tension between them, and it exploded in an ugly way in 1959. Gay Talese recalled the evening: He was working on the night rewrite desk when an editor exclaimed, "Jesus, I just heard from the city desk that there's some problem with John. The cops are over there. John's been breaking plates, and his mother called the cops."

The argument was over his mother's unwillingness to take off her spike heels, which were gouging holes in a new floor. Phillips remembers that they had words and he smashed his fist through a window. He said he never physically threatened his mother, but she summoned the police. "I was taken to Kings County Hospital, and I was essentially held there for six or seven days," he recalled. He was subjected to psychiatric examination. After that, his mother moved to an apartment in Queens. And although they were still on speaking terms and got together with Phillips's younger sister on holidays, they remained somewhat distant for the rest of her life. (She died in 1991.)

Around the newsroom, Phillips kept pretty much to himself. Sometimes he had dinner at the home of Gay Talese and his wife, Nan, or went across the street to Gough's to eat with colleagues. But he never went drinking with the boys. Nicholas Pileggi, who was a police reporter for the Associated Press in the fifties and sixties, remembered that when the police raided a porn parlor, they would confiscate movies. Then the cops and the brass from the old police headquarters, at 240 Centre Street, would join reporters at the *Times*'s office across the street, set up an 8-mm projector, and hang a sheet backed by a blanket over the window to serve as a screen. Every time they did this, Phillips would step outside and take a walk around the block. Pileggi, who says he played poker instead, recalls, "These guys were so retarded. They once forgot the blanket and projected right through the bedsheet. So the outside of police headquarters had a movie of Lucky Pierre in his socks chasing this lady around the bed!"

Phillips rarely dated. Since 1950, he says, he has dated only one woman, a former Associated Press reporter. He stopped seeing her when the Scriptures instructed him that one cannot "yoke" a believer and a nonbeliever. "I am not susceptible to loneliness because I am not alone," he says.

Perhaps the most influential person in McCandlish Phillips's life was a woman he met in 1961, in Miami. He was there on an assignment to search for secret United States government bases where exiled Cubans were training to invade their homeland. Once, on a night off, he got lost and came across a small Spanish mission, where he sat and listened to the service, which was in Spanish. An older woman who spoke English came over and helped him translate. This was Hannah Lowe, who was then sixty-six years old. Her husband, Thomas Lowe, had formed Pentecostal congregations in Baltimore in the late 1920s, and had then gone as a missionary to South America, where he died in 1941. She had continued his work, and had spent much of her life since as a missionary in Colombia and in Israel.

A year later, Phillips again met Mrs. Lowe by chance when she visited New York to preach. Phillips was awed by her devotion. She returned to South America, and they met the next year at a Christian businessmen's breakfast in New York. He persuaded her to stay. Over the next several years, they would pray together, and they organized a church, called the New Testament Missionary Fellowship, recruiting members, spreading the gospel that there was, in his words, "a priesthood of all believers." This church believes that pornography, drugs, abortion, and any form of fornication (including premarital sex and homosexuality) are sins— although, unlike the religious right, it does not champion government intervention to regulate behavior.

In 1963, Mrs. Lowe and another woman moved to a third-floor apartment at 116th Street and Broadway; the following year, Phillips moved to a two-room apartment on the seventh floor of the same building, where he still lives. Often they dined together at the New Asia Restaurant, near 112th Street and Broadway. After dinner, he would go home and sometimes read books; most often, he read Scripture and prayed.

In the morning, a prayer group would convene for an hour at 7:30 A.M. After that, Phillips entered the secular world at the *Times*. He was enraptured by his job. In 1963, when A. M. Rosenthal was summoned from Tokyo and put in charge of the city desk, with Arthur Gelb as his deputy, Phillips and Talese and others were excited. Rosenthal was known to want better writing in the paper. While he was still in Tokyo, he had already decided that Talese and Phillips were the two writers he admired most. Of Phillips, Rosenthal recalls, "He was an original. He had a very telling eye. He had a quiet merriment. His writing wasn't heavy."

Phillips's most celebrated story was written in 1965, when Rosenthal and Gelb assigned him to investigate the life of Daniel Burros, who, at twenty-eight, had become the leader of the state Ku Klux Klan. Rosenthal had received a tip that Burros, who had also been a ranking official in the American Nazi Party, was Jewish. For five days, with help from a team of reporters, Phillips dug.

When he had the facts, he got up early one day and took the subway to Ozone Park, Queens, hoping to stop Burros as he left his apartment. He intercepted him outside a barbershop, and they walked to a luncheonette and found a booth. Burros ordered a Coke, Phillips had scrambled eggs. They talked about the Klan, about how Burros had come to embrace Nazism, about his service in the army and the pictures in his wallet. Then Phillips revealed that he knew Burros had been reared in a Jewish home. Burros demanded angrily, "Are you going to print that?"

Phillips said that it was not within his power to make that decision, but the fact that Burros's parents were married in a Jewish ceremony was a matter of public record.

Burros put his hand inside his coat and told Phillips that he had a vial of acid in his pocket, and that he would kill him in the luncheonette. Phillips nervously glanced down at the knife and fork near Burros's fingertips, then calmly put a dollar down on the table, and rose to leave. Burros followed him outside. As Rosenthal and Gelb later wrote, in "One More Victim: The Life and Death of an American-Jewish Nazi," Phillips "had the story in his notebook" but decided to stay and try to convert this man who seemed so full of hate. "If any man be in Christ, he is a new creature," Phillips told Burros. "Old things are passed away; behold, all things are become new."

"You're trying to con me," Burros snapped. They walked for a while, and before they parted they shook hands. Phillips went back to the office, and all day Burros kept calling, one moment pleading, the next threatening. A security guard hovered while Phillips wrote his story. That night, two detectives drove Phillips home. Gelb and Rosenthal held the story, hoping to confirm that Burros had been bar mitzvahed; when they did, Phillips wrote an insert, and the story was published. When Daniel Burros saw the story, on the front page of the *Times,* he shot himself to death.

These events became a sensation, the more so when the usually tender Phillips seemed to exhibit no guilt at the news that Burros had committed suicide. Rosenthal remembers the conversation this way: "He said, and this was the first time his religion entered into his work, 'It was the will of God'—it gives me shivers to say it!—'and you were the instrument of God!'"

It was common at the time for publishers to turn out quickie paperback books on big news stories, and New American Library wanted to do one on Burros. Hollywood studios expressed interest in a movie. Rosenthal and Gelb invited Phillips to lunch. Phillips brought along Hannah Lowe and his Bible. The two editors outlined the book proposal and discussed movie rights. Phillips, the editors remember, opened the Bible and, in a booming voice, read passages aloud. The crowded restaurant fell silent. Embarrassed, Rosenthal and Gelb slid down in their seats. Phillips, citing Scripture—"Touch not the spoil"—declined the book offer, having decided that he could not enrich himself from a tragedy.

Marvin Siegel, who joined the *Times* as an editor in 1966 and who lives in Phillips's building but rarely sees him, recalled that assigning Phillips to a story was like having money in the bank. "As a combination writer/ reporter, I don't think anyone topped him," Siegel said recently. He did not besiege editors with story ideas, as, for example, Gay Talese did, but he could be depended upon to produce at least three beautifully crafted stories a week.

As the sixties wore on, and as hair lengthened in the newsroom, Phillips seemed an increasingly anomalous figure. "He was definitely regarded as somewhat strange," said a former colleague who had been on assignments overseas and barely knew him. "He was widely said to be a religious fanatic of some sort." This reporter admired Phillips's prose, and the fact that he kept his religion strictly segregated from his work. This separation, however, was becoming harder to maintain.

A sense of mission was building within Phillips. It expressed itself in a book he wrote in 1970, *The Bible, the Supernatural, and the Jews*. Its thesis was that the Devil plotted to get people interested in the supernatural in order to lead them down the "path of spiritual ruination." He denounced the forces of "evil" that encouraged drug use and promiscuity, and warned that these forces were "multiplying and spreading." The book coincided with a new chapter in Phillips's life. He wanted to do something else. He didn't want to move to the Washington bureau or become a foreign correspondent. He aspired to write essays, book reviews, maybe a sports column. Although the *Times* bent the rules for him—granting him a leave to finish the book, for example—he was discontented.

Phillips was obsessed with a story that no one else seemed to take seriously: the life and art of a man named Otto Griebling, a circus clown Phillips had first seen in 1952, when he was in the army in Baltimore. Phillips believed that Griebling was a great artist, and for years he was haunted by the idea that Griebling, although he'd worked at his trade for more than half a century, had gained neither fame nor reward. Whenever the circus came to town, Phillips would pester his editors to assign a story about Otto the Clown. ("Griebling's clown," he wrote, in a 1974 collection of essays, "was harassed and futile, truly pathetic, yet he was also limitlessly patient and persistent and devoted. The things that menaced him were entirely unseen; they were private torments locked within some chamber of his consciousness and showing only on his face. For a circus clown to seek his effects in *implied psychology* rather than in plain and overt acts; for him to rely on a *suggestion* of an inward state rather than an outward showing of things, is virtually a defiance of the form.")

Phillips was particularly incensed in 1972 and 1973 by public accusations by parents that their college-age children were being brainwashed by elders of the New Testament Missionary Fellowship. His church, he believed, was founded on democratic principles. Phillips pleaded with editors to assign stories about what he condemned as a new wave of McCarthyism, this one aimed at born-again Christians. He was bothered by the *Times*'s seeming indifference. In turn, some editors believed that a change had come over Phillips. "He began to filter things through a religious prism," Marvin Siegel says. Editors became nervous as, increasingly, he prayed for guidance while he was working on stories.

Phillips was also tired—emotionally spent by the toll that being an empathetic reporter can take. "If what you are covering is 'moving' and you are not moved by it, you will not move anyone with it," he says. In December of 1973, after twenty-one years at the *Times,* John Phillips told his editors that he was resigning his job, which then paid $26,500 a year.

It was not especially unusual for gifted or ambitious writers to exit the *Times*. David Halberstam, who left in 1967, said recently, "The rest of us sat around and talked about what we wanted to do. He never did." When colleagues in the newsroom learned that Phillips was quitting, they assumed that he wanted to pursue a religious life. This belief was reinforced when Phillips virtually disappeared. God, it was often said around the *Times,* had spoken to Long John.

Phillips himself says that it was not that simple. He says that he was looking for a bigger stage and felt that the institution could not bend enough to accommodate its writers. "I wanted to go higher and have more scope," Phillips said he told Rosenthal. But former associates, including Rosenthal, don't believe that he walked away out of mere ambition. "Phillips is not interested in winning a Pulitzer Prize," Gay Talese said. "He is not interested in demeaning or finding flaws. He wants to redeem people. Talk about marching to a different drummer! Phillips is not even in the same jungle."

Before Phillips left the *Times,* he worked out a freelance arrangement that permitted him to write occasionally. He was contacted about writing for a morning television show, and doing feature stories for a local TV station, but such jobs held no allure. He thought of writing for magazines, of becoming an editor, but he was painfully shy. He had no network of friends and was not a generator of story ideas. He waited for the phone to ring with assignments. It didn't.

In the next eight years, McCandlish Phillips's byline occasionally appeared in the *Times*. His 1974 collection—*City Notebook: A Reporter's Portrait of a Vanishing New York*—was not even reviewed by the *Times*. His income, which he neatly itemized on a reporter's pad, fell to $10,383 dollars in 1976. He stopped writing for the *Times,* he said, because the paper wanted features that took the better part of a week and paid him too little for the effort. For the past fifteen years or so, Phillips has written occasional pieces for church journals. With the exception of Nathaniel Nash, he lost touch with former co-workers. Hannah Lowe, with whom he founded his church, moved to Jerusalem, where she died of a stroke in 1983, at the age of eighty-seven.

———

TODAY, Phillips works out of an office in a narrow bedroom that he rents in a friend's tenth-floor apartment on 116th Street. He sits at a Formica-topped metal folding table. The walls are bare of any adornments except a clock and a calendar; to his left rests a Bible and a small radio tuned to classical music; to his right stands a metal locker. Behind him, on another folding table, is a telephone, a typewriter, a computer that he doesn't use much, and stacks of church literature. A window caked with soot faces north.

Phillips spends part of his time as general manager of Thomas E. Lowe, Ltd., a small religious publishing house that he founded with Hannah Lowe. It buys remaindered religious books and reprints a handful of others, and sells them to Christian bookstores. Phillips estimates that he spends about a quarter of his time managing the firm, and in 1996 his gross pay for this was $2,256.

The bulk of his time is devoted to the Fellowship Church, of which he is an elder and administrator. The church, which relies on contributions from its members, has an income of about seventy thousand dollars a year, and pays Phillips twenty thousand dollars. With Social Security, interest on a savings account, and small stock dividends, his total income in 1995 was just under thirty thousand dollars. He helps prepare for twice-weekly prayer meetings, speaks at about a third of these, does photocopying and other errands, handles correspondence, serves as one of six trustees, and is generally available to listen. "John is like an older brother," explains Jaan Vaino, a CBS News financial executive. Jaan and Sharon Vaino's apartment, on 110th Street, is one of two sites for church gatherings. (The other is in a house the church owns in Yonkers.)

On a recent Tuesday, the group met, as it does every other Tuesday evening, in the Vainos' cramped living room. Nineteen members were present, including an NYU student and eight recent Columbia and Yale graduates, and ten other men and women who would not have looked out of place on Wall Street—except for Phillips, who wore an open, oversized red vest and a muddy yellow shirt with a red tie pinching his collar. For two hours, group members offered spontaneous prayers, sang favorite hymns, recited from the Scriptures, and invoked Jesus' good deeds. Vaino played an electronic keyboard; a professor in environmental medicine from the NYU Medical Center, Roy Shore, played a clarinet; and a pin-striped executive with the Bank of New York, Philip Chamberlain, took Nathaniel Nash's place on strings, with a Colombian instrument called a tiple. There were muted cries of "Praise the Lord!" and arms stretched at times to heaven, much as in a Baptist service. As he once climbed into the lives of people he wrote about, Phillips now showers empathy on the brethren of his church. "John is very tried in God. There is this holiness in him," remarked Helen Sun, a 1995 Yale graduate who works at CBS.

It was a relaxed evening; those present were not unlike Christmas carolers who unwind through song. Holly Vitale, who is a credit manager for a midtown company, said that she looks forward to these meetings as "an oasis, a family gathering." What helps to bind them together, members say, is John McCandlish Phillips.

It was that feeling—a belief in Phillips's largeness of spirit—that led the Nash family to call on him when the journalist was killed in Croatia. Nathaniel Cushing Nash says Phillips was "a great inspiration" as well as a "mentor" to his son. At the funeral in Wenham, Phillips was often the stern preacher, proclaiming that Satan was near. But when he spoke of his friend, he became empathetic and highly personal. "He was a spacious man," Phillips said. "He carried a kind of innocence that had no tincture of naïveté in it. There was nothing narrow or confined—or confining—about Nathaniel."

POSTSCRIPT

When Phillips was at the *Times,* few reporters were celebrities. Their faces were unknown. Their job was to listen, not talk. They did not opine. Television and lecture fees did not beckon. Much has changed, as the next piece suggests.

FEE SPEECH

THE INITIAL HINT of anger from twenty-five or so members of the House Democratic leadership came on an hour-and-a-quarter-long bus ride from Washington to Airlie House, in rural Virginia, one morning last January. They had been asked by the majority leader, Richard A. Gephardt, of Missouri, to attend a two-day retreat for the Democratic Message Group, and as the bus rolled southwest the convivial smiles faded. The members of the group began to complain that their message was getting strangled, and they blamed the media. By that afternoon, when the Democrats gathered for the first of five panels composed of both partisans and what were advertised as "guest analysts, not partisan advisers," the complaints were growing louder. The most prominent Democrats in the House—Gephardt; the majority whip, David E. Bonior, of Michigan; the current Appropriations Committee chairman, David R. Obey, of Wisconsin; the Democratic Congressional Campaign chairman, Vic Fazio, of California; Rosa L. DeLauro, of Connecticut, who is a friend of President Clinton's; and about twenty others—expressed a common grievance: Public figures are victims of a powerful and cynical press corps. A few complained of what they saw as the ethical obtuseness of Sam Donaldson, of ABC, angrily noting that, just four days earlier, *PrimeTime Live,* the program that Donaldson coanchors, had attacked the Independent Insurance Agents of America for treating congressional staff people to a Key West junket. Yet several months earlier the same insurance group had paid Donaldson a thirty-thousand-dollar lecture fee.

By 4:30, when the third panel, ostensibly devoted to the changing role of the media, was set to begin, the Democrats could no longer contain their rage, lumping the press into a single, stereotypical category—*you*—the same way they complained that the press lumped together *all* members of Congress.

They kept returning to Donaldson's lecture fees and his public defense that it was ethically acceptable for him to receive fees because he was a private citizen, not an elected official. The Airlie House meeting was off the record, but in a later interview Representative Obey recalled having said of journalists, "What I find most offensive lately is that we get the sanctimonious-Sam defense: 'We're different because we don't write the laws.' Well, they have a hell of a lot more power than I do to affect the laws written."

Representative Robert G. Torricelli, of New Jersey, recalled having said, "What startles many people is to hear television commentators make paid speeches to interest groups and then see them on television commenting on those issues. It's kind of a direct conflict of interest. If it happened in government, it would not be permitted." Torricelli, who has been criticized for realizing a sixty-nine-thousand-dollar profit on a New Jersey savings and loan after its chairman advised him to make a timely investment in its stock, says he doesn't understand why journalists don't receive the same scrutiny that people in Congress do. Torricelli brought up an idea that had been discussed at the retreat and that he wanted to explore: federal regulations requiring members of the press to disclose outside income—and most particularly, television journalists whose stations are licensed by the government. He said that he would like to see congressional hearings on the matter, and added, "You'd get the votes if you did the hearings. I predict that in the next couple of Congresses you'll get the hearings."

Gephardt is dubious about the legality of compelling press disclosure of outside income, but one thing he is sure about is the anger against the media rising within Congress. "Most of us work for more than money," he told me. "We work for self-image. And Congress's self-image has suffered because, members think, journalistic ethics and standards are not as good as they used to be."

The press panel went on for nearly three hours, long past the designated cocktail hour of six. The congressmen directed their anger at both Brian Lamb, the C-SPAN chairman, and me—we were the two press representatives on the panel—and cited a number of instances of what they considered reportorial abuse. The question that recurred most often was this: Why won't journalists disclose the income they receive from those with special interests?

IT IS A FAIR QUESTION to ask journalists, who often act as judges of others' character. Over the summer, I asked it of more than fifty prominent media people, or perhaps a fifth of what can fairly be called the media elite—those journalists who, largely on account of television appearances, have a kind of fame similar to that of actors. Not surprisingly, most responded to the question at least as defensively as any politician would. Some of them had raised an eyebrow when President Clinton said he couldn't recall ten- or fifteen-year-old details about Whitewater. Yet many of those I spoke to could not remember where they had given a speech just months ago. And many of them, while they were unequivocal in their commentary on public figures and public issues, seemed eager to dwell on the complexities and nuances of their own outside speaking.

Sam Donaldson, whose annual earnings at ABC are about two million dollars, was forthcoming about his paid speeches: In June, he said that he had given three paid speeches so far this year and had two more scheduled. He would not confirm a report that he gets a lecture fee of as much as thirty thousand dollars. On being asked to identify the three groups he had spoken to, Donaldson—who on the March twenty-seventh edition of the Sunday-morning show *This Week with David Brinkley* had ridiculed President Clinton for not remembering that he had once lent twenty thousand dollars to his mother—said he couldn't remember. Then he took a minute to call up the information from his computer. He said that he had spoken at an IBM convention in Palm Springs, to a group of public information officers, and to the National Association of Retail Druggists. "If I hadn't consulted my computerized date book, I couldn't have told you that I spoke to the National Association of Retail Druggists," he said. "I don't remember these things."

What would Donaldson say to members of Congress who suggest that, like them, he is not strictly a private individual and should make full disclosure of his income from groups that seek to influence legislation?

"First, I don't make laws that govern an industry," he said. "Second, people hire me because they think of me as a celebrity; they believe their members or the people in the audience will be impressed." He went on, "Can you say the same thing about a member of Congress who doesn't even speak—who is hired, in a sense, to go down and play tennis? What is the motive of the group that pays for that?" He paused and then answered his own question: "Their motive, whether they are subtle about it or not, is to make friends with you because they hope that you will be a friend of theirs when it comes time to decide about millions of dollars. Their motive in inviting me is not to make friends with me."

Would he concede that there might be at least an appearance of conflict when he takes money from groups with a stake in, say, health issues?

Donaldson said, "At some point, the issue is: What is the evidence? I believe it's not the appearance of impropriety that's the problem. It's impropriety." Still, Donaldson did concede that he was rethinking his position; and he was aware that his bosses at ABC News were reconsidering their relaxed policy.

Indeed, one of Donaldson's bosses—Paul Friedman, the executive vice president for news—told me he agreed with the notion that on-air correspondents are not private citizens. "People like Sam have influence that far exceeds that of individual congressmen," Friedman said, echoing Representative Obey's point. "We always worry that lobbyists get special 'access' to members of government. We should also worry that the public might get the idea that special interest groups are paying for special 'access' to correspondents who talk to millions of Americans."

Unlike Donaldson, who does not duck questions, some commentators chose to say nothing about their lecturing. The syndicated columnist George Will, who appears weekly as a commentator on the Brinkley show, said through an assistant, "We are just in the middle of book production here. Mr. Will is not talking much to anyone." Will is paid $12,500 a speech, Alicia C. Shepard reports in a superb article in the May issue of the *American Journalism Review.*

ABC's Cokie Roberts, who, according to an ABC official, earns between five and six hundred thousand dollars annually as a Washington correspondent and is a regular commentator on the Brinkley show in addition to her duties on National Public Radio, also seems to have a third job, as a paid speaker. Among ABC correspondents who regularly moonlight as speakers, Roberts ranks number one. A person who is in a position to know estimates that she earned more than three hundred thousand dollars for speaking appearances in 1993. Last winter, a couple of weeks after the Donaldson *PrimeTime* incident, she asked the Group Health Association of America, before whom she was to speak in mid-February, to donate her reported twenty-thousand-dollar fee to charity. Roberts did not return three phone calls—which suggests that she expects an openness from the Clinton administration that she rejects for herself. On that March twenty-seventh Brinkley show, she described the administration's behavior concerning Whitewater this way: "All of this now starts to look like they are covering something up."

Brit Hume, the senior ABC White House correspondent, earns about what Roberts does, and is said to trail only Roberts and Donaldson at ABC in lecture earnings. This could not be confirmed by Hume, for he did not return calls.

At CNN, the principal anchor, Bernard Shaw, also declined to be interviewed, and so did three of the loudest critics of Congress and the Clinton administration: the conservative commentator John McLaughlin, who now takes his *McLaughlin Group* on the road to do a rump version of the show live, often before business groups; and the alternating conservative cohosts of *Crossfire*, Pat Buchanan and John Sununu.

David Brinkley did respond to questions, but not about his speaking income. Like Donaldson and others, he rejected the notion that he was a public figure. Asked what he would say to the question posed by members of Congress at the retreat, Brinkley replied, "It's a specious argument. We are private citizens. We work in the private marketplace. They do not."

And if a member of Congress asked about his speaking fee, which is reported to be eighteen thousand dollars?

"I would tell him it's none of his business," Brinkley said. "I don't feel that I have the right to ask him everything he does in his private life."

The syndicated columnist and television regular Robert Novak, who speaks more frequently than Brinkley, also considers himself a private citizen when it comes to the matter of income disclosure. "I'm not going to tell you how many speeches I do and what my fee is," he said politely. Novak, who has been writing a syndicated column for thirty-one years, is highly visible each weekend on CNN as the cohost of the *Evans & Novak* interview program and as a regular on *The Capital Gang*.

What would Novak say to a member of Congress who maintained that he was a quasi-public figure and should be willing to disclose his income from speeches?

"I'm a totally private person," he said. "Anyone who doesn't like me doesn't have to read me. These people, in exchange for power—I have none—they have sacrificed privacy."

In fact, Novak does seem to view his privacy as less than total; he won't accept fees from partisan political groups and, as a frequent critic of the Israeli government, he will not take fees from Arab American groups, for fear of creating an appearance of a conflict of interest. Unlike most private citizens, Novak, and most other journalists, will not sign petitions, or donate money to political candidates, or join protest marches.

Colleagues have criticized Novak and Rowland Evans for organizing twice-a-year forums—as they have since 1971—to which they invite between 75 and 125 subscribers to their newsletter, many of whom are business and financial analysts. Those attending pay hundreds of dollars—

Novak refuses to say how much—for the privilege of listening to public officials speak and answer questions off the record. "You talk about conflicts of interest!" exclaimed Jack Nelson, the *Los Angeles Times* Washington bureau chief. "It is wrong to have government officials come to speak to businessmen and you make money off of it."

Mark Shields, who writes a syndicated column and is the moderator of *The Capital Gang* and a regular commentator on *The MacNeil/Lehrer NewsHour,* is a busy paid lecturer. Asked how much he earned from speeches last year, he said, "I haven't even totaled it up." Shields said he probably gives one paid speech a week, adding, "I don't want, for personal reasons, to get into specifics."

Michael Kinsley, who is the liberal cohost of *Crossfire,* an essayist for *The New Republic* and *Time,* and a contributor to *The New Yorker,* is also reluctant to be specific. "I'm in the worst of all possible positions," he said. "I do only a little of it. But I can't claim to be a virgin." Kinsley said he appeared about once every two months, but he wouldn't say what groups he spoke to or how much he was paid. "I'm going to do a bit more," he said. "I do staged debates—mini *Crossfires*—before business groups. If everyone disclosed, I would."

The New Republic's White House correspondent, Fred Barnes, who is a regular on *The McLaughlin Group* and appears on *CBS This Morning* as a political commentator, speaks more often than Kinsley, giving thirty or forty paid speeches a year, he said, including the *McLaughlin* road show. How would Barnes respond to the question posed by members of Congress?

"They're elected officials," he said. "I'm not an elected official. I'm not in government. I don't deal with taxpayers' money."

Barnes's *McLaughlin* colleague Morton M. Kondracke is the executive editor of *Roll Call,* which covers Congress. Kondracke said that he gave about thirty-six paid speeches annually, but he would not identify the sponsors or disclose his fee. He believes that columnists have fewer constraints on their speech making than so-called objective reporters, since columnists freely expose their opinions.

Gloria Borger, a *U.S. News & World Report* columnist and a frequent *Washington Week in Review* panelist, discloses her income from speeches, but only to her employer. Borger said she gave one or two paid speeches a month, but she wouldn't reveal her fee. "I'm not an elected official," she said.

Like Borger, Wolf Blitzer, CNN's senior White House correspondent, said that he told his news organization about any speeches he made. How many speeches did he make in the last year?

"I would guess four or five," he said, and repeated that each one was cleared through his bureau chief.

What would Blitzer say to a member of Congress who asked how much he made speaking, and from which groups?

"I would tell him 'None of your business,'" Blitzer said.

Two other network chief White House correspondents—NBC's Andrea Mitchell and CBS's Rita Braver—also do little speaking. "I make few speeches," Mitchell said. "Maybe ten a year. Maybe six or seven a year. I'm very careful about not speaking to groups that involve issues I cover." She declined to say how much she earned. For Braver, the issue was moot. "I don't think I did any," she said, referring to paid speeches in the past year.

ABC's *PrimeTime Live* correspondent Chris Wallace, who has done several investigative pieces on corporate-sponsored congressional junkets, said he made four or five paid speeches last year. "I don't know exactly," he said. Could he remember his fee?

"I wouldn't say," he replied.

Did he speak to business groups?

"I'm trying to remember the specific groups," he said, and then went on, "One was the Business Council of Canada. Yes, I do speak to business groups."

So what is the difference between Chris Wallace and members of Congress who accept paid junkets?

"I'm a private citizen," he said. "I have no control over public funds. I don't make public policy."

Why did Wallace think that he was invited to speak before business groups?

"They book me because they feel somehow that it adds a little excitement or luster to their event," he said. He has been giving speeches since 1980, he said, and "never once has any group called me afterward and asked me any favor in coverage."

But isn't that what public officials usually say when Wallace corners them about a junket?

Those who underwrite congressional junkets are seeking "access" and "influence," he said, but the people who hire him to make a speech are seeking "entertainment." When I mentioned Wallace's remarks to Norman Pearlstine, the former executive editor of the *Wall Street Journal,* he said, "By that argument, we ought not to distinguish between news and entertainment, and we ought to merge news into entertainment."

ABC's political and media analyst Jeff Greenfield makes a "rough guess" that he gives fifteen paid speeches a year, many in the form of panels he moderates before various media groups—cable conventions, newspaper or magazine groups, broadcasting and marketing associations—that are concerned with subjects he regularly covers. "It's like *Nightline,* but it's not on the air," he said. He would not divulge his fee, or how much he earned in the past twelve months from speeches.

Greenfield argued that nearly everything he did could be deemed a potential conflict. "I cover cable, but I cover it for ABC, which is sometimes in conflict with that industry," he said. Could he accept money to write a magazine piece or a book when he might one day report on the magazine publisher or the book industry? He is uneasy with the distinction that newspapers like the *Wall Street Journal* or the *Washington Post* make, which is to prohibit daily reporters from giving paid speeches to corporations or trade associations that lobby Congress and have agendas, yet allow paid college speeches. (Even universities have legislative agendas, Greenfield noted.) In trying to escape this ethical maze, Greenfield concluded, "I finally decided that I can't figure out everything that constitutes a conflict."

Eleanor Clift, of *Newsweek,* who is cast as the beleaguered liberal on *The McLaughlin Group,* said that she made between six and eight appearances a year with the group. Her fee for a speech on the West Coast was five thousand dollars, she said, but she would accept less to appear in

Washington. She would not disclose her outside speaking income, and said that if a member of Congress were to ask she would say, "I do disclose. I disclose to the people I work for. I don't work for the taxpayers."

Christopher Matthews, a nationally syndicated columnist and Washington bureau chief of the *San Francisco Examiner,* who is a political commentator for *Good Morning America* and cohost of a nightly program on America's Talking, a new NBC-owned cable network, told me that he gave between forty and fifty speeches a year. He netted between five and six thousand dollars a speech, he said, or between two and three hundred thousand dollars a year. Like many others, he is represented by the Washington Speakers Bureau, and he said that he placed no limitations on corporate or other groups he would appear before. "To be honest, I don't spend a lot of time thinking about it," he said. "I give the same speech."

David S. Broder, of the *Washington Post,* who has a contract to appear regularly on CNN and on NBC's *Meet the Press,* said that he averaged between twelve and twenty-four paid speeches a year, mostly to colleges, and that the speeches are cleared with his editors at the *Post.* He did not discuss his fee, but Howard Kurtz, the *Post's* media reporter, said in his recent book, *Media Circus,* that Broder makes up to seventy-five hundred dollars a speech. Broder said he would support an idea advanced by Albert R. Hunt, the *Wall Street Journal's* Washington editor, to require disclosure as a condition of receiving a congressional press card. To receive a press card now, David Holmes, the superintendent of the House Press Gallery, told me, journalists are called upon to disclose only if they receive more than 5 percent of their income from a single lobbying organization. Hunt said he would like to see the four committees that oversee the issuing of congressional press cards—made up of five to seven journalists each—require full disclosure of any income from groups that lobby Congress. He said he was aware of the bitter battle that was waged in 1988, when one committee issued new application forms for press passes that included space for detailed disclosure of outside income. Irate reporters demanded that the application form be rescinded, and it was. Today, the *Journal,* along with the *Washington Post,* is among the publications with the strictest prohibitions on paid speeches. Most journalistic organizations forbid reporters to accept money or invest in the stocks of the industries they cover. But the *Journal* and the *Post* have rules against reporters' accepting fees from any groups that lobby Congress or from any for-profit groups.

Hunt, who has television contracts with *The Capital Gang* and *Meet the Press,* said that he averaged three or four speeches a year, mostly to colleges and civic groups, and never to corporations or groups that directly petition Congress, and that he received five thousand dollars for most speeches.

William Safire, the *Times* columnist, who is a regular on *Meet the Press,* was willing to disclose his lecture income. "I do about fifteen speeches a year for twenty thousand dollars a crack," he said. "A little more for overseas and Hawaii." Where Safire parts company with Hunt is that he sees nothing wrong with accepting fees from corporations. He said that in recent months he had spoken to AT&T, the Pharmaceutical Research and Manufacturers of America, and Jewish organizations. Safire said that because he is a columnist, his opinions are advertised, not hidden. "I believe firmly in Samuel Johnson's dictum 'No man but a blockhead ever wrote except for money,'" he went on. "I charge for my lectures. I charge for my books. I charge when I go on television. I feel no compunction about it. It fits nicely into my conservative, capitalist—with a capital 'C'—philosophy."

Tim Russert, the host of *Meet the Press,* said that he had given "a handful" of paid speeches in the past year, including some to for-profit groups. He said that he had no set fee, and that he was wary of arbitrary distinctions that say lecturing is bad but income from stock dividends is fine. Russert also raised the question of journalists' appearing on shows like *Meet the Press,* which, of course, have sponsors. "Is that a conflict? You can drive yourself crazy on this."

Few journalists drive themselves crazy over whether to accept speaking fees from the government they cover. They simply don't. But enticements do come from unusual places. One reporter, who asked to remain anonymous, said that he had recently turned down a ten-thousand-dollar speaking fee from the Central Intelligence Agency. A spokesman for the CIA, David Christian, explained to me, "We have an Office of Training and Education, and from time to time we invite knowledgeable nongovernment experts to talk to our people as part of our training program." Does the agency pay for these speeches? "Sometimes we do, and sometimes we don't," he said. Asked for the names of journalists who accepted such fees, Christian said that he was sorry but "the records are scattered."

Time's Washington columnist, Margaret Carlson, who is a regular on *The Capital Gang,* laughed when I asked about her income from speeches and said, "My view is that I just got on the gravy train, so I don't want it to end." Carlson said she gave six speeches last year, at an average of five thousand dollars a speech, including a panel appearance in San Francisco before the American Medical Association (with Michael Kinsley, among others). She made a fair distinction between what she did for a fee and what Treasury Secretary Lloyd Bentsen tried to do in 1987, when, as Senate Finance Committee chairman, he charged lobbyists ten thousand dollars a head for the opportunity to join him for breakfast once a month. "We are like monkeys who get up onstage," Carlson said, echoing Chris Wallace. "It's mud wrestling for an hour or an hour and a half, and it's over."

There are journalistic luminaries who make speeches but, for the sake of appearances, do not accept fees. They include the three network news anchors—NBC's Tom Brokaw, ABC's Peter Jennings, and CBS's Dan Rather—all of whom say that they don't charge to speak or they donate their fees to charity. "We don't need the money," Brokaw said. "And we thought it created an appearance of conflict." Others who do not accept fees for speaking are Ted Koppel, of ABC's *Nightline;* Jim Lehrer, of *The MacNeil/Lehrer NewsHour;* Bob Schieffer, CBS's chief Washington correspondent and the host of *Face the Nation;* and C-SPAN's Brian Lamb.

ABC's senior Washington correspondent, James Wooten, explained how, in the mideighties, he decided to change his ways after a last lucrative weekend: "I had a good agent and I got a day off on Friday and flew out Thursday after the news and did Northwestern University Thursday night for six thousand dollars. Then I got a rental car and drove to Milwaukee, and in midmorning I did Marquette for five or six thousand dollars. In the afternoon, I went to the University of Chicago, to a small symposium, for which I got twenty-five hundred to three thousand dollars. Then I got on a plane Friday night and came home. I had made fifteen thousand dollars, paid the agent three thousand, and had maybe two thousand in expenses. So I made about ten thousand dollars for thirty-six hours. I didn't have a set speech. I just talked off the top of my head." But his conscience told him it was wrong. "It's easy money," Wooten said.

As for me, *The New Yorker* paid my travel expenses to and from the congressional retreat. In the past twelve months, I've given two paid speeches: the first, at New York's Harmonie Club, was to make an opening presentation and to moderate a panel on the battle for control of Paramount Communications, for which I was paid twelve hundred dollars; the second was a speech on the future of the information superhighway at a Manhattan luncheon sponsored by the Baltimore-based investment firm of Alex. Brown & Sons, for which my fee was seventy-five hundred dollars. I don't accept lecture fees from communications organizations.

Like the public figures we cover, journalists would benefit from a system of checks and balances. Journalistic institutions, including *The New Yorker,* too seldom have rigorous rules requiring journalists to check with an editor or an executive before agreeing to make a paid speech; the rules at various institutions for columnists are often even more permissive. Full disclosure provides a disinfectant—the power of shame. A few journalistic institutions, recently shamed, have been taking a second look at their policies. In mid-June, ABC News issued new rules, which specifically prohibit paid speeches to trade associations or to any "for-profit business." ABC's ban—the same one that is in place at the *Wall Street Journal* and the *Washington Post*—prompted Roberts, Donaldson, Brinkley, Wallace, and several other ABC correspondents to protest, and they met in early August with senior news executives. They sought a lifting of the ban, which would allow them to get permission on a case-by-case basis. But a ranking ABC official says, "We can agree to discuss exceptions, but not give any. Their basic argument is greed, for Christ's sake!" Andrew Lack, the president of NBC News, said that he plans to convene a meeting of his executives to shape an entirely new speaking policy. "My position is that the more we can discourage our people from speaking for a fee, the better," he said. And CBS News now stipulates that all speaking requests must be cleared with the president or the vice president of news. Al Vecchione, the president of MacNeil/Lehrer Productions, admitted in June to having been embarrassed by the *American Journalism Re-*

view piece. "We had a loose policy," he said. "I just finished rewriting our company policy." Henceforth, those associated with the program will no longer accept fees to speak to corporate groups or trade associations that directly lobby the government. *The New Yorker,* according to its executive editor, Hendrik Hertzberg, is in the process of reviewing its policies.

Those who frequently lecture make a solid point when they say that lecture fees don't buy favorable coverage. But corruption can take subtler forms than the quid pro quo, and the fact that journalists see themselves as selling entertainment rather than influence does not wipe the moral slate clean. The real corruption of "fee speech," perhaps, is not that journalists will do favors for the associations and businesses that pay them speaking fees but that the nexus of television and speaking fees creates what Representative Obey called "an incentive to be even more flamboyant" on TV—and, to a lesser extent, on the printed page. The television talk shows value vividness, pithiness, and predictability. They prefer their panelists reliably pro or con, liberal or conservative. Too much quirkiness can make a show unbalanced; too much complexity can make it dull. *Time*'s Margaret Carlson told me, not entirely in jest, "I was a much more thoughtful person before I went on TV. But I was offered speeches only *after* I went on TV." Her *Time* colleague, the columnist Hugh Sidey, said that when he stopped appearing regularly on television, his lecture income shriveled. Obey wishes that it would shrivel for the rest of the pundit class as well. An attitude of scorn often substitutes for hard work or hard thought, and it's difficult to deny that the overall result of this dynamic is a coarsening of political discourse.

Celebrity journalism and the appearance of conflicts unavoidably erode journalism's claim to public trust. "My view is that you're going to start having character stories about journalists," Jay Rosen, a journalism professor at New York University and the director of the Project on Public Life and the Press, told me recently. "It's inevitable. If I were a big-name Washington journalist, I'd start getting my accounts together. I don't think journalists are private citizens."

POSTSCRIPT

Journalistic conflicts of interest are not among the foremost problems of our craft. But "fee speech," and the instinctively defensive manner in which these journalists responded when put on the spot, does illustrate one of our foremost maladies: lack of humility. Good reporters need humility to ask questions, to listen, to see ourselves as others do, and to smile more. Humility might keep a Beltway pundit from pontificating, from adopting poses.

There are varied reasons public officials are wary of the press, many of them unavoidable. If we keep our distance and do our job, we will sometimes make their life uncomfortable. No one likes to be checked on, whether his or her profession is government or journalism. But a reason many in public life don't *like* the press in general is because they believe journalists have abandoned a healthy skepticism and replaced it with a cynical pose. We don't just question, we conclude. We mistrust. We generalize about *them*. So they generalize about us. A wall goes up between press and politician, keeping us apart, assuring that we remain strangers. Nowhere is this wall more apparent than in a political campaign, where candidates vie for photo ops and reporters strive for Gotcha! moments.

Once, journalists like Theodore H. White or James Reston—and before them, Walter Lippmann—could tell us what public officials and office seekers were really like, or what they really thought. The first person President Kennedy debriefed after his ugly Vienna summit with Soviet leader Nikita Khrushchev was Scotty Reston of the *Times*. Reston and others often got too close to those they covered. Today the seesaw has swung too far in the opposite direction.

Journalists like Reston or Lippmann were also acutely aware of their personal dignity. It is hard to imagine that either would appear on the Don Imus radio show. I would pay a princely sum to see Jon Stewart conduct a mock-solemn interview with Reston or Lippmann on Comedy Central.

THE DON

T HE DON IS NOT PLEASED when visitors blather. He holds grudges; he is personally insulted when companies don't reward his favorite charity; and if you don't amuse him, you're whacked. Each morning, from 5:30 to 10:00 A.M., he is quick to let loose on "wimps," "jerks," "weasels," and "punks." He bores easily, so he acts on whim. He was once invited to a small Christmas party at the home of a show regular, Jeff Greenfield, then of ABC News. He read his mail on-air, then announced to listeners, "I can't go but you can"—and proceeded to raffle to strangers a visit to Greenfield's home.

From behind his radio microphone, Don Imus looks less like a Don than like an aging cowboy: his eyes concealed by dark glasses, his jaws hammering away at an endless supply of Nicorette gum, his head an unmade bed of wavy sandy hair, his attire often consisting of a black leather jacket, an open-necked shirt, jeans, boots, and a silk bandanna around his neck. A "wrinkled old doofus" is how the producer Bernard McGuirk, who plays the role of bad brother on the show, often refers to his boss. But the fifty-seven-year-old Imus talks like a Don. During his April twenty-fourth broadcast, for example, he stated his displeasure at "those worms" at Simon & Schuster, which happen to be the publisher of his last book—and his next. "It's not like I ever forget," he warned.

The Don has at least two obsessions. The first, the Imus Ranch, is an act of noble passion: an 810-acre working cattle ranch that he launched with a gift of a million dollars, a considerable chunk of what is believed to be a seven-million-dollar salary. The Ranch, which is fifty miles northeast of Santa Fe, New Mexico, and plans to open next spring, will be a camp for children with cancer or with serious blood disorders, and for children who have lost a sibling to sudden infant death syndrome (SIDS), as did the daughter of his longtime WFAN general manager, Joel Hollander. The second Imus obsession is carnal. He wants more Monica Lewinsky and Paula Jones revelations, and has adopted an on-air refrain: *Show me the semen-stained dress!* He talks incessantly about Lewinsky, whom he calls "the fat slut." When there are no new Sex-Gate developments, the I-Man, as fans often refer to him, thinks it a slow-news day. "We want someone down there led out in handcuffs," he bellows. "I don't care whether it's [Senate Majority Leader] Trent Lott, Newt Gingrich, Bill Clinton, or his wife!" Then the Don smiles.

Imus regularly metes out punishment. When he got upset at the way Judge Harold J. Rothwax allegedly treated his wife, Dierdre, when she was on jury duty, he repeatedly pummeled Judge "Sleazewax." When columnist Mort Kondracke complained of Imus's "filthy mouth" and used his weekly platform on the *McLaughlin Group* to question politicians and journalists for "dignifying this show by appearing on it"—something that might be said of the *McLaughlin Group*—Imus called him "a tight-ass wussy." Don't mess with the I-Man.

One thing the Don can't mess with are the commercials on his four-and-one-half-hour broadcast. They consume sixteen minutes an hour on radio, more on MSNBC-TV, which airs him live. Imus can become as tedious as his commercials. Over the past two months, he has mounted a campaign to raise money for the ranch—beseeching individuals to become Ranch Foremen by purchasing one of the 810 acres for five thousand dollars apiece, or for corporations to spend up to one million dollars to sponsor the Ranch infirmary, three barns, six bunk houses, a general store, a radio/TV studio, among other items, each to be named after the company. Imus shilled so shamelessly for this good cause that by late April many of the one hundred stations that carry Imus protested. They wanted more Monica, more insults. General Manager Hollander, as well as station managers, cut Imus some slack because he's entertaining, and because he and his ten million listeners in twenty-three of the top thirty markets generate, according to Hollander's count, nearly half of the fifty million dollars a year in revenue WFAN contributes to its corporate parent, CBS Radio.

The publishing industry takes his power seriously. The onetime disk jockey is a voracious reader, and he loves to plug books. The Simon & Schuster publisher Jack Romanos (whom Imus, inevitably, calls a "beady-eyed little weasel") credits Imus with boosting the company's print order for Howard Kurtz's *Spin Cycle* from twenty-five thousand copies to two hundred thousand. Imus's on-air enthusiasm for books like Pete Hamill's *A Drinking Life* and Jane Mendelsohn's *I Was Amelia Earhart* transformed them into best-sellers. "All you need do," the novelist Anna Quindlen says, "is hear him wax poetic about your book and you say, 'Hell, I'd buy that book.'"

The Mendelsohn book "almost happened in a vacuum," says Paul Bogaards, the vice president and director of promotion at Knopf, the book's publisher. "There was nothing else going on. It was his endorsement that propelled it on the best-seller list. In the span of one month—April to May 1996—we went from thirty thousand copies in print to two hundred twenty-five thousand. For a lot of people in the industry, that was a clear compass point. People were buying the book because Imus recommended it. He essentially bullied people into buying the book."

Imus has even launched the Annual Imus Book Award, which will pay two nonfiction and two fiction book winners an astonishing fifty thousand dollars each, the prize to be financed by various publishing houses and book chains. "He makes all publishers cough up money for the prize," says someone in publishing who has witnessed an Imus pitch. "And if they don't give, he'll attack them."

Imus's best friend and longtime sidekick, the newsreader Charles McCord, once boasted that his boss "is now a fashioner of kings." Imus shot back, "You don't have to suck up to me. Everyone else does."

My own curiosity about Imus was aroused not only by his influence in publishing but also by this matter of courting favor from the Don—this sucking up. Why, I wondered, did so many of my journalistic colleagues flatter him so? And why, I wondered, have so many journalists made donations of five thousand dollars or more to his favorite charity, the Imus Ranch?

Those who are regulars on the show include: Dan Rather, Mike Wallace, and Pat O'Brien of CBS; Barbara Walters of ABC; Tom Brokaw and Tim Russert of NBC; *New York Times* columnists Maureen Dowd, Frank Rich, and Tom Friedman; *Daily News* sports columnist Mike Lupica; Senators John McCain of Arizona, Christopher Dodd and Joe Lieberman of Connecticut, and Bob Kerrey of Nebraska; *Boston Globe* columnist Mike Barnicle; Republicans Laura Ingraham and Mary Matalin, and Democrat James Carville; historian Doris Kearns Goodwin. Often, the Don introduces regulars as his Goodfellas—"our guys." Observed one regular, Mike Wallace: "You get to feel like you're a member of his club. I listen one hour a day." Anna Quindlen, who first started appearing when she was a columnist for the *New York Times* and helped grant Imus a measure of credibility a decade ago when he was shifting from spinning records to talk, said, "I went on because I like him. I like the show. I think it's a great venue. And every fifteen minutes I'm on is fifteen minutes he couldn't put Laura Ingraham on!"

The Don takes care of his "guys," promoting their books, their columns, their public persona. He also plugs his own books, the Auto Body Express shopping-catalogue business he's opened with his younger brother, Fred, as well as their own bottled salsa and Fred's forthcoming book, for which Doubleday has ordered a first printing of two hundred thousand. He lists Charles McCord's wife, Connie, as the travel agent on the Imus Web site. Imus also takes care to plug corporate sponsors of his favorite charity, the Ranch. After it made its $250,000 contribution to fund the general store, Imus praised Mentadent as "the best toothpaste on the planet."

IMUS, who loves to joke about Washington sex scandals, is completely serious about his charitable work. Over the past decade, Imus-hosted radiothons have raised nearly fourteen million dollars for two causes: the CJ Foundation for Sudden Infant Death Syndrome and the Tomorrow's Children's Fund, which helps children with cancer and serious blood diseases. More recently, he has focused his efforts on the Imus Ranch.

When Imus announced in early April that he hoped 810 individuals would come forward and buy one Ranch acre for five thousand dollars, the parcels were gone in four hours. Imus began to thank various media figures for their generosity, calling them fellow Ranch hands. Soon enough, competition to become a Ranch hand got intense. On the April twenty-fourth show, Imus interviewed George Stephanopoulos. Stephanopoulos, who left the Clinton administration after the 1996 election and is now an ABC commentator, has a book contract worth nearly three million dollars to write about his White House years. At the end of their conversation, as Imus was thanking him for appearing on the show for the first time, Stephanopoulos interrupted, saying, "Before I go: I'm not too proud to suck up for a good cause. So count me in for five thousand on the Ranch!"

When I asked later why he had done it, Stephanopoulos told me, "I thought it was a good thing to do." Did he also think about getting invited back next fall to hawk his book? "I suppose," he conceded.

It's unfair, no doubt, to suggest that those who go on the air with Imus, or donate to the Ranch, are doing so solely out of self-interest, or that they are seeking what one regular calls "an insurance policy" against being called a jerk. Journalists who spend airtime with Imus have many motives for doing so. Jeff Greenfield, the senior analyst on CNN, and an Imus regular, says, "For a lot of people, going on Imus is a way for them to be a different person. No one knew Joe Lieberman"—the senator from Connecticut—"was funny." Greenfield says he often gets more comments for his Imus appearances than he does for his own television work. "I think people are on to the political-journalistic dance," he explains. "They know when they watch a press conference or an interview show they are getting predigested stuff—people are saying the same things they always say. With Imus, people feel he's going to ask them blunt things and not take bullshit for an answer."

In that way, people who talk to Imus are selling themselves as personalities, far removed from, say, the confines of a scripted newscast. The television anchors Tom Brokaw of NBC and Dan Rather of CBS are regulars, and enjoy the opportunity to show a little leg. When, in 1992, Imus interviewed then presidential candidate Bill Clinton, the Arkansas governor suggested that Imus call him Bubba because, "It's just another word for *mensch*."

Of course, an Imus appearance is not risk free. Senator Alphonse D'Amato was once introduced by Imus as someone who has "friends with bodies in the trunks of their cars." D'Amato, to demonstrate his hipness, mocked "little Judge Ito"—the judge in the O. J. Simpson trial—by quoting him in a Japanese accent, and evoked howls of protest. President Clinton also discovered that appearing with Imus can be perilous. At the 1996 Radio and Television Correspondents' annual dinner, in Washington, Clinton stood before the audience and gave a flattering introduction to Imus: "All politicians pander to Don Imus because real people listen to him," and he went on to testify that without Imus's support in the 1992 New York primary, he might not have been elected. Imus then made what he later acknowledged to be "a hideous speech"—one filled with sexual innuendo about Clinton and a number of journalists—and delivered it in the presence of Clinton and his wife. After that event, Cokie Roberts called Imus "profoundly rude," and vowed that she would not "ever go back" on the show. Imus retaliated by banning her for life.

DURING THE WEEKS in which I'd been immersed in listening to the Imus program, my plan was to at first maintain a low profile, but Imus found out and announced on the air that I was working on a piece about him. Worse, Imus was talking about me the way John Gotti talked on the FBI tapes about mob boss Paul Costellano (before he killed him). "He was a fucking fish on the desert," Gotti said. I was "a hideous guest," Imus said, recalling that I had been on his show once (twice, actually) and was so "soft-spoken" that I induced sleep.

Imus's office is in the basement of WFAN's space, at the Kaufman Astoria Studios, in Queens, not far from the studio where he performs on *Imus in the Morning*. The office is within a labyrinth of corridors—past an immense tan cowboy hat hanging on a coat hook, past a limited-edition Elvis jukebox alive with lights, past a couch and a chair draped with Indian blankets. In a corner of this dimly lit warren, Imus is surrounded by shelves sagging with books and by tables piled with bound galleys of about-to-be-published works. A muddy-blue industrial carpet covers the floor; the walls, which are paneled, are of a dark wood that is more gray than brown, like the small desk that Imus dwarfs.

Imus, who is more subdued off the air, met me in his office. Although he is quick to dismiss people as suck-ups, he exempts his Ranch hands. "I'd be surprised if they did it for cynical reasons," he said when I brought up the five-thousand-dollar gifts and asked about possible motives. "Maybe I'm naïve. I don't think so." Of his alleged power, Imus says, "It's bullshit."

He said he had no list of Ranch hands, so I produced one that I'd been compiling, and Imus confirmed that it was accurate. The list: *Face the Nation* anchor Bob Schieffer; *60 Minutes* CBS correspondent Lesley Stahl; ABC News anchor Barbara Walters; CNN anchor Judy Woodruff; CNN News chairman Tom Johnson; NBC News correspondent Andrea Mitchell; NBC president Robert Wright; *Boston Globe* columnist Mike Barnicle; author Anna Quindlen; author Mary Higgins Clark; author Carol Higgins Clark; authors Mary Matalin and James Carville; Imus's literary agent, Esther "Lobster" Newberg; publisher Simon & Schuster; WFAN sportscaster Mike Francesa; *Daily News* sports columnist Mike Lupica; *Access Hollywood* anchor Pat O'Brien; Laura Ingraham (she gave a thousand dollars and had a heifer named in her honor); Brokaw (in lieu of a cash contribution, he donated a horse from his Montana ranch); Greenfield; Rather; and Stephanopoulos.

I asked if it was bull for Imus to say, as he has said, that people come on his show because they fear him. "Yes," he replied. Then he smiled slightly and added, "But some people don't like to be made fun of." He added a moment later, "It has some value to them. That's why they come on."

The next morning, on the air, I had become part of my own story. Imus talked about our interview. He called me "charming," but then he proceeded to call me "hideously misguided" and "cynical." He joked about recruiting Bo Dietl, a former detective and show regular, to bend my knees. Then he told NBC's Andrea Mitchell, "He doesn't understand that the only reason people appear on my program is because they just don't want me to make fun of them. It has nothing to do with power. It's fear!"

It wasn't fear that lured Cokie Roberts back. Six months ago, Imus told me, he decided to lift the ban on Roberts and invite her back. "She's a great guest," he explained. "She said fine. She said she'd come in when she's in New York." At the beginning of his April twenty-ninth show, Imus announced that the next day "Cokie Roberts returns to the show."

"Unbelievable!" snickered his sidekick McCord, who was sitting directly across from the I-Man, as he calls him. "She's banned for life! Did she call?"

"Of course she called," Imus said. He went on to explain, "We always liked Cokie Roberts. She was a good guest. . . . She said the reason she was calling was that George Stephanopoulos was very approving."

"You're gullible," the producer Bernard McGuirk declared.

Roberts appeared on April thirtieth. For an exceedingly cordial seventeen minutes and twenty seconds, she and Imus talked about her book, *We Are Our Mothers' Daughters*—about how she wrote it; about her mother, a former congresswoman from Louisiana who is now President Clinton's ambassador to the Vatican; about civil rights; sex discrimination; Ken Starr's investigation of the Clintons; and Viagra. Seeking to melt her Ice Queen image, she also talked about how she and her husband, columnist Steve Roberts, met. "It took me four years to persuade the guy to marry me," Roberts said.

People clamor to get on the Imus show. During his April twenty-seventh show, Imus said of John McLaughlin, the host of Sunday's *McLaughlin Group* on NBC, "He has asked to be on this program. We have declined his offer." Imus, like Gotti, luxuriates in his power. In the privacy of the Ravenite Social Club, Gotti would flaunt his power. "You wanna kill him for what he done, right?" he asked a lieutenant, not knowing the FBI was listening. "I mean, right or wrong, he's got to whack the kid down." In our interview, I told Imus that Simon & Schuster's Jack Romanos had praised him as "the second most powerful person in the country in terms of selling books"—after Oprah Winfrey. Imus professed outrage at this lack of respect, and during his May sixth show he declared, "Oprah Winfrey couldn't have put *Spin Cycle*"—about the relationship between Clinton and the press—"on the best-seller list if she'd bought all the copies herself. If you said, 'Have you read *Spin Cycle*?' she would have thought it was a washing-machine manual!" The more Imus talked, the more agitated he became. Looking at his sidekicks, he announced that they would murder both Romanos and Simon & Schuster: "So here's the new policy: We are never, ever, in the history of this program—ever!—going to have an author on this show who has a book at Simon & Schuster. . . . Why would you want to go on the number-two show?"

Another lifetime ban? When I later asked Imus how long the ban would last, he said, "It lasts until the photography book my brother and I are doing for them comes out!"

To listeners who enjoy the act, Imus appears to be a man who says whatever he pleases. He won't build a church on the Ranch, and to hell with listeners who ask him to. He makes fun of Jews, blacks, Italians, feminists, Cardinal O'Connor. On April twenty-seventh, he shook a bottle of pills, and announced that he would conduct an on-air experiment with the impotence drug Viagra; he handed one tablet each to various male employees (exempting himself), and kept asking how things were going. "I'm pretty much a no-bullshit deal," Imus told me.

Listeners always know that at any minute he might do something outrageous—or hilarious. Each week he has private investigator and former detective Bo Dietl and his sidekick, Joey Pots and Pans, whose occupation is a mystery, in the studio to offer their reviews of the latest movies. On April twenty-ninth, Dietl, who is built like a fire hydrant and talks like a capo, just happened to bring a client to the Astoria, Queens, studio. The client, Joe Malone, is the treasurer of the state of Massachusetts. Malone, Dietl announced, has made millions for the state through shrewd investments of taxpayers' money. Now Malone is seeking the Republican nomination for governor, Dietl said.

Imus asked Dietl to summon Malone, and Dietl beckoned him to enter the cramped studio. There appeared a tall man in a dark suit with slick black hair. Imus gave him the once-over before announcing, "This guy looks like a gangster!"

Mike Wallace compares Imus to Howard Stern, seeing both men as shock jocks and sometimes sophomoric jokesters. But Wallace also notes an enormous difference. "Stern is a crass vulgarian," he says. "Imus in his soul is a much gentler person." Imus reaches only about half as many listeners as Stern, but he is proud that his audience, unlike Stern's, is largely white-collar. "We have a more upscale audience than NPR," he said. During the April twenty-third show, Imus blurted out that he had received an invitation to critique the *Times* at a luncheon with editorial-page editor Howell Raines and other executives from the newspaper. The invitation came from Sam Tanenhaus, a staff editor on the op-ed page, whose recent biography of Whittaker Chambers Imus has plugged. Imus, Tanenhaus wrote in the invitation, "might give us an idea or two for our sections and also give us a read on how the pages are doing."

The Don won't go, but he was pleased by this show of respect.

POSTSCRIPT

Quiet, thoughtful discourse is discouraged on the Imus program. The show is fun. It is also a show with attitude, and expects its guests to exhibit attitude. Imus welcomes sharp opinions, but he wants guests to join him in a good sneer. It's all a pose, and one with a spillover effect. Talk-show hosts and talking heads increasingly display disdain for those in public life. Without having done the hard work of digging up information, reporters shout questions at press conferences that substitute attitude for information. Straight journalists are interviewed on cable news shows and *Meet the Press,* where they express opinions and attitudes that would be edited out of their daily copy. Network newscasts search for stories that show citizens are getting *screwed,* stories that are usually heavier on attitude than reporting. It doesn't really matter whether the target is big business or big government, the medical establishment or class action lawyers. Even those who are thought to be ideological—like "conservative" Bill O'Reilly on Fox News—express more an I'm-on-the-side-of-the-little-guy populism than a consistent ideology.

There are those who believe the dominant media bias is liberal. I don't. The most persistent press bias is one that favors conflict, not ideology. And this bias is usually unconscious, and as likely to infect a liberal at the *New York Times* or *The New Yorker* who gives Al Sharpton a free pass as it is an anchor at Fox News who thinks it permissible to snidely dismiss France as "the axis of weasel" for opposing the U.S. in Iraq. Nowhere does this bias for conflict better express itself than in a presidential campaign, which is explored in the next piece.

GOTCHA: CANDIDATES VERSUS PRESS

W HEN THE 1996 presidential race ended—when the last "bridge to the twenty-first century" had been proposed and the last "He's a liberal, he's a liberal" had been uttered—the press called it an awful, dispiriting campaign. President Clinton and Bob Dole, many wrote, were negative and cynical and had become slaves to the latest poll.

From behind the lines of the two campaigns, the press was viewed in similarly unflattering terms. Michael McCurry, the White House press secretary, and John Buckley, Dole's communications director, saw the press as negative and cynical and infatuated with poll numbers. They regarded the press as one adversary in a daily three-front war.

In battling each other, McCurry and Buckley used the traditional weapons of a modern campaign, such as sneak attacks. Against the press, they relied more on seduction, employing humor, fact sheets, gentle rebukes, charm, hot food, cold beer, access. But even as Buckley and McCurry tried to cajole the press, they found themselves caught up in a third struggle—with the candidates themselves. Among the things that Dole and Clinton have in common is a deep loathing for the press, a tendency to generalize about "them," and this created special problems for Buckley and McCurry.

Clinton "likes Mike personally, but he treats him as a necessary evil," a senior White House aide confided recently. "He sees him as an agent of the press. He lectures him about sticking up for the press." Whenever Dole granted an interview and it came off poorly, he blamed Buckley and his staff for encouraging him to do it. In the final weeks of the campaign, Dole could not contain his hatred of the media. Pushing aside texts prepared by his staff, he ad-libbed attacks on "the elite liberal press," especially the *New York Times.*

During the campaign's last two months, McCurry and Buckley spoke to me about the frustrations they experienced in their jobs and about the men who employed them. Although McCurry, unlike Buckley, was confident of victory in a campaign that lacked suspense from start to finish, there were few moments of joy for either man.

THROUGHOUT THE CAMPAIGN, McCurry worried less about Dole than about what he called "an atom bomb"—perhaps a Whitewater-related explosion or a press storm over some new character issue that would cause a majority of voters, who had already told pollsters that they didn't trust Clinton, to take the next step and decide not to vote for him.

Clinton's strategy was to float above the fray by "being presidential and campaigning as president," said Donald Baer, a former lawyer, reporter, and editor with *U.S. News & World Report,* who is now the White House communications director. No more jogging in shorts, and no more pit stops at McDonald's. "One of the lessons we learned is that even when the message was strained through the filter of skeptical press coverage, the public heard it," Baer said. "What we learned was the corollary of Michael Deaver's old rule that all that mattered was the picture, and you could turn down the sound. We realized that you had to turn up the sound. Deaver was wrong. The substance mattered. If the headline was CLINTON PANDERS ON EDUCATION, the public heard CLINTON SUPPORTS COLLEGE SCHOLARSHIPS."

In this campaign, Clinton displayed a restraint that he had not shown before. It no doubt helped, White House aides say, that Ann Devroy, of the *Washington Post*—the most aggressive, the most feared, and possibly the best White House reporter—was seriously ill and on the sidelines throughout the campaign. Although Clinton himself made few overtures, his fractious relations with the White House press corps improved.

Meanwhile, the Dole campaign often scheduled—and then canceled—interviews with the local press. Dole complained that his message was not getting out, but he repeatedly turned down chances for press coverage. Although Dole's camp, like Clinton's, believed that the three network nightly newscasts were the most important medium, reaching thirty-two million viewers each day, in September, Dole or his staff spurned every offer that Jeff Zucker, the executive producer of NBC's *Today* show and the network's political producer for the campaign, made to have Dole appear on an NBC news program. "It says something about a campaign at this stage, that either the candidate's comfort level is not there or his staff is incompetent," Glenn Kessler of *Newsday* said. "His staff should be able to say, 'Do the interviews.'"

But Buckley and the Dole staff knew very well that Dole didn't want to do the interviews. He was so enraged at what he thought was the media's eagerness to catch him making a mistake that he was unwilling to risk the exposure. He was a man who, in Buckley's words, "likes to move in his own orbit." Buckley would send Dole memos suggesting interviews, with "yes" or "no" boxes next to each name. "Often they would come back with question marks," said Buckley, who grew to admire Dole but became frustrated as the question marks accumulated. In early September, Buckley told me, "There is still a candidate belief that you keep reporters far away."

By the second week in October, relations between Dole and the press had become more relaxed. The détente, pushed by Buckley, who was not close to Dole, was the result of a recommendation by Margaret Tutwiler, a senior adviser to the campaign, who had been enlisted to travel with Dole and help evaluate his press strategy. She told friends she was appalled that the campaign was not availing itself of relatively safe press opportunities: inviting local reporters onto his plane the day before he visited their city so that he would get a story in the local media the day he arrived; hooking up with local drive-time radio talk shows; and granting interviews to local TV anchors. She blamed inexperience for these failings.

But there was another explanation for Dole's seemingly irrational press policy, and it remained a closely held campaign secret. Dole had learned in early September that Charles Babcock, an investigative reporter for the *Washington Post,* was pursuing a charge that in the late 1960s, when Dole was married to his first wife, he had had an affair. Babcock, it seemed, had interviewed the woman, who had confirmed the story. All at once, Dole—not Clinton—was fretting about "bimbo eruptions."

Dole and his second wife, Elizabeth, became apoplectic. In September, Mrs. Dole phoned Donald Graham, the *Post*'s publisher; Mari Will, who is the wife of the columnist George Will and had been Dole's press secretary during the 1988 campaign; got in touch with the *Post*'s executive editor, Leonard Downie, Jr. Both women urged the newspaper to respect Dole's privacy. As long as Dole was uncertain whether the *Post* intended to publish the story, the situation "totally froze his willingness to submit to television interviews," a senior campaign aide said. "It was like the sword of Damocles. He never knew whether the day he granted the interview would be the day the *Post* broke the story." Dole feared a media frenzy that would doom his candidacy. So, for much of September—and then again in late October—he erected a wall between himself and the press.

Because Dole's motivations were not known to the press or the public, the campaign often assumed baffling contours; at times, no one was more mystified than the beat reporters who were covering the candidate. Blaine Harden, who followed Dole for the *Washington Post,* and who has been a foreign correspondent, told me in October, "I've never been around one of these strange things before. My experience of elections is Eastern Europe and Africa, where campaigns are about what the candidates truly believe, and not these nuanced, poll-driven, photo-op things." In Croatia, he said, "Franjo Tudjman, a demagogue, holds press conferences. There are open questions from the foreign press: 'Are you a dictator? Why are you subverting the Constitution?' The last Dole press conference"—other than the one at which he announced his retirement from the Senate— "was in the Florida primary, in March."

MIKE MCCURRY AND JOHN BUCKLEY, adversaries in the presidential campaign, were, as it happened, also friends. They had become acquainted in the late eighties, when each was the spokesman for his party organization; and during the early nineties they had become better acquainted at the Washington public relations firm then known as Robinson, Lake, Lerer & Montgomery. Each was a senior vice president there, with McCurry concentrating on clients like MTV, and Buckley on clients like IBM. "I helped recruit Mike," Buckley said.

Buckley was well-known to reporters. A nephew of William F. Buckley, Jr., he was a former reporter and music critic for the counterculture *SoHo Weekly News* and the author of two novels. He had been deputy press secretary in Ronald Reagan's 1984 campaign, press secretary to Representative Jack Kemp, and, in 1989, director of communications for the National Republican Congressional Committee. McCurry, who had worked for Democratic presidential contenders since 1984, opposed Clinton in the 1992 primaries as press secretary for Senator Bob Kerrey of Nebraska. He then became the State Department's official spokesman, and Clinton brought him to the White House in January of 1995— replacing Dee Dee Myers, who had replaced George Stephanopoulos. The change was dramatic, Laurence McQuillan, the Reuters White House correspondent, recalled. "When George Stephanopoulos was press secretary, we would bring complaints to him, and George would sit there chewing bubble gum and blowing bubbles, slouched in his chair," McQuillan said. "It seemed like a deliberate sign that he wanted the meeting to get over. McCurry is one hundred eighty degrees different. He seems to enjoy reporters, and it creates a different response."

During this year's campaign, Buckley and McCurry kept up their friendship, speaking from time to time. In October, when a former college roommate revealed that Buckley had smoked marijuana as a student at

Hampshire College, in the late seventies, a small media tempest ensued. McCurry, who had once confessed to smoking pot while a student at Princeton, in the midseventies, stood on the podium of the White House briefing room and complained that Buckley had "been done an injustice."

The two men, according to Kenneth Lerer, their supervisor at the public relations firm, "have almost identical personalities"—calm and self-effacing. They are close in age: McCurry is forty-two, Buckley is thirty-nine. Each has battled the establishment wing of his party—McCurry, when he worked for Senator John Glenn, in 1984, opposed liberals like Walter Mondale, and Buckley, as a Kemp supporter, opposed traditional Republicans like George Bush. Both voted for Clinton in 1992. And among reporters who need straight answers both are unusually popular. "They've actually been a pleasure to deal with," NBC's Jeff Zucker said.

Considering that the president has had such a triumphant year, it seems odd that he (like Dole) should have felt such Nixonian rage toward reporters. Stephanopoulos, the senior adviser to Clinton, who has been by his side since 1991 and displays the same rancor, traces Clinton's hostility to the 1992 primaries, when Gennifer Flowers told a supermarket tabloid that she had had a twelve-year affair with Clinton while he was governor of Arkansas. "He's had more attention to his past and his personal life than any other public official ever, from an unflattering light, based on sources that are suspect but are treated as credible," Stephanopoulos said. "You'd be upset, too."

A more complex explanation is offered by McCurry. "His view of the press is that there is a unique political culture in Washington, defined by establishment figures in the press and figures in Washington, and those figures have never been able to accept him for what he is," McCurry said. "That is why from the minute he arrived here they tried to destroy him."

McCurry's observation evokes memories of Lyndon B. Johnson. But Clinton is, in some ways, the more sophisticated of the two, for Johnson was always sensitive about his rural background, especially when he was in the company of Ivy Leaguers. Clinton, as a Rhodes Scholar and a Yale Law School graduate, has built a network of establishment friends. Yet, according to McCurry, Clinton sees Whitewater and Gennifer Flowers and all the assaults on his character as arising from Washington's contemptuous attitude toward his Arkansas origins. "He feels he's been rejected by Washington society," McCurry said. "The press belongs to an axis that he has not been able to charm."

Perhaps because he maintained a comfortable lead over Dole throughout the campaign, Clinton kept his anger camouflaged. Dole did not. In three previous bids for national office, Dole thought that the press had caricatured him as Mean Bob. As his campaign limped into October, advisers were still livid over what they saw as reporters' anti-Republican bias. Buckley swam against this current. When he was asked whether he agreed that the press was biased, he answered, "I can't allow myself to believe it's true because it distorts my ability to get my job done. My job is to persuade reporters of the rightness of my cause. If I go in persuaded that they are persuaded by their liberalism, I hurt my cause."

MCCURRY AND BUCKLEY are personally fond of many reporters, but they also share a sometimes savage view of the press. Both know that the press is not so much ideologically biased as simply in favor of conflict, that too often reporters prefer a quick headline to a deeper understanding. McCurry and Buckley cite some familiar complaints: that all too often the lighter burden of proof that is acceptable among tabloid newspapers and television has become acceptable in the mainstream press as well, and that reporters are too cynical, too conspiracy minded, and too caught up in polls and punditry, and therefore skimp on coverage of what the candidates say. Both, however, make a fresh claim: Reporters and editors have allowed news to surrender to opinion.

"The hard-news lead and story have been replaced by the analytical story," McCurry said in mid-September. Because editors are aware that by morning their readers will have already learned from television and radio what the candidates did the day before, McCurry explained, they demand more "context," which can be a synonym for attitude or opinion. "My guess is that one-third to one-half of every story written about the campaign reflects some level of analysis," McCurry said. "Look at the *New York Times* and the *Washington Post.*"

That same day, John Buckley, sitting in his office at Dole campaign headquarters in Washington, echoed McCurry's lament. "The margins have widened for political coverage," he said. "The way it should work is: Cover what he did, what he said, but don't lead with the context and the interpretation. I may be naïve, but I believe that a presidential candidate has the right to deliver a message."

McCurry complained about the adoption by "Ivy League and upper-income reporters" of a more cynical, and even "bratty" attitude, which leads to a more adversarial relationship. Buckley attributed the preoccupation with process, polls, and handlers to Theodore H. White's first campaign book, *The Making of the President 1960,* which grafted a dramatic narrative onto campaigns. Robert Lichter, a codirector, with his wife, Linda, of the nonprofit Center for Media and Public Affairs, in Washington, traces the trend toward opinionated reporting to the 1988 Bush campaign, when the press felt that it was being manipulated by photo opportunities.

Throughout the campaign, both sides complained of press bias. In May, Buckley wrote to Joseph Lelyveld, the *Times*'s executive editor, saying, "I think it's important to bring to your attention concerns we have about the *Times'* coverage of Senator Dole's candidacy. I do so with respect, and in the spirit of a ballplayer stating, early in the game, that he thinks the ump's strike zone may be a bit too narrow." The letter went on to discuss the previous day's front-page coverage of the two candidates, which he thought was skewed toward Clinton.

Lelyveld called Buckley after receiving the letter. "His response was 'We blew it,'" Buckley said. "It was totally gracious." Lelyveld invited Buckley to get in touch with him directly if he had any subsequent complaints about *Times* coverage. Lelyveld told me recently, "We dropped the ball that day. We had been snookered that day. We took Clinton a little too seriously and Dole not seriously enough."

Nevertheless, over the next few months, Buckley said, the *Times* concentrated on Dole's mishaps, leaving his speeches "virtually uncovered." The *Times* reported on the candidate but, Buckley complained, "always in the context of 'How's he doing?'" And the *Times,* he believed, "drives the news coverage" of other reporters. He protested often, not to Lelyveld but to the *Times*'s Washington editor, Andrew Rosenthal, and to the two principal reporters on the Dole campaign, Adam Nagourney and Katharine Q. Seelye.

Lelyveld insisted, "I'm really proud of our campaign coverage," and he defended the trend toward more contextual reporting. "We're not a headline service," he told me. "We used to spend a lot of time in hotel ballrooms covering the speeches of candidates. . . . We've converted our space to more enterprising reporting." He acknowledged that having fewer strictures posed a risk that opinion could infiltrate news columns, then added, "But the risk is under very great control. I think we're very straight." Reporters, who like to think of themselves as members of a profession, rebel against the idea that they are stenographers. Jeff Fager, the executive producer of *CBS Evening News,* said, "If we don't go out and report that Clinton is talking about campaign-finance reform and that the record shows he did almost nothing in his four years for campaign-finance reform, we are not doing our jobs."

THE CLINTON ADVISERS privately agreed that a majority of the reporters who cover Washington are at least moderately liberal, but they felt no less beleaguered than the Dole camp, claiming that the press had given excessive emphasis to Clinton's personal life and Whitewater and other so-called ethical lapses. "We are, I believe, held to higher standards on a range of issues than Dole," Stephanopoulos said, arguing, for example, that Clinton's fund-raising was continually placed under a microscope while Dole's was not.

Reporters write "within paradigms," the presidential assistant Rahm Emanuel said. "Bob Dole said he took positions in the primary that he totally disagreed with. Nobody picked that up. The reason nobody picked it up is that the paradigm is that 'Bob Dole is a principled person, who only operates on principle.' Had Bill Clinton taken similar positions, I think reporters would have grabbed on to it."

It was another sort of paradigm—a belief among many reporters that the president has something to hide—that led to one of McCurry's more surreal encounters with the press, on the morning of September twelfth. Dole had called for Clinton to release not just summaries of his medical exams but the complete records. And, sure enough, at a regular briefing, in Fresno, California, McCurry was asked a total of thirty-six questions about Clinton's health and only fifteen about Iraq, which the United States had just bombed and was poised to bomb again. The exchanges showed McCurry's good humor and patience, as well as his exasperation.

During the briefing, McCurry repeated that Clinton had made his doctors available to reporters and had released more detailed medical summaries than either of his two predecessors. Even presidents, he said, deserved a zone of privacy and dignity.

"So there's nothing in any of these medical records that a normal person might consider embarrassing to the president?" one reporter asked.

"I wouldn't say that," McCurry responded, unwittingly arousing suspicion. Some tests had to be summarized by physicians because laymen wouldn't understand the charts. And "all of us undergo tests that I'm not sure that any of us would want to have spread out and printed on the front page of the newspaper."

Reporters' imaginations ran wild. What tests? Could he characterize a test that might be embarrassing? McCurry deflected the questions, urging the reporters to "just think for a minute."

According to the White House transcript, the following exchange erupted:

Q: Does he have a sexually transmitted disease? I mean, what is—
Q: Jesus!
Mr. McCurry: Good God, do you really want to ask that question?
Q: No, I'm just asking what is embarrassing.

Had the president demanded that his medical records be sealed? No, McCurry answered. Clinton had instructed his staff to tell reporters "what they need to know."

"But that's not the same thing, Mike," a reporter said.

"The astonishing question—did you answer that, or say that it's inappropriate to be asked?" one semibaffled reporter asked.

"If there was anything related to a disease or health condition the president had, it would have been accurately and timely reported to you," McCurry countered.

"So you're saying that he's in perfect health and—"

"No, I did not say that," McCurry protested. He was trying to indicate that no one is in perfect health, but instead he fueled suspicion that he was hiding something.

Again, he was asked if in the past four years Clinton had had a sexually transmitted disease. After gasping again, McCurry said, "It's obvious he has not, because that would have been reported at the time he had his annual medical exam."

Since he would have disclosed the fact if Clinton had had such a disease, a reporter persisted, "What level of privacy are you trying to protect?" What chart was he worried about releasing? None, McCurry answered. The briefing continued:

Q: Mike, you seem to be saying that even . . . taking a test for HIV, or some other sexually transmitted disease, is in and of itself embarrassing.

Mr. McCurry: Look, I'm trying to keep some level of dignity here. I'm talking about things like rectal exams, O.K. Do you want to have all those things spread out to here? . . . You guys are really bored. It's hard to know that there is a campaign under way here.

A month later, on October eleventh, McCurry was worried that the atomic blast he had dreaded might be coming. That morning, the *Times* carried a story by Jeff Gerth and Stephen Labaton exploring President Clinton's ties to James Riady, an Indonesian businessman who had known Clinton since 1977, when Riady was working as an intern at an investment bank in Little Rock. He was the son of a billionaire who founded the Lippo Group, a Hong Kong- and Jakarta-based multinational financial and real estate empire. The *Times* reported that Indonesia's ambassador had asked Riady to help "arrange a rare meeting" with the president, and that the Riadys were a source of campaign cash for Clinton. A *Los Angeles Times* story two weeks earlier had explained how a former Lippo executive, John

Huang, who was the vice chairman of the Democratic Party's finance committee and a recent high-ranking trade official in Clinton's Commerce Department, had illegally solicited a $250,000 contribution from a South Korean magnate, which was returned only after the reporter started asking questions.

October eleventh, a Friday, was what McCurry called "a slow news day," which could heighten interest in the Riady story. The night before, he had prepped himself on the Riady-Clinton tie and on the Clinton administration's attitude toward the Indonesian regime. The day the story broke, McCurry said to me, "I came to work today thinking, Will Indonesia become a frenzy and will the press decide to hang me out to dry? Sometimes the press does that just to remind us that we're hired help."

Since September, the press has reported that Huang was in hiding, that the South Korean magnate had seemingly disappeared, that Vice President Al Gore had attended a fund-raiser in a Buddhist temple that was orchestrated by Huang. McCurry and the president's handlers tried to change the subject or confuse the issue by attacking Republicans, by producing new negative TV ads charging the Dole campaign with corruption, and by ignoring reporters' shouted questions.

The issue wounded Clinton, but it did not become what McCurry feared. "It did not go thermonuclear," he said. "It stayed conventional." This made Republicans all the more certain that there was a press double standard. "They don't put any anti-Clinton stories in the *New York Times*," Dole cried on October twenty-fourth, even though the *Times* had broken the Whitewater story and was now pursuing the Riady connection. Polls showed that this story, like Whitewater, was not registering with the public. John Buckley knew this, but he maintained that the press treated influence peddling in the Clinton administration as "separate, discrete events" rather than as part of a pattern. "The press is not tying it together," he told me.

In the final weeks of the campaign, it was Dole who fretted about a major surprise. Two weeks before Election Day, he learned that the tabloid press was investigating a rumor of yet another decades-old affair. Dole began to worry, as he had worried in September, that his own character as the pro-family-values candidate was about to be shredded. He was convinced that the tabloids could put pressure on America's mainstream press to run with the story, as had happened in 1992 with Gennifer Flowers's charges. Suddenly, in mid-October, Dole once again began declining interviews, including even relatively safe appearances on *Larry King Live* and *The NewsHour with Jim Lehrer*. And he increased his attacks on the media, imploring voters to "rise up" against them.

As it turned out, the *Village Voice* published parts of the story in its October twenty-ninth and November fifth issues, while the mainstream press all but ignored the allegations. Dole's assault on the press in the closing days of the campaign was decoded by a top campaign strategist: "We are really saying to the *New York Times* and the rest of the media, 'If you follow the *National Enquirer* and the *Village Voice,* you are out to get me.' It was a preemptive strike."

JOURNALISTS SEEMED to admire the efficiency of the Clinton machine even as they mistrusted it. "They feed the beast better than the Dole campaign," the *New York Post* correspondent Thomas Galvin observed. An army of Clinton aides regularly showered reporters with briefing materials: Anytime reporters joined the campaign somewhere or were expected to explain legislation signed by Clinton, they found they had the information at their fingertips. McCurry and the campaign spokesman Joe Lockhart mingled easily with reporters, conducted regular briefings, and allowed the reporters plenty of time to file their stories. By hanging around reporters, Clinton's aides learned what stories reporters were working on. McCurry liked to say, "I'm in sales, not product development."

McCurry's office made a sale on September sixteenth, when the White House tried to upstage Dole in announcing an anticrime effort—and largely succeeded. Television pictures that night showed the president surrounded by policemen in their blue uniforms as he was endorsed by the nation's largest police union.

On the press plane, most reporters saw one thing clearly: Clinton "was about to kick Dole's ass," as one of them put it. That afternoon, I asked Bill Plante, the CBS White House correspondent, if he felt trapped by Clinton's handlers. "For the most part, we set the agenda rather than let them set the agenda," he said. After a pause, he added, "I don't mean that to sound arrogant, but we follow what we think news is. Generally, we develop our own take on it. So I don't feel trapped."

Television coverage of the crime issue was considered "good" by the Clinton staff. A daily memorandum circulated by campaign aide Mary L. Smith to McCurry and seventeen other senior officials reported that on the three network newscasts Clinton had received nine minutes and sixteen seconds of "good" coverage and only two minutes and fifty seconds of "bad" coverage. Many newspapers, notably the *Times* and the *Washington Post,* packaged the Clinton and Dole crime initiatives as a single story. Mike McCurry was pleased, thinking that the campaigns got a fifty-fifty split in the coverage. John Buckley, for his part, admitted that the Dole campaign had been set back by "the symbolism of the cops" endorsing Clinton and hurt by combined coverage of the two stories.

Again, one reason Dole lost this particular battle was that Clinton's team was more attuned to the media. McCurry conducted at least one daily briefing because, he explained, "I usually take the temperature of the press to see if they're anxious." Sometimes he found the press anxious about matters that were other than weighty. On the afternoon of the anticrime announcement, for example, McCurry entered a pressroom in Cincinnati, stood on a podium, and asked for questions. There were none, which was unusual, prompting McCurry to joke, "OK. Brain-dead." Off to the side a moment later, McCurry attributed the dearth of questions to an upcoming Clinton campaign trip. "No one wants to make today too complicated because tomorrow they start a four-day trip, and they want to get home and pack tonight," he remarked, his tone a mixture of affection and resignation.

By contrast, the press held the Dole operation in contempt. Early in his campaign, Dole had made a mistake by instituting a two-tier press system. A select group of reporters from CNN, the networks, the newsweeklies, and a handful of major newspapers were allowed to ride in the back of Dole's 727. The rest of the press corps was orphaned on another airplane—dubbed the Bullship—with no senior aides in attendance. This arrangement produced resentment. Dole's press secretary, Nelson Warfield, told me in October, "There's a lot of feeling, with justification, of inequitable treatment."

Until early October, the most senior Dole official on the separate press plane was usually Charley Cooper, who is in his twenties. Few briefings had been held on the plane and few materials distributed, and reporters moaned about not having enough time to file stories. Warfield saw it as his job to stay close to Dole, and doing so meant that he was less available to reporters.

The days of the boys on the bus—when politicians and reporters felt relaxed enough around one another to schmooze off the record—were gone. "People who are younger than I am are more intense, more serious," said the *Boston Globe* political reporter Curtis Wilkie, who has been covering presidential campaigns for two decades. "They are less forgiving. They don't have a good time, and they don't allow politicians to have a good time." And an old-school politician like Bob Dole no doubt found this change of tone hard to get used to. When he was interviewed, he often meandered or got testy. Last summer, when he tried to finesse the abortion controversy within the Republican Party, his ineloquent, verb-free lingo, combined with the news-hungry press pack's eagerness to catch the candidate making a gaffe, ensnared him in further controversy. When, on June seventeenth, he joked to reporters on the plane that a compromise was a "piece of cake," various newspapers led their coverage with it, suggesting, as Katharine Q. Seelye wrote in the *Times,* that perhaps "he was making an effort to appease the abortion opponents whom he alienated last week."

Looking back on the summer, Buckley thinks that for Dole the coverage of the abortion controversy was a significant moment in the campaign. "He had an epiphany the time he went to the back of the plane," Buckley said. "It became a front-page story. The reporters on his plane were younger and had no clock ticking beyond November fifth. And they had a tendency to play Gotcha! So Dole's traditional Republican distrust of the press came out."

After that, "the curtain came down," Buckley said, unapologetically. It was the only way, he said, to escape the tar baby that Dole's gaffes had become—for example, his saying first that he wanted to overturn the assault-weapons ban in the Senate, then refusing to say whether as president he would do so, and shifting again by hinting that he would keep it. He had stubbornly resisted when Peter Jennings of ABC, and then others, pressed him to say whether or not he believed tobacco was addictive: He insisted that it was for some and not for others, and then he blamed "the liberal media" for trying to make him look silly.

By mid-July, Dole was no longer associating with reporters. He did not grant the traditional preconvention interviews to the newsweeklies, and he did not offer "exclusive" interviews to the local press on his visits around the country. Bringing down the curtain meant that Dole's gaffes were fewer, and the press's Gotcha! game ended. But in a larger sense Dole failed because he had wasted much of the summer, doing little to combat a mind-set that was developing in the press, which manifested itself in a campaign narrative that allowed reporters to portray the hapless Dole versus the Clinton juggernaut.

On July twentieth, Dole permitted a peek into his own thinking in a rare interview with Blaine Harden. Explaining why he had stopped chatting with the press, Dole said, "I'd like to go back and have fun and have little cracks here and there. But they are going to be misunderstood. . . . There isn't an ounce of humor in the back of that plane. . . . I like to talk to the media. In the Senate, you can banter back and forth. Nobody takes it seriously. . . . But here when you say it, somebody is going to write it. I don't know, maybe it's because they don't know me."

Dole's press secretary, Warfield, recalled, "Twice I tried to arrange for Dole to go to the back of the plane" and speak informally to reporters— an account confirmed by journalists. Twice, though, a handful of reporters objected. "Yes, we can do it off the record," a *Times* reporter said the second time, "unless he makes news." For the candidate, the risk exceeded the reward, even though both he and the press suffered a penalty.

The press felt imprisoned. One week this fall, as the press bus transported the *Times* White House correspondent Alison Mitchell from plane to filing center and on to a hotel in Chicago—another day in which she hadn't seen Clinton except on the TV monitor in the press filing center— she looked around at her colleagues on the bus and asked, "Is this an anachronism? If you can watch the guy on TV, if you can read his speeches pretty fast on the Internet, what are we here for? It's the old assassination watch. I'm not sure what we add. . . . In covering the president, I don't see anything different from what I see on TV."

McCurry and Buckley knew that the presidential debates would be a critical source of information for voters, and both campaigns began planning—and even spinning—before the first words were spoken at the first debate, in Hartford, on Sunday, October sixth. On October second, for example, Buckley's 8:00 A.M. meeting with his staff on the communications strategy for the debate outlined a detailed schedule: On Thursday, the Dole campaign would launch negative television ads "designed to set off news at the debate"; Friday, they would "engage local political reporters by announcing state debate-watching parties." Privately, Buckley said that on Saturday, Dole would create news that would spill over into the debate by announcing his cabinet choices, including Colin Powell and William Bennett. (Dole did not do this.) On the day of the debate, Buckley and his staff would be plugged into the database at the Republican National Committee, so as to be ready with an instant debate scorecard of misleading Clinton statements; they would also have a bevy of prominent Dole supporters ready to offer upbeat spin. "On Monday, we'll have the Big Mo press conference," said Buckley, describing their intention to claim total victory whether they achieved it or not.

Meanwhile, McCurry and Stephanopoulos were discussing a radical idea: "We're toying with the notion of no spin," McCurry said. He went on, "It's almost absurd what happens afterward: 'Our guy won!'" Maybe they would say nothing, and just invite reporters across the street for a beer.

In Hartford, conclusions about the first debate were in play even before Clinton and Dole took their places on the podiums. At 8:40 P.M. the Clinton press office distributed to the hundreds of reporters gathered in the Hartford Civic Center what was labeled "Prebuttal: Dole vs. the Facts"—a six-page single-spaced memo that followed the formula "Dole might say the following, but these are the facts."

David Broder, the *Washington Post* veteran who has been covering campaigns for four decades, remarked that this was the first time he'd ever seen predebate spin. Some of the spinners seemed to hate it. Laura D'Andrea Tyson, Clinton's national economic adviser, looked bewildered by the sight of hordes of reporters, pads ready, charging at her fellow spinners. I asked whether she was embarrassed to be in this position. "A little bit," she said.

At 9:10 P.M., Tabitha Soren, of MTV, walked up the center aisle toward a camera in the basement arena where reporters were gathered, taping a segment in which she told viewers about a debate she was not watching. She did this seventeen times, or until 9:45 P.M., before she and her producer were satisfied. At 9:50 P.M., a commotion occurred when Dole aides rushed from table to table with a single sheet of paper citing three Clinton misstatements of fact so far in the debate. Fifteen minutes before the debate ended, there was a buzz from behind the curtain leading to the rooms where the spinners were watching. Reporters swarmed behind the curtain and found the chairman of the Republican National Committee, Haley Barbour, and Dole's campaign manager, Scott Reed, moving forward.

"What's happening?" one reporter asked.

"They're spinning before the debate is over," another reporter answered, and notepads and microphones soon engulfed the two men. Just a few feet away, another swarm formed around the chairman of the Democratic National Committee, Christopher Dodd. Buckley later credited his camp with being the first to get out fact sheets and to enter Spin Alley, while acknowledging that his opponents had more spinners and better signs. "As in so many things they do, it was a joke," he said. "A little bit crass."

Was it difficult for Buckley to smile and spin when, privately, he knew that his candidate was doomed? "This has not been a fun campaign since April," Buckley admitted. "Throughout the campaign, people felt, How do I get out of bed this morning?"

THE INCREASINGLY impersonal relations between the press and the candidates was worrisome to Buckley and McCurry and, as the campaign wore on, McCurry was doing a lot of thinking about how to improve the often chilly relationship between the president and the press corps in a second term. "If he gets reelected, that's the only reason I would really want to stay around here much longer—to work on that and to try and see if you could get his head in a different place about that," McCurry told me this fall, while rubbing his eyes in his White House office, halfway between the pressroom and the Oval Office. "There's an element in every president— I know the Bushes felt that way, too. They felt that they were always being pounded."

McCurry has already suffered some wounds in this battle. When he tried to place Clinton in less formal settings with the press on Air Force One at the end of a long day in late 1995, Clinton, wearing jeans and relaxing with reporters, talked expansively about his own and his party's mistakes, and at one point he used the word *funk* to describe the anxiety of citizens regarding the economy. The next day, Clinton's philosophical musings were translated into Gotcha! headlines, (CLINTON PLANS TO LIFT PUBLIC OUT OF "FUNK"), so Clinton, like Dole, called a halt to such get-togethers.

For the American voter, the campaign of 1996 was oddly distant—and distancing. In its last weeks, polls dominated the coverage, yet the gap between the candidates yawned so wide that there was less press reliance than in the past on reciting poll numbers. What the polls provided was a context for coverage. Omnipresent polls also meant endless stories about the "stumbling" Dole campaign, which drowned Dole's message. Dole planned to devote the final days of September to advancing his economic plan, starting with a speech in Detroit, but that speech, and its theme, received scant press notice. Instead, the press focus was on judging Dole's performance.

In seeking a cease-fire between the media and the candidates, what would the campaign operatives like to say to the press? "I don't think I'm a credible carrier of that message," Stephanopoulos answered, laughing. But he nevertheless continued, "It's very simple—be reporters, not psychologists. Yes, we spin. Yes, like everyone else, we're not perfect. But it wouldn't hurt to give elected officials a little bit more of the benefit of the doubt. And in return, maybe we can do the same. Maybe that's the way you deescalate the spin cycle."

Christina Martin, Dole's deputy press secretary, was both complaining and pleading when she said, in October, that what bugged her about the press was a "lack of empathy." She went on, "Members of the press always plead with us to understand their lives. Every once in a while they need to turn around and think about the candidates' lives and what they're asking. Things such as acknowledging a certain right to privacy . . . and allowing a certain degree of spontaneity in these candidates' lives—allowing them the flexibility to go home thirty minutes early without reflecting on their health or their state of mind or the condition of the campaign's health. . . . Not everything—every movement, every breath—has a deeper meaning to it."

Buckley believes that in the future reporters will continue to be quarantined, leaving them with even less understanding of the individuals they cover. If the press doesn't end the humorless "Gotcha! atmosphere" it's created and begin to cut the candidate "a millimeter of slack," he said, then the candidates' "only response will be to slap on a bulletproof vest and try to communicate over the heads of reporters or through them."

McCurry believes that the power of the press will inevitably decline as it becomes easier to circulate information. "There will be a decline of the old media's dominance," he said. "Things will be infinitely more complicated. We are in the twilight of the days where you can control information by giving it to a few newspapers." But such changes also mean that handlers like McCurry will lose their ability to control, say, rumors. "So," McCurry concluded, unhappily, "rumors and access to information lessen our power and lessen the power of the dominant news organizations."

As technology speeds the news cycle, press secretaries routinely brief the wire services and the radio reporters the night before, in order "to get the story moving overnight," McCurry said. "We basically don't let presidents make announcements anymore." Or if he tells reporters in the morning what the president plans to announce at 2:00 P.M., that story will circulate immediately and not only go over the wires but be heard on the radio and on the all-news cable channels, leaving print and nightly news editors to think of the 2:00 P.M. announcement as old news.

Similarly, McCurry sometimes goes out to the briefing room to slow the news cycle, as he did to stall a rumor that Iraq had fired missiles at

American planes in September, or that terrorists had blown up TWA Flight 800 in July. Two enemies of good reporting—thoughtlessness and lack of time—will loom larger. "Everyone feels the pressure for shorthand; everything is about politics," the CNN White House correspondent Claire Shipman said. "That's a convenient way to avoid substance." Shipman, who has a master's degree in international affairs from Columbia University, was covering her first campaign. "Cynicism has been adopted as a way to be seen as fair, as a way to view both sides," she said. "In a larger sense, it's laziness. But no one on this beat is lazy. Everyone works very hard. But there is so much so quickly that there is no time."

ON ELECTION DAY, Buckley said that he couldn't imagine working on another campaign. "This is not an experience I'd chalk up as one of the happiest of my life," he told me. "It was very painful to go through a campaign where every day we had to roll a rock up another hill"—that is, try to make an impression on reporters whose frame of reference did not include candidates like Ronald Reagan, who came from behind to win the presidency in 1980—"and every day it seemed that it rolled right back down again."

The day after the election, McCurry said that this was his last campaign as well. "This is it for me," he said. "I want to quit while I'm ahead." McCurry had one more campaign engaging him, however: his plan to bring about a truce between his client the president and his client the press. He was thrilled that Clinton had recently chatted with reporters on the way back from Little Rock on Air Force One. When Clinton was pressed about Huang and the Lippo Group and told reporters he'd like to wait until his Friday press conference to answer, the press relented, and McCurry could sense that Clinton was pleasantly surprised.

Will Clinton change his attitude about the press? "Intellectually, he knows it's the right thing to do," McCurry said. "But to do it well he has to feel it in his heart." The press secretary wasn't sure of the outcome, but he was sure that if the press remained hostile to Clinton, the Republican majority in Congress would be emboldened to step up its attacks—an argument that ought to appeal to Clinton. "There's not going to be a press honeymoon," McCurry said. "But there's a brief opportunity here to reach a new relationship."

POSTSCRIPT

My first piece about press coverage of presidential campaigns was for the *Village Voice*. The year was 1976; and in the years since, the way campaigns are covered has been transformed. The different attitudes of reporters and candidates account for this change, but so does technology. Reporters now file stories on the run using cell phones and wireless laptops; their editors hunger for something new, for they are exposed in the office to more live news, which generates many more news cycles. A vehicle that delivers instant news is the Internet. While many journalistic business ventures on the Web, such as Inside.com, have plunged back to earth, the impact of the technology is enduring.

INSIDE OUT

THE IDEA CAME to Kurt Andersen and Michael Hirschorn in early 1999, at the height of what has come to look like the Internet gold rush. Print was doomed, it was said; revolutionary forms of online journalism were at hand, and would also make you rich. As they remember it, Hirschorn telephoned Andersen, his former boss at *New York,* and excitedly proposed an online magazine devoted to the media and entertainment industries. Hirschorn had just been fired as the editor of *Spin,* and was in search of something new.

Andersen was finishing a novel, *Turn of the Century,* and had suggested a similar idea to the hedge fund manager James Cramer, a former Harvard acquaintance and the cofounder of TheStreet.com, whose stock price had risen more than 200 percent on its first day of trading. Hirschorn's call to Andersen led to dinner with Cramer, who arranged for them to meet venture capitalists at Flatiron Partners. Flatiron then took the lead in providing capital. On the business side, Hirschorn, who had been an editor at

Esquire, enlisted Deanna Brown, a former ad-sales director he had worked with there.

The three became equal partners, and in the summer of 1999 went to work producing a business plan for what was then called InsideDope.com. The plan bemoaned the lack of what it called a "must-read online site for members of the cultural elite." InsideDope was to fill that void; it would be a place where insiders could get inside information and data that had never been easily obtained. It would provide a way to keep track of book and movie deals, music-industry sales, and advertising spending. It would watch for personnel shifts and gossip in what the partners called "the new entertainment economy." Unlike other online content providers (the *Wall Street Journal* being one notable exception), InsideDope expected to make money by charging for subscriptions, and it was widely reported that the partners anticipated a hundred thousand paid subscribers within three years. Subscriptions would account for about 40 percent of revenues, with another 40 percent coming from advertising and the rest from conferences and the sale of exclusive information. The stakes held by Andersen, Hirschorn, and Brown at the start would eventually be reduced to 5 percent apiece. To recruit good journalists, they would set aside 25 percent of the ownership for the staff.

Flatiron agreed to put up two-thirds of the initial $5 million start-up cost for the company, which would be called Powerful Media; its online name would be changed from InsideDope to Inside.com. The "name journalists" who were hired, Brown boasted, would bring "brand awareness" to the enterprise. Had Andersen still been the editor of *Spy*, which he cofounded in 1986, he might have smirked at the language: Andersen, a forty-six-year-old who favors black jackets and open-necked shirts, and who displayed a cool wit in columns for *Time* and for *The New Yorker* and as the editor of *New York*, was now described without evident irony by his partner Hirschorn as Inside's "ambassador, building relationships in New York and Los Angeles." *Ambassador* is not a word that springs to mind as a description of Andersen, for he tends to look off into the distance when he speaks; he is more astringent observer than cheerleader. The thirty-seven-year-old Hirschorn, who has a considerable girth and wears polo shirts and sneakers, would run the operation from the inside.

He had served as editor of *Spin,* executive editor of *New York,* and features editor at *Esquire;* and he brought an inclusive management style.

Prior to Inside.com's electronic debut, in the spring of 2000, Andersen and Hirschorn e-mailed to the staff a six-page, single-spaced "first installment of our editorial playbook." Inside.com, they said, must be both "fresh and definitive":

> We are neither lapdogs nor pitbulls. Of course we must be willing to piss people off, but pissing people off is not our raison d'etre. We will [seek]. . . . Juicy detail—but also context, context, context. . . . We are creating a genuinely new journalistic form. We are not reporters or columnists or analysts. We are hybrids: reporters as smart, frank, entertaining columnists, columnists as hard-working shoe-leather reporters. This is a great opportunity to really help invent a form, not unlike magazines at the beginning of the 20th century, or even newspapers and the novel in the 18th and 19th. . . . Our key journalistic goals: Correctness. Insiderness. Juiciness. Utility. Honesty. Smartness.
>
> Go kill.

And "kill" they did, raising a total of $35 million in little more than a year. Raising money was "easier than getting laid in 1969," Andersen famously joked. The partners rented loft space alongside other dot-coms in an old warehouse in West Chelsea and hired a staff of about ninety, the majority of them journalists. Inside held a media launch party attended by Courtney Love, among others, at a New York nightspot, Eugene, and a kickoff party in Los Angeles attended by the director Curtis Hanson, who was planning to direct a movie of Andersen's novel, for which Andersen would write the screenplay.

In its first year, Inside scored some scoops on the media beat: Stephen Battaglio's account of how Jeff Zucker would become the new president of NBC Entertainment, replacing Garth Ancier; David Carr and Lorne Manly's account of the closing of *George;* Sara Nelson's real-time account of the $8 million auction of Hillary Clinton's book; Roger Parloff's early dissection of Napster's weak legal case. In addition, Andersen, especially, proved masterly in attracting publicity for Inside, and for a while he and his partners were ubiquitous in the media. But, even as it found its footing as a presence in the increasingly crowded journalism world, Inside failed as a business. "The partners figured if they were out there and visible, Inside would go public and they'd make money," an investor who studied their books says. "They never had a business plan." And their timing was off, unlike such Web-content companies as GeoCities. "If all the meetings to raise money had occurred in 1996," James Cramer says, "they would have gotten a one-and-a-half-billion-dollar offer from Yahoo! a year and a half later."

ANDERSEN, Hirschorn, and Brown designed a vast, nonpartitioned space, part newsroom and part commune, with views of the Hudson River. The new staff included David Carr, who moved up from Washington, where he had been the editor of the *City Paper.* "I was afraid of missing out on something cool," he says. "I was mostly attracted to the cult of personality around these two guys"—Andersen and Hirschorn. "No one who worked for them ever came out for the worst." Stephen Battaglio, who had been the New York bureau chief of *The Hollywood Reporter,* says, "My sources knew who I was, but my publication had no visibility in New York. These two guys were New York media guys, and I knew that if I went with them my work would get attention. And it did." Michael Cieply, who had covered Hollywood for the *Los Angeles Times* and the *Wall Street Journal* before becoming a film producer, joined as the West Coast editorial director because "I was unexpectedly swept away by the charisma of the thing."

The Insiders shared a pioneer spirit, a desire to break out, and maybe even get rich on the day they went public or sold the company. The trade publications they tended to admire were those that approached their industries broadly, and with some skepticism, such as *The American Lawyer,* which appeared in the late seventies, and *The Industry Standard,* which appeared in the late nineties. They had respect for *Brill's Content* but thought that it suffered from what one recruit called a pious, "church-lady tone." (Andersen, in his novel set in the near future, described a cocktail party where among the guests were "people with no interest in discussing . . . the thirty-one-page pundits' roundtable critique of pundit-on-pundit punditry that appeared in the final issue of *Brill's Content.*")

Few seemed to be troubled by the fact that online magazines like *Slate* had abandoned paid subscriptions, or that advertisers disdained the kind of banner advertising that Inside banked on selling. In the madness of that moment, venture capitalists were chasing dot-com ideas and in the winter of 2000, Andersen recalls, "One of the name banks in New York was going through our building in Chelsea cold-calling people and asking, 'Who wants money?'" The Internet revolution was more transformative than the Industrial Revolution, it was said, as if the Web represented a more profound change than, say, Thomas Edison's invention of electricity, without which PCs and the Internet could not live. The Net would make us free, enthused writers such as Jon Katz of *Hotwired*—free of advertising, free of stockbrokers, free of old think, free of controlling oligarchies, free of old-media control. James Cramer unabashedly predicted that TheStreet.com would supplant Dow Jones and Reuters as the foremost source of financial news. The Net, futurist George Gilder predicted, would free us from crowded cities and "revitalize public education." Tech and new-media magazines—*PC Magazine, The Industry Standard, Wired, Business 2.0, Fast Company, Red Herring, Yahoo Internet Life*—were phonebook-thick with ads. In the euphoric milieu in which Inside was born, those who questioned the dot-com rage were treated as old-media fogies— brick-and-mortar types who just didn't get it. Jonathan Weber, the editor of *The Industry Standard,* suspended his skepticism when it came to what he called the "revolution"—a "struggle" between "the Eastern establishment," or "old order," and "the renegades of the West."

By the time Inside appeared, in May of 2000, the signs of decline were everywhere. Dot-com stocks were beginning to collapse. Venture capital money was drying up. And yet the downturn in the stock market did not immediately have an impact on Inside. It raised $23 million more in April, bringing its total to $28 million. Andersen and Hirschorn were ecstatic.

They were bucking the trend, and their staff, caught up in the spirit of the endeavor, concentrated on the sheer fun of almost instant reporting on the Web and of writing in a conversational style. "It was like journalistic heroin to be able to report something that was true and get it right out there," Michael Cieply says. Andersen and Hirschorn won the loyalty of their reporters, Steven Battaglio says, because they treated them like "experts. If they came to you with a nutty idea and you told them it was nutty, they'd say, 'OK.'" Sara Nelson, who had written book reviews for *Glamour,* worked on an AOL consumer book site, and now covered the book industry, remembers, "We were ebullient. People were calling me back who never called me before. People were calling me whom I used to be afraid to call." When Inside broke a story, or was credited in the *Times* or elsewhere, a flashing red police light that was kept on David Carr's desk would be turned on. Hirschorn, often the first to arrive at the office and the last to leave, edited most of the pieces and was much loved by the staff.

Andersen's presence was more complicated. Those who worked with him would probably recognize Andersen in the description he offers of George Mactier, the protagonist of his novel: "Even when George feels blissful, he never radiates a glow of inner peace or smiles infectiously—another reason he was not a very good hippie in the seventies." While staffers remember being surprised at Andersen's accessibility and modesty, they also found him to be a Buddha-like figure. Surprised at this accessibility and this modesty, they also found him to be elusive. "Writers were always eager to have him edit their stories, because it was a compliment," the managing editor, Chris Peacock, recalls. "There was an eagerness on everyone's part to perform for him."

In the summer of 2000, despite the problems in the Web economy—other dot-com content sites were laying off personnel and folding—the staff of Inside seems not to have been worried. "It's amazing how strong denial can be," Sara Nelson says. Nor was the business side yet alarmed. Deanna Brown had worked for start-ups, including *Brill's Content,* where she had been president. By the fall of 2000, she had raised $7 million more for Inside, bringing the total to just under $35 million. "We raised enough to carry us through 2001," she says, "which would get us in striking distance of profitability."

In retrospect, Fred Wilson, the managing partner at Flatiron, says, "the critical mistake" was to start a biweekly print magazine in December 2000, on the cusp of what turned out to be an advertising recession. It consumed, according to various estimates, between $8 million and $15 million of capital. And although the editors proclaimed that Inside was an antispin publication, the partners were not always forthcoming—and not always in agreement—about some of Inside's own business data. A senior Inside executive told me that Inside had about twenty thousand paid subscribers. In an e-mail exchange, I mentioned to Andersen that press accounts had put the number at ten thousand. Andersen replied, "I can live with that." When I asked if the number was lower, Andersen said, "I'm afraid I'm not going to comment." Was ten thousand an accurate number? "No, it isn't," he finally conceded. One person who knows Inside's finances intimately says that the highest number of subscribers at any point was approximately twelve hundred. Confronted with this low number, one of the partners admitted that the peak subscriber base "was closer to five thousand," and has now fallen to about half that.

"To wake up every morning and have people who work with you ask if you're going to go out of business—which is a legitimate question—is a real burden," recalls Hirschorn. "We were out there without a net." By the end of 2000, Kurt Andersen knew that Inside would not become profitable in the foreseeable future and would need to find a partner or a buyer sooner than anticipated. In the commentary he offers during a weekly public radio show he has (*Studio 360*), Andersen said of the presidential campaign, "I am a sucker for the fantastic surprise ending. I like O. Henry stories. . . . I like twist endings."

He got one. In early January of this year, Steven Brill, the chairman of Brill Media Holdings, and Brill's friend Tom Rogers, the chairman of the media company Primedia, announced that they were merging. Brill would continue to run, independently, the monthly *Brill's Content,* and also Contentville.com, an e-commerce venture he owns. The two companies would acquire a substantial minority interest in one another, and Primedia would place 172 of its Web sites, newsletters, magazines, databases, conferences, and other products that cover the media industry in a subsidiary, Media Central, which Brill would run; these outlets reach around sixty thousand subscribers, who pay an average of about six hundred dollars per year. Later that week, Brill phoned Kurt Andersen and invited him to lunch to discuss how their two companies could work together.

Brill is Andersen's temperamental opposite—a heated personality. He is barrel-chested, wears ties and suspenders and cufflinks, and chomps on cigars. He had a baseball diamond constructed behind his house in Westchester, where he plays softball and doesn't hide his hatred for losing. He phoned James Cramer, who had invested in Brill's company as well as in Andersen's, and recruited him to lobby Andersen. "I don't believe that anyone is going to give the company more money," Cramer remembers telling Andersen.

Brill recalls that at lunch he told Andersen that Media Central "had a lot of paying customers but not enough talent, and he had talent and not enough customers." Brill said that he wanted to establish a central hub for his various media Web sites, and Inside.com could be it. Andersen did not say yes or no, but agreed to talk again. (Andersen and I were colleagues for a few years at *The New Yorker,* although we rarely intersected. I know Brill better, having worked with him at *New York* in the seventies.)

Andersen, Hirschorn, and Brown caucused and agreed to survey other prospective partners or buyers. Andersen or Brown spoke with executives from NBC, Advance Publications (which owns Condé Nast), AOL Time Warner, Ziff Davis, Cahners (a division of Reed Elsevier, which publishes *Variety* and *Publishers Weekly*), and the Washington Post Company, but these organizations either were not interested or would not move quickly enough. Powerful Media had an in-depth conversation with one of its own investors, Standard Media International, which owns *The Industry Standard.* Throughout these negotiations, Brill kept in close touch with Andersen, Cramer, and the venture capitalists, particularly Fred Wilson at Flatiron.

"We had this quiet moment," Brown recalls, "the three of us, where we asked, 'Do we take the bird in hand?'" The Brill deal was their sole firm offer, and thus "the best decision for the legacy of the brand and the staff." On the other hand, Brown says, "Personally, it was tough for me, because I knew there was no role for me at the new company." Like Brill, she was the CEO. And Brill was openly critical of Brown.

By March, rumors of a possible sale had begun to appear in print. The revenues the partners had been counting on from conferences organized by Andersen were not materializing. That month, they were down to approximately $9 million; the venture capitalists were growing impatient. Deanna Brown says she knew that another round of financing was needed, which was probably out of the question.

AN ANNOUNCEMENT of the sale to Brill was made on April second. Around a small table at a press conference at the Palace Hotel, Brill extolled Inside's journalistic product, and vowed that his own magazine, under a relatively new editor, David Kuhn, would become more like Inside, with greater emphasis on the business side of the media. Flanking Brill at the table, Andersen, Hirschorn, Rogers, and Kuhn talked about what a good deal this was. Certainly, Brill Media could now claim the talent assembled by Powerful Media, and the Inside.com brand name, Web site, and magazine. It also got what Fred Wilson says was approximately $8 million in wire transfers. Deanna Brown said that she would leave, and Andersen and Hirschorn said that they would sign contracts to stay for at least two years, but these had escape clauses. David Carr, who covered the press conference for Inside, asked the core question in his dispatch: "Is this a return of synergy or just an amassing of crippled assets?"

The staff at Inside took some comfort in Brill's career as a fiercely independent journalist. It soon became clear, however, that the two cultures did not easily fit. Inside moved from Chelsea to a warren of offices in Rockefeller Center. Almost fifty Inside employees were laid off. Staff members worried that Andersen and Hirschorn would not stay, and that Brill, who was known for yelling at employees and fellow softball players, would be his usual combative self. When Andersen invited Brill to address the staff, Brill told them that Inside would become a marketing and delivery vehicle for his other trade sites, and when questions were raised, he said bluntly, "You are in the trade business." David Carr says, "We didn't want to hear that. People acted like he was the Antichrist."

On the day the remaining staff of Inside moved uptown, Sara Nelson invited the old gang to a party at her apartment in SoHo. About fifty people, including Andersen, Hirschorn, and Brown, drank wine and beer and ate a six-foot-long hero from Katz's Delicatessen. David Carr, with help from Whitney Joiner, a young reporter at Inside, performed a puppet show. The puppets were Andersen dressed as a king; Hirschorn as a lovable teddy bear; Brown as a lady; and Brill as a lamb. The show opened, Carr recounts, with Inside's launch party and its high hopes, and this scene ended with Hirschorn knocking over Andersen when he spots Courtney Love and races to greet her. The second scene takes place ten months later and reveals Andersen at his desk, taking a phone call and talking in a hushed tone. "Who was that?" Hirschorn asks.

"Steve Brill," Andersen says. "He wants to buy the business."

They look at each other and say, in unison, "He's not cool enough."

In another scene, Sara Nelson recalls, Hirschorn reassures the staff about the sale to Brill: "It's cool. It's cool." Andersen says, "This is a way to keep the DNA of Inside alive." Then Andersen escorts the lamb—Brill—to meet the staff, and he begins by saying, "I love what you guys do. This is what I want in my company." Brill says that Inside will become a successful trade publication because the only way to guarantee revenue streams is to have a trade publication.

"What Steve really means," Andersen explains, "is that we will report on the media and entertainment."

Nonsense. Brill yanks off his sheep costume to reveal that he is a wolf.

The final scene features Hirschorn asking Andersen what he's doing. "I'm the vice chairman and I'm in charge of strategic initiatives," Andersen says. As he speaks, he morphs into a grasshopper and hops away.

The puppet show was over, but so was a special period in their lives. "What Inside had, more than any place I ever worked at, was a camaraderie," Lorne Manly, Inside's media editor, says. "We really felt we were doing something that was new and that had impact." Although Inside.com failed as a business and the staff feared for their livelihood, few of them had a bad word to say about Andersen, Hirschorn, or Brown. They thought that the nice guys had lost.

A reason they lost is that they were too nice. They didn't make some tough-minded decisions. There were differences between Andersen and

Brown, who wanted to restrict how much information they gave away for free, and Hirschorn, who wanted to attract a bigger audience. These were never resolved. Nor was the tension between building a business and building a brand. Nor was there a dominant business leader. Andersen genuinely admires Deanna Brown but, he says, she "is not a strong numbers person." As a result, in October 1999, the partners hired "a strong chief financial officer." One senior staff member of Inside, speaking anonymously, says that Andersen is "fabulously charismatic," and that "people naturally want to follow him," but "the flip side of this" is that he lacked the "next step" of leadership: a take-charge personality that gets in the trenches. "We had a three-headed leadership," this person says. "In crunches, Kurt tended to disappear. Michael thus became the dominant operating presence." Michael was good, and Deanna Brown was good. But "what they were trying to pull off required brilliance," he says.

PERHAPS IT IS the nature of the Internet to be unfriendly to the sale of content, observes Thomas Phillips, who was an investor in Powerful Media and has had his share of victories and losses as an Internet entrepreneur, starting at Starwave in 1993, then at ABC.com, ESPN.com, and at deja.com. "I've learned that trying to build ad-supported journalism sites is not fruitful. I don't think journalism is well consumed in an ad-friendly way online. There are several elements to that: The medium is not conducive to sitting back and digging in for information. You're leaning forward and your finger is the trigger all the time. Because you're not sitting back and receiving a message, it is not ad friendly." Nor is it subscription friendly, he continues: "The Web is a self-directed and limitless medium. Any user can find whatever his interest level and appetite demands. Searching is the dominant mode of the Internet. So the mentality of the information seeker is: I can find it if I keep looking. Why should I pay for anything? That's the phenomenon that has not been overcome with time."

That's the phenomenon Steve Brill, joined now by Kurt Andersen and Michael Hirschorn, confronted as they strove to build a business. Before they sat down for their first business plan meetings, Brill had some difficult business decisions to make: What to charge? Do they charge per day? Month? Year? Per piece? What information will be free? How much free information is needed as a promotional or marketing tool to expand the site—one free story per day? Two? Three? Is it the top story, the one that generates the most interest? How do they devise a simple sign-up subscriber process that is quick, yet secure? How do they design a user-friendly site that will also cross-promote many of the 172 other Media Central trade sites and publications?

To address these and other issues, on May second, Brill called a meeting, which he chaired, and which was attended by Andersen and Hirschorn, among others. Brill's starting premise, he said, was that Inside.com had to be thought of as a newsstand, one that displayed and sold an array of Media Central's publications.

Implicit in Brill's comments was a hope that Inside would produce revenues not just from pay-per-view or monthly subscriptions but by luring subscribers to his other trade publications. An annual subscription to a Media Central newsletter called *Inside Book Publishing Report,* for example, is nearly seven hundred dollars, and some newsletters cost a thousand dollars, so this is a potentially lucrative source of revenue for Brill. Tom Rogers, Brill's partner and Primedia's CEO, explains in the language of the business world: "The point of Inside was to give Brill an online vehicle . . . through which to drive subscription revenue . . . , which is what we think in the business-to-business space is the biggest opportunity for business-to-business information." That was not what the people at Inside had set out to do.

Mostly through layoffs, there has been a 40 percent decrease in Inside's editorial staff, according to Hirschorn, from fifty-three to thirty-three; David Carr, Michael Cieply, Kyle Pope, and Richard Siklos are among those who chose to leave. Steve Brill "has to woo people," Hirschorn says. But Brill does not woo people in the accustomed manner. He says that part of his job "is figuring out how to keep good people," and he has awarded broader responsibilities to some Inside staff members, including Sara Nelson, Lorne Manly, Stephen Battaglio, and Scott Collins. Nevertheless, he admits, "I have a style that is different." As an executive, he is abrasive. "Sometimes paying attention to them is asking, 'How come you didn't call this person before writing this story?' Some people think that's bad for morale. What about the morale of the person they're writing about?" Andersen, on the other hand, cautions that one thing he learned from his experience at *Spy* is that good people "are not replaceable."

Brill's Content, meanwhile, has gone from a monthly to a quarterly, and Brill has announced that he plans to reduce its circulation from "about three hundred seventy-five thousand if it were audited today"—not four hundred thousand, as is usually proclaimed—to about two hundred twenty-five thousand. By cutting back, Brill says, he will break even. Gone are the plans to merge its editorial mission with Inside's. Gone as well is *Brill's Content*'s projected December deficit of $1.7 million, which Brill says he feared would swell to twice that, thus prompting him to seek outside financing.

Brill has involved Andersen and Hirschorn in decision making (the two, along with Kuhn, have been named vice chairmen of Brill Media). Andersen says that Brill is "intellectually nimble" and has praised him for acting with "mind-bending speed, which is great." He and Hirschorn agree with the decisions Brill made about charging $3.95 for a monthly subscription to Inside and 40 cents per article. "I don't think we could have made them," Andersen graciously says of these decisions. "We would have temporized." Hirschorn is staying on as the editor of Inside, and Brill says of Andersen, "I think he'll end up staying." Andersen himself says he won't. "There's relatively little for me to do," he says. He wants to concentrate on a second novel, screenplays, and his weekly radio program.

The brief marriage has already had its share of spats. During the week of May fourteenth, for example, Deanna Brown and Fred Wilson, representing Powerful Media, exchanged e-mails and angry words with Brill, who says that he is being asked to come up with hundreds of thousands of dollars to cover unrecorded accounts payable and inflated accounts receivable. "It turns out that the people running the business side there never kept good books so they could pay writers." He also says that promised ad revenues turned out to be phantom. But he adds, "I don't think there will be litigation," because he and the Inside people are "working it out."

Deanna Brown says that it is "absolutely untrue" that Inside did not keep good books, but she wants to avoid a confrontation. These are the normal kinks of "two companies in transition," she says. As for Brill's assertion that he is suddenly burdened with hundreds of thousands of dollars in costs, she concedes that "the payables are probably higher than on the day the deal was signed, because we didn't have all the invoices in." At the same time, she says, Brill is "underestimating receivables" from advertising. Fred Wilson, like Brown, has implicitly acknowledged many of Brill's facts but places them in this context: "In the process of doing the deal at lightning speed, some things didn't get done that should have gotten done."

ALL THIS IS taking place as the Web culture itself evolves—or doesn't. The Internet, Hirschorn says, "feels like a transitional medium." If the Internet remains central, as Eric Etheridge believes it will, then the business model Brill is fashioning may clash with the sociology of the medium. Etheridge has worked as vice president of content for Deja.com, a software company that archived and made Internet discussion boards searchable, and as executive producer for Sidewalk, Microsoft's since abandoned online city guide. "What the Internet is really good at is people making their own medium," he says. "Inside is really a very old model—forty to fifty smart people contributing stories." It's hierarchical. "The new model is more people contributing on a peer-to-peer basis," he says, digging down for information they want. And the old model is expensive. "What the Web is really good at is people sharing information." Thus when Etheridge, who is a camera buff, wants information about cameras, he links to and exchanges information with fellow camera owners because this information "is better than anything you can get from a camera catalogue."

An offshoot of this personalized Web model is a site like journalist Mickey Kaus's Kausfiles.com. Daily, Kaus posts his quirky opinions on subjects ranging from welfare reform to journalistic conflicts of interest. "The imperative is to put it up even if it's a bit raw," he says. "The raw stuff is what people like best." Partly because he writes for *Slate*, he attracts what he says is up to six thousand visitors a day and up to twelve thousand visitors each week. He says his monthly costs are a hundred dollars for a server to store and send his newsletter; two hundred dollars for a subscription to Lexis-Nexis for research; and twenty dollars for Internet access. After an initial six-hundred-dollar payment for a software designer, his upgrade expenses have been small. He does not include the cost of his time, which he estimates at four hours a day. His revenue depends on "the tip jar," with people sending him about seventy-five dollars a week, and on advertisers, of which he has had one. A site like Jim Romenesko's poynter.org/medianews.com allows readers to see press-related stories each day, including the free stories that appear on Inside. But if you can do this for nothing, will anyone be willing to pay for Inside.com?

Yes, Brill says, because Inside's information has value and will not be available elsewhere. Bloomberg Professional Service has been able to charge $1,285 a month for electronic information it says cannot be replicated on the Web. As of March thirty-first, according to a *Wall Street Journal* spokeswoman, the *Journal*'s online version had grown to 574,000 paid subscribers, with those who subscribe to the paper paying $29 per year and those who don't paying $59. James Cramer believes that a second generation of Web users is less hostile to paying for content. "When I started, no one used a credit card on the Web," Cramer says. "Now everyone does." The key ingredient, Steve Brill believes, is good content. "The business plan is the editorial plan," he says. Build it and, if it is good content, they will come. But perhaps they will not pay.

In an Inside piece last December entitled "The Revolution Is Glorious, and the Sky Is Falling—Get Used to It," Kurt Andersen wrote that one could look at Christopher Columbus as a failure: "His business model did not pan out: no western route to Asia, hardly any gold, abandonment by his investors, not much of an enduring first-mover advantage for Spain . . . *but he fucking discovered America.*" Andersen, looking back, and forward, from the second floor of Wu Liang Ye, a bustling Chinese restaurant across the street from his temporary office on West Forty-eighth Street, couldn't be sure what he had discovered. He didn't know whether Inside.com would be seen as a pioneer or as a failure. But of this he was certain: "People are making it up as they go along. There are no precedents, and no comparables." And, so far, few good business models.

POSTSCRIPT

In the end, Kurt Andersen chose to leave, as did most of his former colleagues. After a nasty spat with his old friend Thomas Rogers, the CEO of his corporate parent, Steve Brill also exited. Inside.com died (as did *Brill's Content*). In April 2003, Rogers lost his CEO job. An advertising recession crippled the traditional magazine business, and nontraditional Web ventures as well. By mid-2003, few if any business models had surfaced to instruct how money could be made off Web journalism. The heirs to Kurt Andersen and Michael Hirschorn's vision gather not in a collective journalistic entity like Inside.com but individually, using the Web to disseminate their own bloggery. The word—*blogging*—was invented to describe this democratic outpouring of opinion made possible by the Internet. That is its virtue. Its drawbacks are the lack of editors and fact checkers—and a few moments to reflect—that come with instant news.

The next piece, I'm afraid, also explores journalism's future. It does not involve the Web or blogging, but it does involve a vision. Fox News has attitude, edge, noise—and, above all, a niche as the patriotic news channel. Fox News makes money. Just as vital to Rupert Murdoch, its owner, is that Fox News has synergistic impact—on his business, or our politics, on our public discourse, and, based on its imitators, on the media's behavior.

FOX NEWS:

WE REPORT. WE DECIDE.

O NE MORNING not long ago, the cohosts of *Fox & Friends,* the Fox News network's raucous and right-leaning version of the *Today* show, were promoting Fox-branded merchandise such as baseball caps and soap-on-a-rope when Steve Doocy, a coanchor, turned to his partner, E. D. Hill, and said, "You know who's really jealous about our merchandising?" Doocy, who doubles as the weatherman, answered his own question: "My dentist is so jealous. You've seen him on TV—Aaron Brown. You know, the guy on CNN—he does that show at night? He just works nights over there. But during the day he's our dentist. Do we have a picture?"

Up popped a grim photograph of CNN's principal nighttime anchor, Aaron Brown. "That man looks just like a dentist, doesn't he?" Doocy said, and soon he and Hill were chatting about whether Brown was a good dentist and what he charged for a cleaning. Brown's picture lingered on the screen for a full minute, over bold, block-lettered captions: AARON BROWN DDS, followed by MOLAR MAN, followed by ARROGANT BROWN.

That bit of intramural japery, which aired on December 13, 2001, was choreographed by Roger Ailes, the chairman and CEO of the sometimes raucous and right-leaning Fox News. Ailes was trying to strike back at Brown for publicly "putting us down," he says. "I don't ignore anything. Somebody gets in my face, I get in their face." Ailes requires enemies the way a tank requires fuel, and as he contemplated retaliation he kept thinking, I know someone who looks like Aaron Brown. Then it came to him. He telephoned Doocy, telling him, "Steve, just say that Aaron's your *dentist.* Then have your coanchor say, 'He's not a dentist. He's on CNN!'" Ailes, a man of Falstaffian girth, roared with laughter, and continued, "I said, 'Doocy, no matter what happens, even if they torture you, say he's your dentist!'" For two days, Doocy followed the script, and for two days, Ailes recalled fondly, "I'm sitting here laughing my ass off."

Aaron Brown, for his part, was not laughing his ass off. I thought it was sort of juvenile," he said. "This is a little game they play. It's Roger's game. Roger seeks to define his political or journalistic opponents and destroy them."

There have been many such memories for Ailes, some playful, some brutal, all purposeful. In March, when antiwar protesters blocked traffic on Fifth Avenue and paraded in front of the Fox News offices on Sixth Avenue between Forty-seventh and Forty-eighth streets, the electronic news ticker that wraps around the building suspended Iraq-war headlines to respond: ATTENTION PROTESTERS: THE MICHAEL MOORE FAN CLUB MEETS THURSDAY AT A PHONE BOOTH AT SIXTH AVENUE AND 50TH STREET. Marvin Himelfarb, a former sitcom writer, wrote the ticker copy, but Ailes was his happy abettor. Of the announcements, Ailes says, "I helped with a couple." Paula Zahn recalls that when she told Ailes she was moving to CNN in 2001, "he made it very clear to me that he was not going to make life easy for me. He told me I was allowing myself to be drawn into what he called a holy war between CNN and Fox News, and that I was going to have to pay a price for that." (Ailes brought a lawsuit charging that Zahn's agent interfered with Fox's contract; it was dismissed by two state courts.) Subsequently, *Fox & Friends* disparaged Zahn, whose *American Morning* aired at the same time. Mancow Muller, the Chicago-based radio shock jock who appears regularly on the morning show, said of Zahn—screamed, actually—"I kick your ass, Paula! You take on us, we'll kill you, Paula! We'll kill you! *We will kill you, Paula!*" Walter Isaacson, who was then CNN chairman, acknowledges that Ailes's approach "constrains your action. You wake up aware of Roger. He's always on the attack." Ailes doesn't deny that he tries to intimidate people: "I'd say half of it is because people let their heads be played with and half of it is just my sense of humor."

AILES IS SIXTY-THREE and does not look immediately fearsome. He says he is five feet nine inches tall and weighs 225 pounds; his jowls droop over his collar. With his pallor and barely perceptible eyebrows, Ailes looks like someone who has spent a lifetime under fluorescent lights. In many ways, he is a throwback—to the fifties, perhaps. He slathers a morning bagel with butter and cream cheese; he often wears white shirts with French cuffs and a tie clip. Nine years ago, on the Don Imus radio program, he referred to Mary Matalin and Jane Wallace, then the cohosts of a CNBC show, as "girls who, if you went into a bar around seven, you wouldn't pay a lot of attention, but they get to be 10s around closing time."

Roger Ailes is also a television pioneer, someone who had no background in news and yet created something different in the TV news business. In large part because of Ailes, Fox News, in its short life—it debuted on October 7, 1996—has established an unmistakable identity: it is opinionated and conservative, and its news is delivered by people who themselves are often unabashedly opinionated and conservative. When Ted Turner launched the Cable News Network in 1980, CNN took the idea of all-news radio and transferred it to television. The Fox News idea was to make another sort of transition: to bring the heated, sometimes confrontational atmosphere of talk radio into the television studio.

The rise of Fox News has been swift. By 2002, it had overtaken CNN as the leader in cable news ratings. The audience for the four other cable news networks—CNN, MSNBC, CNBC, and CNN's Headline News—was generally flat last year, but Fox's expanded by more than 40 percent over the previous year.

The trend has been particularly troubling to CNN, which has always claimed that during major events viewers turn in greater numbers to CNN, which calls itself "the most trusted name" in cable news. But on March nineteenth, the first night of the Iraq war, Fox News bested CNN in the ratings, and did so every day for the duration of the war, according to Nielsen Media Research. On most nights, Fox's top-rated show—*The O'Reilly Factor*—attracts almost as many viewers (around three million) as all its cable news competitors combined. On its best night during the war in Iraq, the O'Reilly show reached seven million viewers. For the first time ever in a crisis, the audience for the network newscasts on CBS and ABC dropped—2.5 percent for ABC, 9 percent for CBS (NBC's rose slightly)—while the five cable news networks climbed by more than 350 percent. Fox News set the pace. Last October, when Fox's business anchor Neil Cavuto asked the chairman and CEO of General Electric, Jeffrey Immelt, how he planned to improve his own cable news network—MSNBC—Immelt replied, "I think the standard right now is Fox. And I want to be as interesting and as edgy as you guys are."

ROGER AILES went to Fox from NBC, which he joined in 1993, to run CNBC, its business-news channel. Journalists at NBC had worried that Ailes would be too partisan; he was, after all, a former Republican media consultant (for Richard Nixon in 1968, Ronald Reagan in 1984, and George H. W. Bush in 1988), and was known for producing Rush Limbaugh's television show. But over the next two and a half years Ailes won over many dispirited employees who had been banished to the dreary CNBC headquarters in Fort Lee, New Jersey. He placed a neon sign on the building, ordered fresh coats of paint and new furniture. He treated business news as a sport. He placed the reporter Maria Bartiromo on the floor of the New York Stock Exchange, and she became known as the Money Honey. He helped make Ron Insana a star. Jack Welch, who was then the chairman and CEO of GE, says, "He made the network a combination of ESPN and the *New York Post*." On a second NBC cable channel, America's Talking, he programmed fourteen live hours a day of mostly talk shows. By 1995, CNBC alone was generating profits of about $100 million annually.

Ailes, however, did not thrive in NBC's corporate culture. He was overweight. He was profane. Welch remembers that after he had bypass surgery he instructed the GE executive dining room to produce healthful meals. Ailes demurred. "I'm not eating this crap!" he announced, and ordered a double cheeseburger and french fries. "Everyone wanted a cheeseburger, but he was the only one with the guts to ask for it," Welch says.

Although America's Talking went on the air in July of 1994, and Ailes signed a new contract in June of 1995, Bob Wright, the CEO of NBC, had another idea: He decided to parlay America's Talking into a new cable network, MSNBC, and he wanted the new network (a collaboration between NBC and Microsoft, which paid half the start-up cost) to report to the president of NBC News, Andrew Lack. Ailes thought that he had lost a power struggle to bureaucrats who "probably doubted my ability to run a business." NBC officials thought he was too volatile—not, it was said, a team player. Ailes quit.

Thinking about what to do next, Ailes phoned Rupert Murdoch, the chairman and CEO of News Corp. A secretary called back to say that Murdoch was arriving in New York that afternoon and could see Ailes at five. At News Corp.'s office on Sixth Avenue, Murdoch told Ailes that he was impressed by his record at CNBC and confessed that he was frustrated. "I've been trying to get a news channel started," Ailes recalls Murdoch saying. "I've had a bunch of guys try." The two men shared a conservative political viewpoint; when Murdoch brought up CNN, Ailes agreed, "It's too liberal." Ailes explains, "I think the mainstream media thinks liberalism is the center of the road. I really think that they don't understand that there are serious people in America who don't necessarily agree with everything they hear on the Upper East Side of Manhattan." Murdoch, too, believed that CNN and the other networks and major newspapers were strongly biased.

News Corp. saw an opportunity. The Fox entertainment network, with programming like *The Simpsons* and *Married . . . with Children,* had competed successfully with the broadcast networks, and Fox also owned the world's most extensive satellite distribution system. But News Corp., which owns more than 175 newspapers on three continents, including the *New York Post,* had neither a network news operation nor a cable news division. Despite Murdoch's business triumphs, few took the idea of Fox News seriously. But when Murdoch told Ailes he had a business plan to start the Fox News network in eighteen months, Ailes said that was too slow: MSNBC would debut before then, and Fox News ought to be on the air by the end of 1996.

Ailes realized that the assignment was difficult. "We had no studios," Ailes later told me. "No programs. No talent. No ideas. No news-gathering capabilities, weak stations in news, no history of news. And we had two— and looking like three—very tough competitors, with a generic product. So it was daunting when you looked at it. And we had no distribution."

Ailes had always thought that if he was running a local news station he would run ads that said, "We may not always be first. But we will always be fair." He explains, "There is an underserved market in news. . . . What I meant was 'fair and balanced.' I think I can create a market for the news." He believed that, "up until the Fox News channel, if any conservative or even libertarian got his opinion on the air, it was viewed as right wing." To Ailes, "the elimination of anybody's point of view is biased." Friends later worried that Ailes would be accused of blatantly promoting right-wing viewpoints, and he responded, "Good! That'll drive my ratings up!"

In retrospect, it was a perfect joining of politics and business; a more conservative news channel would create another niche in a fragmented marketplace. At a 1998 Sun Valley management retreat, Peter Chernin, the president and chief operating officer of News Corp., declared that media companies have "to seize the edge, because the most dangerous thing in the antibland world is to play it safe. And it must leap out with brand identity."

ON JANUARY 30, 1996, Ailes stood next to Murdoch at the public announcement of a Fox News channel and was introduced as its chairman and CEO. "I told Wright in 1996," Jack Welch remembers, "'We'll rue the day we let Roger and Rupert team up.'"

MSNBC hurried to create a news channel that they said would harness technology and "revolutionize" news coverage. Ted Turner vowed that CNN would squish Murdoch "like a bug." CNN's corporate parent, Time Warner, then the second-largest cable company in America, at first denied Fox News any access to its cable system, provoking a Murdoch lawsuit. Ailes fought back, and eventually eighty-two employees left NBC for Fox; when an NBC lawyer phoned to suggest that by recruiting its employees Ailes was tampering, Ailes responded, "You don't know the difference between recruitment and a jailbreak."

The promotional tag lines that Ailes wrote were as snappy as any he had designed for a candidate: "Fox News. Fair and Balanced" and "We report. You decide." Ailes borrowed one other technique common to political campaigns: He lowered expectations. Five days before Fox's scheduled debut, he called fifteen executives to a staff meeting at 4:00 A.M. He wanted to jolt them, one Fox executive recalled, and "he wanted the world to think, Hey, Fox may not launch in five days."

It was not an auspicious launch. Fox News had access to seventeen million homes; CNN had seventy million, and MSNBC twenty-two million. There were embarrassing glitches. To inaugurate the news channel, Israeli Prime Minister Benjamin Netanyahu agreed to an interview, but midway through the segment Fox lost the feed from Israel.

From the start, Ailes and his team say they knew what Fox News would look and feel like. America's Talking was the idea, acknowledges Jack Abernathy, who worked for Ailes at NBC and joined Fox News as chief financial officer. "I knew we could come in here and create a credible news service at a fraction of the cost that people had expected," he said. Ailes, too, acknowledged that his model had been America's Talking, but that's not what he told the *Los Angeles Times* in October 1996: "We're going to be basically a hard-news network," providing "straight, factual information to the American people so that they can make up their own minds, with less 'spin' and less 'face time' for anchors." Neil Cavuto, a business anchor at CNBC, had been among the first to sign on. "A lot of people thought I was a little crazy leaving all that," he said. "NBC and CNBC matched the money. But I really thought the opportunity was great here and I really like Roger. I felt he was an exciting guy to work for. And he was a funny guy to work for." Cavuto added, "I don't worry about things like 'Will I have a job or job security.' I have multiple sclerosis. I had cancer. . . . If I'm living, I wake up in the morning and I'm still breathing, that's a good start." John Moody, who had spent fourteen years at *Time* and seven years overseas for UPI, signed on, too, as vice president in charge of news. Moody is usually as understated as Ailes is brash. But he had come to believe that *Time,* like other media outlets, had succumbed to an unconscious but powerful liberal bias. Another important hire was Brit Hume, who was for years the White House correspondent for ABC and became Fox News's Washington editor.

Ailes also recruited Bill O'Reilly, a former CBS and ABC correspondent who was the anchor for the gossipy syndicated show *Inside Edition.* O'Reilly had left the show and was studying for a master's degree in public administration at Harvard's Kennedy School. Ailes, who liked O'Reilly's style and his directness on camera, is very clear about what he believes works on television. In his hybrid memoir, *You Are the Message: Getting What You Want by Being Who You Are,* he writes that a key lesson is to be a "proactive—not a reactive—communicator." It takes seven seconds to make an impression on others, he calculates, so the passive communicator will fail. Often, Ailes writes, when he was evaluating talk-show hosts as a broadcasting consultant, he would watch television with the sound off. "If there was nothing happening on the screen in the way the host looked or moved that made me interested enough to stand up and turn the sound up, then I knew that the host was not a great television performer."

Ailes's—and Fox's—moment came more than a year later, in early 1998. In much the way that the O. J. Simpson trial helped to create an audience for Court TV, Fox News found its perfect story in President Clinton's affair with a White House intern, Monica Lewinsky. A few months earlier, Ailes had told Brit Hume that he wanted him to anchor a political hour at 6:00 P.M. When the scandal broke, Kim Hume, who is the Washington bureau chief, told her husband that they should get the show on the road. The Humes consulted Ailes, who startled them by saying, "We'll do it tonight!" That night, Ailes moved Bill O'Reilly, who until then had conducted an interview program with relatively weak ratings, to 8:00 P.M. Thus began *The O'Reilly Factor.*

This was a significant moment, NBC's Bob Wright says. "Talk-radio shows started to go crazy with it"—the widespread resentment at Clinton's misdeeds. "We were not paying as much attention to it at NBC News. And MSNBC wasn't. CNN wasn't. And what Fox did was say, 'Gee this is a way for us to distinguish ourselves. We're going to grab this pent-up anger—shouting—that we're seeing on talk radio and put it onto television.'"

Ailes insists, "We covered impeachment 'fair and balanced.'" But the Clinton impeachment tapped into a core conservative base. "Here is the issue we faced when we started," Brit Hume says. "There were a certain number of people out there that had given up on network news, because they just couldn't take it. . . . What we needed was a story they simply couldn't take their eyes off." More important than the Lewinsky scandal, he believes, the 2000 election and the Florida recount were "of such pressing, passionate interest that people couldn't stop watching. It was a little like the [1991 Gulf] war was for CNN. It would change two or three times a day, and be reversed three hours later. We immediately put our top political correspondents in Florida—we took them away from the candidates and put them in Florida and went after that story as hard as we could with the best people we could." Fox News was the first network to declare George W. Bush the victor.

By then, Ailes had many reasons to be pleased. He had got married for the third time—to Beth Tilson, who had been the vice president of programming at America's Talking—and in January 2000, they had a son, his first child. At about the time of the 2000 election, Fox News was in fifty-five million homes and had broken even, much earlier than expected. Ailes got a new three-year contract from Murdoch. By the spring of 2001, Fox News often bested CNN in both the morning and the evening ratings.

THE CLINTON SCANDALS helped Fox to find its political base, but the attacks of September 11 had a more profound effect: Fox, far more than any other television enterprise, went to war. And in doing so it defined itself. To be sure, news coverage in wartime tends to be less reflective, more emotional; in the aftermath of the deadliest attack on American soil, this was particularly so. But Ailes and Fox News went further. Geraldo Rivera, whom Ailes had recruited from CNBC to be a war correspondent, armed himself with a pistol and proclaimed that he would be honored to kill Osama bin Laden. Fox anchors and reporters spoke not of "United States troops" but of "our troops." Fox graphics identified the captured American Taliban recruit John Walker Lindh as "Jihad Johnny." Ailes wrote to the president, urging him to strike back hard. Fox News dramatized its presentation with whooshing sounds heralding new headlines and flashing titles—BREAKING NEWS or NEWS ALERT. (In February, when the United States raised the terror-alert level from yellow to orange, every cable news network used the bottom of the screen to warn viewers of a TERROR ALERT HIGH and a NEWS ALERT. On a visit to New York, Laura Bush scolded the networks for "frightening people.")

A former correspondent told me that it was common to hear Fox producers whisper, "We have to feed the core." In an interview last December with the *New York Observer,* Al Gore described Fox as a virtual arm of the Republican Party. "Something will start at the Republican National Committee, inside the building, and it will explode the next day on the right-wing talk-show network and on Fox News and in the newspapers that play the game," Gore said. "And pretty soon they'll start baiting the mainstream media for allegedly ignoring the story they've pushed into the zeitgeist." Former House Speaker Newt Gingrich, a Fox News commentator, refers to CNN as "the Clinton News Network"; he describes his employer as if it were a closed circuit to fellow insiders: "If I go on the Fox network, no question that people in the administration see that. If there's one channel on in a Washington office that I visit, it will usually be Fox."

BY THE FALL OF 2001, Ailes was already fighting a private war. In response to Paul Zahn's defection to CNN, he hired CNN's Greta Van Susteren to host a nightly talk show. He also accused CNN of being overly solicitous to America's enemies. "Suddenly," Ailes told Jim Rutenberg, of the *Times,* "our competition has discovered 'fair and balanced,' but only when it's radical terrorism versus the United States." His criticism was aimed at all the other networks, although CNN remained his primary target. Ailes's fervor attracted more viewers to Fox News, and he made clear to his own troops that one bias was acceptable: "The one thing I say to our folks is 'This is a pretty good country. Before you make the conclusion that America's wrong first, always leave an open mind that there might be something good here.'"

Many journalists resented the insinuation that journalistic independence—reporting, say, on Afghan civilian deaths or military mistakes—was somehow unpatriotic. "Coming out of 9/11, something happened that made people feel that if you questioned anything you were liable to be labeled unpatriotic," Marcy McGinnis, CBS's senior vice president for news coverage, says. "It was kind of scary to me." The ABC News president, David Westin, says, "I like 'We report. You decide.' It's a wonderful slogan. Too often, I don't think that's what's going on at Fox. Too often, they step over the line and try and help people decide what is right and wrong."

In a survey by the Pew Research Center, 40 percent of CNN and 46 percent of Fox News viewers regarded themselves as "conservative." What is different at Fox, according to Andrew Kohut, the director of Pew Research, is the "intensity" of its viewership. Nielsen Media Research does not dissect political views when measuring audiences, but it did find that, typically, Fox viewers between the ages of twenty-five and fifty-four watched 70 percent more news than CNN viewers. Ailes insists that people watched not because they were conservative but because Fox was the "most interesting" network.

To be sure, when one considers the entire television audience, the share that belongs to Fox and its cable cohorts is minuscule. Prior to the war in Iraq, on a typical weekday the thirty-minute evening newscasts on NBC, ABC, and CBS reached more than thirty million viewers—twelve times the audience at that hour of the five cable news networks combined.

VIEWERS OF FOX NEWS quickly discover a Niagara of opinion, which is consistent with Ailes's view. "Cable is an edge business," he explains, alluding not just to attitude or opinion but also to Fox's faster pace. "Brian Williams has no edge, so he sits there and mumbles in his nice shirts and can't get through." According to Ailes, cable disdains "pompousness" and values sharp opinions. Such opinions come regularly from the hosts of *Fox & Friends,* which drew a bigger cable audience from 7:00 to 9:00 A.M. in 2002 than CNN's Paula Zahn or MSNBC's simulcast of the Imus radio show. From 9:00 A.M. to 3:00 P.M., Fox features stories and reports from its bureaus and covers government press conferences. (Fox, to its credit, devotes more time to the workings of government than its rivals do.)

Unlike its competitors, however, Fox lets its daytime anchors intrude with opinion—usually opinions consonant with the Bush administration's. Fox News became a magnet for conservatives much as Al Jazeera, the Qatar-based satellite station, did for its more than thirty million Arab viewers. On January twenty-seventh, John Gibson, an afternoon anchor, described a war protest in Davos, Switzerland, as composed of "hundreds of knuckleheads." On February eleventh, Steve Doocy talked about those in Congress who favor some exceptions to strictures on immigration—for instance, for the families of victims of the September eleventh attacks. "Guess who's giving sympathy to illegal immigrants linked to terrorists," he said, and showed a video of Senator Hillary Clinton: "You're looking at her." On February twenty-third, when it was clear that France would oppose an American resolution at the UN, the anchor Bob Sellers described France as a member of the "axis of weasels." This phrase, first published in the *New York Post,* became a refrain on Fox News; it often appeared in a banner at the bottom of the screen. (Asked if he approved, Ailes told me, "We shouldn't have done that, if we did. I would call that bad journalism." The practice didn't stop.)

In the weeks leading up to the war, Fox anchors kept announcing, "The coalition of the willing continues to grow," saying that some thirty countries now supported the United States, but rarely noting that this was a distinct minority of the world's nations. (On CNN, the senior White House correspondent, John King, pointed out that the coalition of the willing essentially consisted of the three nations whose troops were engaged in combat—the United States, the United Kingdom, and Australia.) Fox placed the conservative talk-radio host Oliver North with a marine unit as an embedded correspondent. On the eve of war, North passed along to Fox viewers "rumors" that French officials at the embassy in

Baghdad were destroying documents proving French complicity in Iraq's chemical- and biological-weapons programs. These "rumors" proved false, and a spokeswoman for Fox, Irena Steffen, described North to the *Times* as "a military contributor to Fox. He is neither a reporter nor a correspondent." When Fox anchors assured viewers that images of Saddam Hussein's statue falling would let the Arab world see America as a liberator, the correspondent Simon Marks, in Amman, Jordan, warned that "the Arab street" was angry and that it would take diplomacy to convince people that this was not "an American war of occupation." This prompted the anchor David Asman, a former *Wall Street Journal* editorial writer, to say, "There's a certain ridiculousness to that point of view!" Neil Cavuto ended an interview with Republican House Majority Leader Tom DeLay this way: "You know, a lot of your loyal fans, Mr. Majority Leader, say, That has a nice ring to it, but they like 'President DeLay.' You interested?"

As Fox News has pulled further away from the cable competition in the ratings race, no one piles up higher ratings than—or outshouts—Bill O'Reilly, who announces that his program is a "no-spin zone." When I met with him recently, in his office on the seventeenth floor of the News Corp. Building, O'Reilly, who is six feet four, was sitting at a small desk cluttered with clippings and research material. Besides his weeknight Fox program, he has a syndicated radio show and a newspaper column. He sees himself as a victim of stereotype, surrounded by a press corps that is 70 percent hostile and "vicious." O'Reilly delights in deprecating the "elite" press. "These people, not only in the print press but other network people, and some powerful people in boardrooms, are basically frightened of the Fox News channel," he said. "They understand that the power has shifted into an organization that is right center."

O'Reilly did a little spinning himself when I asked if he was often rude on the air. "If you count the times I've shouted in the last six months—maybe ten," he said. He turned the question around: "I have six minutes per segment. If you don't answer the question, I think that's rude."

Asked why Fox does so well, O'Reilly had a ready answer: "Because we're daring. Because we're entertaining and interesting and different—stimulating." The other networks, he went on, are "too timid and hide-behind—'CNN: We're the journalists.' Oh, bullshit." O'Reilly called

Connie Chung's canceled program "a tabloid show that rivals what I did at *Inside Edition*—I mean, we were tougher, we did investigative stuff on *Inside Edition*."

O'Reilly says that Fox owes much to Ailes. "Roger Ailes is the general, and the general sets the tone of the army. Our army is very George Patton-esque. We charge. We roll. The other armies that we're competing against are very Omar Bradleyesque. They're defensive players. They're cautious. They don't go into uncharted territories. They don't outflank. They play it the way it's been played for forty years. Those days are over." O'Reilly did not spin *Advertising Age*. Asked whether a more accurate tag line for Fox might be "We report. *We* decide," he replied, "Well, you're probably right."

ROGER EUGENE AILES, who was born on May 15, 1940, comes from Warren, Ohio, a tiny factory town near Youngstown. He was one of three children, with an older brother and a younger sister. His father worked at first as a laborer at Packard Electric, which made wiring for General Motors; his mother was a housewife who embroidered handkerchiefs and dispatched Roger, at age ten, to sell them door to door. During high school and college, Roger worked summers for the state highway department, sometimes digging ditches. His mother would tell him, he remembers, "'You always have to have goals.' My mother in some ways was sort of difficult. Because my brother was such a good student, she was always on my ass because I didn't love school. If I got a B, she'd say, 'Why didn't you get an A?' . . . If I got an A-plus, she'd say, 'Did you get the highest grade in the class?' You couldn't please her." He adds, "My mother would have been a CEO of a corporation in today's world."

When Roger was eight, he was hit by a car and hospitalized. During his convalescence, he had to learn to use his legs again. His father would take him to a track to practice. Once, he fell and landed in a pile of horse manure. His father had no patience. "Don't fall down and you won't get that crap on you!" he said. Roger has another vivid boyhood memory of his father. "I used to see college boys"—he spits out the words—"give my dad orders in the shop in an inappropriate manner." He once asked his father why he let them talk to him like that. After a long pause, his father said, "Son, because of you, your brother, and your sister. I need the job, and you kids have got to go to college so you don't ever have to put up with this."

Roger enrolled at Ohio University, in Athens. He spent four years at the college radio station, as a disk jockey and a sportscaster, and dreamed of making a living that way. He was nineteen when his parents telephoned to announce that they were getting a divorce. It was abrupt. "I went home and everything was gone," he said. "My house wasn't there. My room wasn't there. My stuff wasn't there. . . . I never found my shit!" He rarely went home on holidays or in the summer, volunteering to work "the holiday shifts" at school. His mother soon moved to San Francisco and remarried. His father eventually remarried, too. Roger talked to his parents on the phone but lost touch with his hometown. "Their attitude was, when you get to be eighteen, you go to college and you're on your own," Ailes said matter-of-factly. Around the time of his parents' divorce, he married a classmate, a marriage that lasted fifteen years.

When Ailes was a senior, he had a job interview with the program manager of a Cleveland television station. The manager, Chet Collier, remembers him as a slender, self-confident young man. "I was impressed with his enthusiasm, his willingness to think in different ways," Collier recalls. Collier was helping to launch a local talk-variety show, *The Mike Douglas Show*, on KYW-TV, and hired Roger as a production assistant at sixty-four dollars a week. The show caught on and was soon syndicated nationally. One of Roger's chores was to meet guests at the airport— celebrities like Jack Benny, Bob Hope, and Pearl Bailey—and drive them to the studio. Soon he was writing the cue cards for Douglas, which was much the same as posing the questions.

Collier now works from his home in Florida but remains close to Ailes; he was the second person Ailes recruited to devise programming for America's Talking, and was a key programmer at Fox News. "Standing there, he looked like most people," Collier recalls. "Then he talked, and he got you excited." Sometimes Ailes got too excited. Once, he threw a bullying advertiser off the loading dock into the snow. And once he slammed the executive producer up against a wall. In both cases, Ailes says, he erupted because someone "had abused little people." To this day, he says, he follows this code: "Don't mistreat people who work for you." (He doesn't *always* follow it, observes a Fox executive who knows him well. "He can be really mean. . . . He yells at 'little people' unnecessarily.") Three years after Collier hired him, Ailes became the executive producer of *The Mike Douglas Show,* which had by then moved to Philadelphia.

RICHARD NIXON ENTERED Ailes's life in 1967, when Nixon was booked to appear on the Douglas show. Any prominent figure passing through town might be invited onto the show, and it fell to Ailes to come up with a good mix. Nixon hated being on television. Ailes knew that he didn't want the former vice president sitting in the greenroom with Little Egypt, a belly dancer who performed with a boa constrictor, so he put Nixon in his own office. When Nixon learned that he was to follow Little Egypt, he said, "It's a shame a man has to use gimmicks like this to get elected."

"Television is not a gimmick," Ailes, who was then twenty-seven years old, replied. Furthermore, he said, the candidate who mastered television would win. They discussed this for about ten minutes, and a few days later Nixon's staff invited Ailes to New York. They met for three hours on a Sunday. Ailes, who describes his father as a Taft Republican, says, "I never thought too much about politics." When he was invited to join the campaign, what appealed to him was the challenge. "Everyone said the man could never get elected because of television," Ailes says. "The challenge was more to me—it had nothing to do with politics. In fact, all my work with Nixon had nothing to do with politics. It was a media problem. It wasn't a political problem."

The first writer to get inside a modern media campaign for president was Joe McGinniss, at the time a columnist for the *Philadelphia Inquirer.* His 1969 book *The Selling of the President* quotes Ailes on his thinking at the time: "Let's face it, a lot of people think Nixon is dull. Think he's a bore, a pain in the ass. They look at him as the kind of kid who always carried a bookbag. Who was forty-two years old the day he was born. . . . Now you put him on television, you've got a problem right away. He's a funny-looking guy. He looks like somebody hung him in a closet overnight and he jumps out in the morning with his suit all bunched up and starts running around saying, 'I want to be president.'" Ailes's task was clear: "To make them forget all that." He created a "man in the arena concept," in which Nixon didn't have to read from a TelePrompTer or stand at a podium but instead fielded questions from what looked like a wide range of citizens but was, in fact, a prescreened audience. He did not believe it was possible for viewers to warm to Nixon. This format allowed people, Ailes says, "to respect him by showing that he was smart."

Nixon was already president when the McGinniss book was published, but he was appalled that a reporter had infiltrated his campaign. McGinniss says that Nixon's aides all denied that they had cooperated with him, except Ailes. Not surprisingly, Ailes was not invited to mastermind Nixon's 1972 reelection effort.

Ailes says that he respected Nixon's intelligence and many of his policies, but adds, "I felt sort of sorry for him. He was socially uncomfortable." If Nixon were a candidate today, Ailes adds, "he would be allowed to go on *Oprah* and plead that he was an abused child. And the liberals would have to love him!"

After Nixon's victory, Ailes formed Ailes Communications, and consulted with corporations and Republican candidates. He coproduced Broadway and Off Broadway plays, among them *Hot L Baltimore,* and television specials. He was a commentator on the *Today* show. Ailes returned to presidential politics in 1984, when he was brought in to coach Reagan for his second debate with Walter Mondale.

In 1988, Ailes signed on for Vice President Bush's effort to succeed Reagan and helped to orchestrate one of the nastiest media campaigns ever. Ailes agreed with Bush's campaign manager, the late Lee Atwater, that Bush needed to overcome his "wimp" image and do more than lower his own negatives in the polls; he had to raise the negatives of his Democratic opponent, Michael Dukakis. One night, according to an account by Peter Goldman and Tom Mathews, of *Newsweek,* Ailes had a dream about a recent disastrous campaign appearance in which Dukakis had been filmed riding in a tank. Ailes got up, jotted the word "tank" on a pad, and went back to sleep. Within two days he had started production of a spot with a voice-over enumerating the defense-spending programs that the governor of Massachusetts opposed. As the voice cited the programs, one saw Dukakis's head sticking out of the turret of a tank and capped by a helmet with headphones that looked like Mickey Mouse ears. Dukakis became the wimp—a liberal elitist who was pro taxes, pro criminals, pro defense cuts, and even pro polluter. Ailes "has two speeds," Atwater told *Time:* "Attack and destroy."

Ailes knew that he had muddied his own reputation. His adversaries, he said, tried "to smear me with racism" for devising anti-Dukakis television spots that featured a black felon, Willie Horton. Ailes denies responsibility for those ads. By 1991, he had quit working with political clients. He says he was tired of the travel and of the political game. "I hated politics. The candidates were getting weaker and younger and dumber, and I was getting older and wiser." He did take on more corporate clients, and some overseas political clients, including Jacques Chirac, who was then the mayor of Paris. When NBC recruited Ailes in 1993, he eagerly turned the consulting business over to his partner, Jon Kraushar.

FOX NEWS has alarmed its competitors. In 2001, Jamie Kellner, who helped Barry Diller launch the Fox broadcast network in the mideighties and later designed the youth-oriented WB network, became chairman and CEO of Turner Broadcasting. Kellner says that his charge was to focus "on television presentation and promotion skills" and to build more "stars," though "without in any way changing the journalism." More people watched CNN, he says, but the people who watched Fox continued to stay tuned for longer periods.

CNN copied Fox's whoosh sound to introduce breaking news; it explored the idea of talk shows featuring the conservatives Rush Limbaugh and Pat Buchanan and the liberal Phil Donahue—then worried that this might dilute the CNN brand. Rather than successive newscasts that once filled an estimated 70 percent of CNN's schedule, the network moved toward programs like Zahn's *American Morning, Late Edition with Wolf Blitzer, Talk Back Live,* and Connie Chung's 8:00 P.M. interview show. CNN correspondents complained that it was harder to get airtime for actual news. Walter Isaacson, the CNN chairman, disputed this, and said that what CNN was doing differed from what Fox did: "You make the programs dependent on news, not the opinion of the host."

By 2002, morale at CNN was down. Ailes not only put a movable Fox billboard in front of Zahn's studio on the day of her debut but bought a large billboard across from CNN's Atlanta headquarters. "I heard it was available and that everyone who walks in the building has to look at it," Ailes explained. When Greta Van Susteren's 10:00 P.M. Fox show went ahead of Aaron Brown, or *Fox & Friends* got better numbers than *American Morning,* Ailes put a fresh message on the billboard to remind CNN. Kellner could see the billboard from his office. "It's not nice," he says. "You're in the news business. It should be a higher playing field." (Nevertheless, CNN bought a billboard on Sixth Avenue across from Fox News to tout Zahn's show.)

Morale was also hurt by budget cuts and by the sharp drop in the valuation of AOL Time Warner stock. Allan Dodds Frank, who is fifty-five, had been a CNN correspondent for eight years, and before that he was a correspondent for ABC, *Forbes,* and the *Washington Star.* He was the investigative correspondent for *Moneyline* and won the Gerald R. Loeb Award in 2002. He was laid off last December, as was Brooks Jackson, an expert on campaign contributions and influence peddling in Washington. "They are overreacting to Fox and deciding that everything has to be live, no matter how little sense it makes," Frank says. "The first rule of zoology—or journalism—is: You can't outape the monkey."

There was a growing sense that CNN was doing just that—imitating Fox but not getting it right. There were complaints about the perceived superficiality of Connie Chung's program; the most hurtful of these came from Ted Turner himself, who told a reporter that Chung's show was "just awful." Privately, CNN correspondents complained that Lou Dobbs, on *Moneyline,* was declaring conservative opinions. ("Isn't it time someone said something straightforwardly?" he said on February eleventh, before denouncing France as "obstructionist.")

Ailes believes that CNN faltered because it got too comfortable: "I don't think they trained for competition. They also built a huge bureaucracy. They're still operating on four times the number of people that I have. Yet I don't see a lot going on up on their screen that we're not doing at least as well. They have a little more coverage in various locations, but they have a lot of people sitting around playing checkers, waiting for something to happen."

It is a measure of CNN's strategic confusion that in March of 2002 Isaacson held a full-day retreat in Atlanta, inviting about forty senior CNN executives. Isaacson told me that the proposals discussed came down to two options: Reduce the network's forty-two bureaus and move toward an opinionated talk format, or keep the emphasis on news. The consensus was to stay with news. To all this, Kellner said, "You're right. You have to go with your strength and stay a classy network." Isaacson added, "MSNBC went the Fox way. CNN reacted slowly—too slowly—but we did go the other way."

Nevertheless, in early 2003, Kellner resigned and Isaacson, exasperated with television, accepted an offer to head the international Aspen Institute. Isaacson says of the television business, there was "not much time to pause and reflect and look ahead. I like knowing what the third paragraph will be." Isaacson was replaced by his deputy, Jim Walton, who had joined CNN a year after it went on the air. The journalists at CNN would be pleased to hear Walton say, as he did to me, "We want to be accurate and timely. . . . Notice that I didn't say I wanted to be first." He also said, "It's not enough to have higher ratings" if CNN "dumbs down" to get them.

FOX NEWS seemed also to rattle MSNBC. When MSNBC went on the air, in July of 1996, three months before Fox, it relied on NBC News talent, it drew upon its rich video library, and it recruited a great many on-air commentators. Then it switched formats. It promoted an hourlong newscast anchored by Tom Brokaw's designated heir, Brian Williams, then switched his program to CNBC. It promoted Ashleigh Banfield, a relatively inexperienced reporter, sent her to Afghanistan, then gave her a nightly program, which was later canceled. Phil Donahue's hourlong show was canceled, although it was their top-rated program. Asked if there were too many formats and changes at MSNBC, Bob Wright, the CEO of NBC, concedes, "That certainly is true recently. Probably in the last two and a half years. That's a criticism, and it's a fair one." MSNBC's president and general manager, Erik Sorenson, who oversaw these changes, says, "I think we've lacked directional consistency. We overexperimented." MSNBC's ratings today are about a third of Fox's and half of CNN's.

The president of NBC News, Neal Shapiro, who has nineteen television monitors in his office, appears to see the competition as one between the hedgehog and the fox, with Fox as the hedgehog. Shapiro praises Fox for "sticking to a few things" while noting that MSNBC did not. He said he now planned to put more NBC News talent on its cable network and build up its identification with the network. "By day it will be much more association with NBC. By night it will be smart analysis"— led by Chris Matthews and a new roster of talk-show hosts, including former Minnesota Governor Jesse Ventura and conservative commentators such as former Congressman Joe Scarborough and former House Majority Leader Dick Armey. "The premise of all these people is that our people don't just talk—they know what they're talking about," Shapiro said. He did not mention the right-wing radio talk-show host Michael Savage, who recently got a weekly show and does "just talk"—so intemperately that Procter & Gamble and Dell withdrew their advertising.* "Cable news," Ailes says, "is beginning to change the agenda of what is news."

As for allegations of partisan coverage, Ailes will not admit that Fox is "right of center," and insists, "I think I've forced the entire world to deal with 'fair and balanced.'" He portrays himself as nothing less than a high-minded news executive: "I'm not saying I'm the answer. But . . . there hasn't even been a story where we've been accused of tipping some big story to the right in seven years. Why hasn't it happened? Because we're honestly trying to do a good job."

CNN executives and others believe that Fox tips right all the time. In a thinly disguised slap at Fox, a marketing slogan touted CNN as "News. Not Noise." Dan Rather, of CBS, concedes that he doesn't watch much Fox News, but he thinks Fox is a reflection of Rupert Murdoch's political views. "Mr. Murdoch has a business, a huge worldwide conglomerate

*After still another rabid outburst, the network fired Savage in the summer of 2003.

business," Rather says. "He finds it to his benefit to have media outlets, press outlets, that serve his business interests. There's nothing wrong with this. It's a free country. It's not an indictable offense. But by any clear analysis the bias is towards his own personal, political, partisan agenda . . . primarily because it fits his commercial interests."

Neal Shapiro believes that the networks are now more sensitive to any ingrained liberal bias. "We talk about it constantly," he says. "I think it's sensitized newsrooms, and that's a good thing." It is widely supposed— and hard to document—that reporters at major news organizations tend to be more liberal, which inevitably influences coverage. "I think the traditional broadcast media does have a slightly left-of-center bias," concedes Paul Friedman, who has produced NBC's and ABC's evening newscasts and was most recently the executive vice president of ABC News. "It's not so much in what is said. It's in the choice of what to cover." The networks, he went on, tend to choose "social-agenda stories"—AIDS, poverty— "rather than stories about the flag or religion."

Some conservatives believe that liberals deliberately promote an agenda. Brit Hume's view is that the alleged liberal bias in mainstream media is unconscious. "My sense is that very few reporters, if any, that I've ever known are closet political activists or actually have agendas," he says. "There is, however, a very widely shared set of assumptions and values. It's very unusual to find reporters who are pro life. It's unusual to find reporters who don't think more gun control is a good idea. It's not common to find reporters who are enthusiastic about the idea of a tax cut."

Todd Gitlin, of the Columbia School of Journalism, frames it somewhat differently. He believes that Fox and the conservatives have bullied a "lazy" and servile press into submission. Of Ailes, Gitlin observes, "I think that his talent is percussive. Fox News has a tone. The tone is what it delivers. The tone is urgency—crashing noise. Occasionally, this entails interesting debate. More likely, it entails bluster. . . . Fox certainly accelerated the sense of panic at CNN." Fox's greatest influence, he says, is "felt in Washington. I find it hard to believe many Fox viewers believe Bill O'Reilly is a 'no-spin zone,' or 'We report. You decide.' It's a joke. In Washington it reinforces the impression of 'we happy few who are members of the club.' It emboldens the right wing to feel justified and confident they can promote their policies."

Certainly the success of Fox has permitted Rupert Murdoch to promote his own agenda. When New York Governor George Pataki denounced proposed new state taxes, the April thirtieth front page of the *Post* read like an editorial: AT LAST, A LEADER WITH GUTS. Last year, Murdoch wanted the Bush administration to block, on antitrust grounds, the merger of the two largest satellite operators, which the administration did. This let Murdoch reenter negotiations to buy America's largest satellite operator, DirecTV, a deal that went through in April (it awaits the approval of the Bush administration). Murdoch also wanted the administration to lift the cap on the percentage of American households that one company's TV stations can reach; earlier this month, the staff of the Federal Communications Commission proposed the change.

In part because of the success of Fox News, Murdoch—with DirecTV, British Sky Broadcasting, Star in Asia, and satellite systems in Latin America—has created a worldwide competitor to CNN and the BBC. Jack Welch, for one, is deeply impressed: "If Rupert gets DirecTV, his whole position in the communications arena changes. He now has all the distribution. He has programming assets. And his options are now as big as his appetites."

FOR AILES, a typical day begins when he is chauffeured from his northern New Jersey home to his office, arriving before 8:00 A.M., having already read the *Post,* the *Times,* and the *Wall Street Journal.* Ailes's office on the second floor has seven TV monitors, but few personal items; there are no pictures of his wife or their three-year-old son—in fact, there are no photographs at all. On the wall opposite his desk is a picture of George Washington's Valley Forge headquarters. The windows provide an unobstructed view of Sixth Avenue, but to the north the venetian blinds are drawn so that he won't have to look toward the electric CNN and NBC signs two blocks away. A huge open file cabinet behind his desk is dedicated to "evidence" Ailes has collected of the press's liberal bias. His curved cherry-wood desk is free of papers, and his "in" box is usually empty. Buttons on his phone connect him to various news executives, including the news chief, John Moody, who says that a long beep is "not my favorite sound." Also on his desk are two Bibles—"They're old friends," Ailes says.

The first meeting of Ailes's day is usually the 8:00 A.M. news meeting, which he hosts in his office. Moody puts together a list of the stories to be pursued and is accompanied by a team of news executives; they were joined on February twenty-fifth by Brit Hume, on the speakerphone. Ailes hung up his suit jacket and sat at his desk. He listened as Moody started with an overview of the big news stories. Moody mentioned that British Prime Minister Tony Blair had dismissed the French resolution before the UN to extend the arms inspectors' deadline. "It's a scam," Ailes said, and added that he was looking at some numbers last night showing that France, Russia, and China had major trade ties with Iraq. "We ought to look at the import-export situation there."

Geraldo is in Turkey, Moody said.

"Do you have him under control, so he's not going to do any hotdogging?" Ailes asked.

"'Under control' is a relative term," Moody replied.

"He has understood that any wild moves over there can get our other guys killed, right? Have we made it very clear?" Ailes asked. "Geraldo is a good journalist and he's a team player, but you do have to speak to him very directly." He added, "Just tell him no hotdogging."

Moody said that, in an interview to air that night on CBS, Saddam Hussein told Dan Rather that he would not destroy the missiles that UN inspectors said he must. Ailes asked if Rather was required to turn his tape over to the Iraqis and let them edit it. Although the answer was unclear, Ailes worked himself into a lather. Voice rising, he said, "Did they have prelook at his questions? . . . Was anybody in the room with a weapon?" He added, "I have less of a problem in getting in a room with Saddam Hussein with ground rules as long as those ground rules are disclosed." He complained that *Time* did not disclose the ground rules of what he called an "anti-American interview" with Jacques Chirac that it carried that week, and said it was "a total setup." He went on, "Nowhere in the *Time* magazine interview do they say, 'Mr. Chirac, do you have any business dealings with Iraq? Mr. Chirac, is there a $120 billion oil contract with Iraq? Mr. Chirac, weren't you the guy that went over and set up a nuclear reactor? . . . How about the seven million Muslims down the street that are going to blow up the Eiffel Tower? Does that bother you?' There are a few other questions that a few other *good* journalists would work into the interview."

Ailes discussed coverage of the tension between the United States and North Korea and its implications for Asia. Throughout the meeting, Ailes would interrupt with something he had read or heard, in a style that was part oracle and part stand-up comic. He mentioned that he'd heard that MSNBC had allegedly set up a small team to seek out more conservative, populist stories. "They'll fuck it all up," he said. He couldn't believe, he told me after the meeting, that MSNBC had failed with Chris Matthews. Ailes hired Matthews at America's Talking, but thinks he talks too much: "If Chris Matthews worked for me, he'd be doing better. . . . I wouldn't let him answer everybody's question for them. He asks the question. Then he answers it. Then he asks you what you think of his answer. Then he goes on to another question. At some point, he's got to let the guest answer. I'd say, 'Chris, if you don't shut the fuck up I'm going to fire you!'"

Later that day, someone told Ailes that MSNBC had just fired Phil Donahue, and Ailes was pleased to learn that his senior vice president for corporate communications, Brian Lewis, was prepared to attack. "We're putting it out that Donahue's numbers were higher than Matthews's," Lewis said. To the news that MSNBC had lined up Jesse Ventura and Joe Scarborough, Ailes said, "It's their attempt to move right." Ailes said that Chris Matthews, in MSNBC's 7:00 P.M. slot, often does monologues. "The last guy to do a good monologue on TV was Fulton J. Sheen," he said.

"And he had a good writer," an executive said.

"Yeah—God!" Ailes said.

FOX NEWS is capable of solid work and straightforward reporting, as when it covered the devastation caused by the recent tornadoes in the Midwest. In Iraq, Rick Leventhal and Greg Kelly, embedded war correspondents, broke more than their share of exclusives from the front and provided vivid pictures. Brit Hume asks acute questions, listens to the answers, and usually tries to be balanced. Correspondents like Eric Shawn and Jim Angle, at the White House, are industrious. And although the culture at Fox is partial to the Bush administration, it was Fox News that broke the story on the eve of the election that George W. Bush had once been arrested for drunk driving. "I knew it would hurt him," Ailes said. "They said we should hold it. We ran it. We're in the news business and we do what's news." During the murder trial of Michael Skakel, the correspondent Eric Shawn recalls that Fox titled one of his pieces "Kennedy Cousin Trial." Ailes "thought it wasn't fair," so he called the control room and had it changed to "Skakel Trial." On other occasions, Ailes says, he killed a story about Al Gore's son getting a speeding ticket—he thought a teenager deserved some privacy—and a story in 1998 exploring how Bill Clinton, as governor, had used state troopers to do more than protect him, which Ailes thought was "piling on."

At the same time, CNN, which once called itself "the world's news leader," saw the Iraq war largely through American eyes. And MSNBC, like Fox and the Bush administration, called the war "Operation Iraqi Freedom" and duplicated Fox's display of an American flag in a corner of its screen. In mid-April, the MSNBC anchor Natalie Morales read a report that said the French foreign minister had cautioned the United States not to start a war in Syria, saying, "We have to concentrate on giving the Iraqi people the victory they deserve." Morales then looked into the camera and seemed to ad-lib: "The minister might want to save 'we' for countries that actually fought to give Iraqis their freedom!" Watching this, Ailes called out, "They've gone right wing!"

MSNBC had a major embarrassment in late March when Peter Arnett, a correspondent for *National Geographic Explorer,* who doubled as NBC and MSNBC's eyes in Baghdad, let himself be interviewed by Iraqi television, saying that America's "first war plan has failed because of Iraqi resistance" and that "our reports about civilian casualties" and Iraqi resistance help "those who oppose the war." Fox feasted on Arnett's bad judgment, and Arnett was quickly fired. Around the same time, Geraldo Rivera, who was embedded, drew for his viewers a diagram in the sand, letting them know where his unit was and how it planned to attack an Iraqi position. That gave MSNBC the chance to report that the military was furious and planned to expel Rivera. At first, Rivera denied that he had been ordered out of the country, but later said that he would be relocating to Kuwait. When MSNBC produced a promotional ad declaring that it would never "compromise military security or jeopardize a single American life," Fox ran an ad, approved by Ailes, attacking Peter Arnett: "He spoke out against America's armed forces. He said America's war against terrorism had failed. He even vilified America's leadership. And he worked for MSNBC." It didn't matter that none of it was true. Ailes says he pulled the ad after it aired once because the spat was unseemly.

FOR THE IRAQ WAR, Fox News had 1,250 full-time and freelance employees and 17 bureaus, only 6 of them overseas, and operating costs of about $250 million. Last year, a senior Fox News executive told me, its revenues were $325 million and its profits were $70 million. (This year, the profits are expected to double.) By contrast, CNN had 4,000 employees and 42 bureaus, 31 of them overseas, and total news costs of about $800 million. Its revenues, according to a senior executive, climbed above $1 billion last year, and its profits totaled $250 million. MSNBC, according to Bob Wright, essentially breaks even; CNBC with its business audience and its cable subscriber fees, generated profits last year of about $300 million.

Neal Shapiro, of NBC News, saw the war in Iraq as an opportunity to rebrand MSNBC by benefiting from its pool of NBC News stars. Shapiro dispatched 125 journalists and crew members to the region; CBS sent a team of 100, and at one point ABC had twice as many in the region. The BBC also sent 200 people to the Gulf.

Ailes knew that Fox had to rely on only fifteen correspondents in the region. "We don't have the resources overseas that CNN and other networks have," said Rick Leventhal, who was with the 1st Marine Light Armor Reconnaissance unit. "We're going in with less money and equipment and people, and trying to do the same job. You might call it smoke and mirrors, but it's working." CNN had forty-nine correspondents in the region, eighteen of them embedded with American troops. Ailes told his financial staff that the challenge is "not to let this war be a win for CNN. If I have to, I'll go upstairs and argue for extra money. I'm not going to let these sons of bitches beat us!" He wanted the financial people to understand that a war with Iraq was also a war between Fox and CNN.

This degree of involvement reflects Ailes's enormous competitiveness. Rick Leventhal described a Christmas party at the home of Shepard Smith, who anchors the 3:00 P.M. and 7:00 P.M. news hours. Smith has an eight-foot pool table at his loft on the Lower East Side, and he and Leventhal, who are skilled players, attempted to hustle Ailes. "I haven't played in twenty years," Ailes said. A crowd of about forty Fox News employees gathered to watch the boss get taken by two pool sharks. Ailes says he was "pissed off," and remembered the time he and his brother challenged their father to a race home. Their father let them get ahead and tire, and then he sped past them. By the time they got home, he was sitting on the grass, laughing. "You know the difference between an average horse and a champion?" he asked his sons. "A champion always has something left when it comes around the last turn."

Of the pool-table challenge, Ailes said, "They had no understanding of how important that game of pool suddenly became to me." When it was his turn to shoot, Leventhal recalled, Ailes proceeded "to make a series of ridiculous shots and to win the game." Ailes said, "Every time someone thinks I'm beat, I always have something left."

MY FOUR-MONTH IMMERSION in Fox News left me dismissive of its claims of "fair and balanced." When I asked Ailes about what seemed one-note coverage and the disproportionate number of conservative commentators, he said that he beseeched his staff to "book Democrats," but they told him, "They won't come on. They're hiding." Fox does have a stable of liberal commentators, including Sean Hannity's partner, Alan Colmes, and NPR's Mara Liasson, who appears with Hume, but they are often overpowered by the conservatives around them. And there is Susan

Estrich, who was Michael Dukakis's campaign manager. Ailes likes her but calls her "hard core," a term he does not apply to right-wing Republicans.

Looking back on Fox's coverage of the war, Ailes acknowledged that mistakes were made, and blamed many of them on fatigue and on the speed it takes to produce 168 hours a week of live television, which inevitably leads to "sloppiness." He said that he played a watchdog role during the war and would call the control room or news desk at any time of day or night to ensure balance. "If I see bias of the left or right, I will complain about it," he says. It is possible that this was one of the rare times in his sixty-three years that no one was listening to Roger Ailes.

Ailes's contract is up at the end of this year, and a source close to him says that it wasn't until early April that his lawyer was approached about a new one. Ailes and Murdoch have an easy rapport, but Fox executives say that his relationship with the chief operating officer, Lachlan Murdoch, is not so relaxed. Ailes battles often with Fox's owned-and-operated broadcast-station group over when and how to air Fox News, and this group reports to Lachlan Murdoch. Friends say that Ailes sometimes fears he will grow stale and should try something new, such as running a television entertainment division or even a network. In recent weeks, negotiations between Ailes's lawyer and News Corp. have accelerated.

Ailes is a wary man, but not in the way most journalists are wary. "Roger's sort of thesis of the world is that they're out to get us," Brit Hume says. "It makes him the most alert competitor you've ever seen. He's not always right about that, but he's always alert. And it makes him very hard to sneak up on—it's very hard to do anything that Roger hasn't already anticipated." What surprises colleagues is that Ailes appears actually to disdain journalism; Ailes says that he detests what he thinks of as "elite" journalists with "a pick up their ass" who treat journalism as "a from-the-Mount profession." Some senior executives at Fox express private puzzlement that Ailes seems, in the words of one, to "hate journalists so much. . . . I've never seen him use the word 'journalism' and smile at the same time."

Over lunch one day, I suggested to Ailes that although he bridles at being stereotyped as a former political operative, he stereotypes others—

"Thirty percent of New York City teachers are too stupid to teach!" he told me. And he stereotypes journalists. "I do," he replied, ripping a hunk of bread from a loaf and spreading butter on it. "And it's unfair, because they're not all like that. . . . There are some journalists I will talk to, there are other journalists I won't talk to." He insisted, "If I hated journalism that much, or had that little confidence in journalism, or thought that it had made that little contribution to the republic, I frankly would walk away from it and ignore it and make money and say, 'Screw it. You can't fix it.'" Asked to identify his journalistic heroes, Ailes paused for several seconds, before saying "I've never thought of journalists as heroes. I think of journalists as very bright people with enormous responsibilities that they often don't live up to. Now that I'm doing this job, I can't live up to it every day, either, because I have ratings pressure, financial pressure—all the things that I have. But there are certain things that I just won't do."

I asked if he would have published the Pentagon Papers, and his response revealed not only an aversion to the press but an uncharacteristic uncertainty: "I won't do anything that will jeopardize national security. . . . Does that mean I will cover up for America? No." Reminded that the papers were, essentially, the Pentagon's own history of the Vietnam War, he said, "I never thought there was a huge problem with the Pentagon Papers," and he conceded that the Nixon administration was paranoid about the press. Finally, he said, "Maybe the story should have been reported, and Ellsberg"—Daniel Ellsberg, who leaked the papers—"should have had the shit beat out of him for stealing. Of course, the press would never beat the shit out of him for stealing, and that's sometimes why the press lacks morals. The end justifies the means as long as the end justifies their political view."

At the core of Ailes's journalistic philosophy, he says, is a belief that the press should "seek to be watchdogs, not attack dogs." He says he dislikes journalists who are "gratuitous brutalizers"—an odd sort of fastidiousness from the man who sponsors such verbal gunslingers as Bill O'Reilly and Sean Hannity. "I try to force Bill to be more fair," Ailes says. "I try to force all my people to be fair." But to Ailes fairness doesn't mean selecting the stories or the amount of time devoted to the victims; it means giving them airtime. Ailes says, "If anybody has a complaint, we put them back on another show to have their say. But we are in a time medium that depends on outgoing, aggressive talent to get ratings."

Although he has never worked as a journalist, Ailes believes that his campaign-consulting work and his years as a producer prepared him to run Fox News. "You learn the issues from everybody's point of view, left and right," he said. "I actually have a broader and deeper knowledge of most issues than probably some news guys because I've actually read position papers on a lot of this stuff, both left and right. I've learned you don't move Election Day back, but I knew that from broadcasting—in other words, whatever you do, you better make your decision and get it done, you better get your show on the air . . . because you don't get any second chances."

Seated behind his clean desk, the television monitors silently running, Ailes sounded less like the man who created a fierce, right-leaning news network than like someone who sadly bears the burdens of a journalistic reformer. "The hardest part of my job now is to maintain any kind of journalistic standards, because they're being weakened all over the country by newspapers and magazines," he says. Once more, he brought up the *Time* interview with Chirac, then moved on to other targets: "*Newsweek* is just an anti-Bush publication put out by the DNC every week. . . . Dan Rather is over there letting Iraq edit the tape. At some point, you've got to say, 'What are we doing here?' "

Aaron Brown, whose face is on the CNN billboard outside Ailes's window, believes that he understands what Fox is doing. "I honestly think they do something quite different from what we do," he says. "I hesitate to say this, because I don't want to create a sense that they're in the same business we're in. . . . They've done a very good job with marketing slogans. They came up with two good slogans. To me, they lead with their opinions. There's room for conservative talk radio on television. But I don't think anyone ought to pretend it's the *New York Times* or CNN." It would not make Roger Ailes happy to know that his "dentist" got the last word.

ACKNOWLEDGMENTS

I'm always amazed at writers or lawyers or professors who seem to give up their day jobs to spend entire afternoons and evenings in cable television studios, as if being on television was of great moment. I know statistics say most Americans get their information from the TV, but to me it seems so transitory, as if the images just disappear into the air. Yes, I know everything can be stored and saved digitally. But to me a book feels permanent.

Which is why I was pleased when my editor, Scott Moyers, and publisher Ann Godoff agreed to sandwich between two covers some of my print journalism pieces. My hope, and theirs, was that they might serve as a kind of State of the Fourth Estate. I thank them for their efforts and support. I would also like to thank Tracy Locke; Sophie Fels for keeping this train running; and copy editor Susan Johnson for her fine work.

With one exception these pieces were done for *The New Yorker,* where I was first recruited, in 1977, by William Shawn. The current editor, David

Remnick, has in five years proven as gifted an editor as he was a writer. He is also, just as important, a good man. The editor who made most of these pieces better is Jeffrey Frank, who is my editor at the magazine as well as a pal. His assistant, Lauren Porcaro, was helpful in myriad ways and ever cheerful. Tina Brown, the talented former *New Yorker* editor, first asked me to write about the media, and I remain grateful to her. The magazine is a team enterprise, with everyone pitching in to make the work better. Among those I'd especially like to thank are the executive editor, Pamela McCarthy, and her assistant, Daniel Cappello, and managing editor, Dorothy Wickenden. The fact checkers at the magazine are, simply, the best anywhere, which they never fail to prove; first Mauri Perl, and then when she went upstairs to bigger things, Perri Dorset, who have effortlessly helped me field press calls.

The one non-*New Yorker* piece in this collection was commissioned by Gene Roberts as the first in his series on newspapers. Gene is a great mumbler, and I always wondered how he motivated generations of journalists at the *Times* and the *Philadelphia Inquirer.* Now I know. For their help on this project, I am grateful as well to Tom Kunkel and Caroline White.

I have had one agent throughout my career, Esther Newberg of ICM, and one wife, Amanda Urban.

INDEX

ABOUT THE AUTHOR

Ken Auletta has written "Annals of Communication" for *The New Yorker* since 1992. He is the author of eight previous books, including four national best sellers. In ranking him as America's premier media critic, the *Columbia Journalism Review* concluded, "No other reporter has covered the new communications revolution as thoroughly as has Auletta."

He has written for various newspapers and magazines and appeared regularly as a television interviewer and analyst. He started writing for *The New Yorker* in 1977.

He grew up on Coney Island and now lives in New York City with his wife and daughter.